PRAIS

WE N..

ROBOTS

How apropos is a book entitled *We're Not Robots: How Leading with Humanity Creates High-Performing Organizations*, during an age and time when artificial intelligence (AI) is the "soup du jour" of a generation! General Lynch—a West Point "Star Man" and an MIT graduate with a Master's in Robotics—who led the Army's robotics program in the second half of the 1980s, is at the intersection of the human dimension and AI. He correctly views AI as a complement to the human experience. Within this opus he masterfully argues that what separates man and machine is empathy—the ability to feel and to make adjustments based on human emotion. In this age of self-driving cars, spacecraft that needs humans only as occupants, and unmanned drones, Lynch makes a compelling case for oxygen-breathing, blood-pumping, compassionate, and empathetic human leaders. A phenomenal and timely must-read volume.

—**BARRYE L. PRICE, PHD**, Major General US Army (Retired),
President and CEO CADCA

Rick Lynch provides a unique perspective on leadership by weaving together his experiences in the military and corporate America. Whether you are just starting out or are an experienced professional with decades of experience, *We're Not Robots* is a tool to have in your toolkit. Leadership is universal, and Lynch's book lays out those timeless lessons.

—**JOSEPH KOPSER**, President of Grayline Group,
Chair of the Board of Sustainment

Rick Lynch has translated 35 years of distinguished service in the Army (retiring as a 3-Star General) and more than a decade as a corporate leadership consultant into a readable, valuable guide for leaders and aspiring leaders. *We're Not Robots* is filled with wisdom, wit, and practical examples for us all. A must-read!

—**JIM SPANIOLO**, President Emeritus,
University of Texas at Arlington

General Lynch shares his wealth of knowledge and experience as a proven military leader, business leader, and executive coach, in a way that is straightforward, candid, and honest. This is his fourth book, and I have read them all. His no-nonsense approach to high-performance leadership skills is refreshing. I particularly enjoy his humility, caring heart for people, and deep faith. This is a must-read for any leader at any level who wants to achieve success with any reputable organization.

—JEFF THOMAS, Retired Senior Vice President and
General Manager, HEB Central Texas Region

Lt. Gen. Lynch does an exceptional job of sharing his unique insights from his days in the military, working with C-Suite professionals and then marrying those with historical examples pulled from some of America's most important battlefields. The book provides actionable insights that every professional can use to make themselves better leaders and to improve the culture of their respective companies. This is a must-read!

—BOB JANSEN, President/CEO Zensights

In a time of increasing concern over the rapid pace of technological advances, especially AI, General Rick Lynch's new book *We're Not Robots* could not be better timed. Highly readable with numerous personal and historical examples, it clearly examines the indispensable role empathy plays in effective leadership. Every leader from entry level to the C Suite should read this book and reflect on its message. As Rick rightfully maintains, leadership is a contact sport, and to be effective, you must make it personal.

—MIKE MILANO, Major General, US Army (Retired),
President, Milano Leadership Services, LLC

Lots of folks claim to have written "Self-Help" books, but Rick Lynch has actually done exactly that! Rick has had an extraordinary career, which he gladly shares. Through powerful personal teachings from this well-practiced, compassionate leader, you can't help but become a far more successful individual and respected leader.

—SANTO J. COSTA, retired President and Chief Operating Officer,
Quintiles Transnational Corp.

Of all the great books Rick has written, this is the best! In *We're Not Robots*, he gives substantive recommendations on how to become a high-performing leader in a high-performing organization. His ten recommendations should be carefully considered and implemented by leaders who want their organization to perform better.

—**DAN WALLRATH**, Founder, Operation Finally Home

WE'RE
NOT
ROBOTS

WE'RE NOT ROBOTS

How Leading with Humanity
Creates High-Performing Organizations

LIEUTENANT GENERAL RICK LYNCH
U.S. ARMY (RETIRED)

with Mark Dagostino

For information about this title, contact the publisher:

Lieutenant General Rick Lynch U.S. Army (Retired)
www.rlynchenterprises.com
ricky.lynch55@gmail.com

ISBNs:
978-1-7378833-4-0 (hardcover)
978-1-7378833-5-7 (softcover)
978-1-7378833-6-4 (eBook)

Printed in the United States of America

Cover and Interior design: 1106 Design

I give all glory to God, and all thanks to my Family
(Sarah, Susan, Lucas, JW, Rex, and Piper)
for their love and support.
None of this would be possible without you.
You are my everything!

ACKNOWLEDGMENTS

I could not have finished this book without the help of so many people. Every conversation I have had with friends, peers, and colleagues over the past several years has contributed immensely to the content of *We're Not Robots*. They are too numerous to mention, but I would like to thank each one. I hope I correctly captured our thoughts and ideas. I would like to single out two folks, Sandy Costa and Steve Suttles. Candidly, I would not have written my fourth book without Sandy's constant urging and encouragement. Our monthly calls have become so very important to me . . . and I leave each call more enlightened and a better man. Steve tolerated my constant questioning during our weekly breakfasts and had amazing insights into each topic in the book. His input was invaluable. As always, I can't do any of this without the help of Mark Dagostino. We have been together 12 years now, and this is our fourth book together. His passion, insights, and amazing skills and professionalism are a joy to work with. Last but certainly not least I would like to thank one of my mentors, Lieutenant General Walt Ulmer, US Army (Retired). Walt has taught me so very much about leadership since we first met at West Point more than 50 years ago, when he was the commandant of cadets, and he is still helping me a become better leader to this very day. I am indeed still a work in progress.

TABLE OF CONTENTS

AUTHOR'S NOTE

While the stories and examples I'm about to share with you are drawn directly from my experience spent working with more than thirty companies all across America over the past twelve years, I have chosen to leave out the names and specific details of the companies in question as a means to protect the innocent—and, I suppose, as a means to protect the guilty. Because while some of these companies might enjoy seeing their names in print when I reference their moments of triumph or good practices for all the world to see, publicly sharing the names of certain leaders and companies who failed their employees—and/or failed their shareholders—would simply be rude and untoward.

So while names, pronouns, circumstances, etc., have been altered to maintain anonymity, please know that the stories and outcomes shared here are true. They actually happened. What matters most is how the lessons learned from the examples you're about to read can be applied to what you and your organization choose to do from here on out.

INTRODUCTION

Back in the mid-1980s, I acquired a nickname: They called me "The High-Tech Redneck." Why? Because the Army had the foresight to send me from my comfortable position as a captain in Fort Knox, Kentucky, to the hallowed halls of MIT—the Massachusetts Institute of Technology, perhaps the most prestigious technology school in the country—to study an emerging field called robotics.

I didn't know what "robotics" meant. I had to look up the word in the dictionary. But as someone who sees every challenge as an opportunity, I took the assignment happily. My wife, Sarah, and I moved up to Boston, and while the two of us struggled together to get through the harsh winter weather, I struggled through the most difficult academic environment I'd ever encountered.

Two years later, I passed my coursework, earned my master's degree, and went back to Fort Knox with a high-tech expertise that was light years ahead of that of my peers, and light years ahead of most of my superiors; so much so that the General Officer in charge of Fort Knox sent me, still a young captain and only eight years into my Army career, to meetings in his place. Soon, I became one of the leading voices on adapting robotics technology to use to our advantage on the battlefield.

Today, whether you bring up a YouTube video of a modern-day, fire-breathing, combat-ready robot dog, or watch an intricate performance of coordinated drones lighting up the sky over Disney World, what you're seeing is built on a foundation of some of the technology I helped to design and put into action, way back when. Including a system that would eliminate the need for one of four human crew members to ride in a tank—a system that would adjust to conditions, damage, and more while loading 60-pound rounds into the chamber, while moving 45 mph on the battlefield. A robotics system that would be perfected by others over time in order to save human lives on our side while giving us a strategic advantage in combat.

People talk a lot about Artificial Intelligence these days, and we were talking about it then, too. But what we created in the 1980s wasn't really intelligence, and it's still not intelligent now, if you ask me. Programming robots to learn and adjust on the fly has always been a matter of creating algorithms that mimic the rote-learning techniques we humans sometimes use. Just because you can watch a TikTok video and learn how to solve a Rubik's Cube doesn't make you smart, does it? It just means you can follow a flowchart. It doesn't come close to the full human experience of "learning" and "intelligence" at all. But I'll get back to that point in a bit.

Upon retiring from the Army as a three-star general after 35 years, my first position in the civilian world centered on robotics research, too: I was hired to lead The University of Texas at Arlington Research Institute (UTARI).

Back when I took the reins of that large research institute near Dallas, UTARI had spent 25 years achieving less than a million dollars a year in terms of research expenditures. And the president of the university set a lofty goal when he hired me: He wanted to increase our research expenditures to $100 million a year over the next 15 years. So, immediately I was tasked with creating a work environment where all of my people had to work together to look for better, more innovative ways of doing business. We had no choice but to turn ourselves into a High-Performing Organization, or there was no way we were gonna make it. How did I accomplish that? To start, I had to step back, listen, and learn. I got everybody at UTARI together—I didn't care if it was the janitor or the Senior Research Scientist—and we all started brainstorming: "What should we be doing that we're not doing? What are we doing that makes no sense? What are we doing that's wasting time and energy, and consuming our resources?"

I listened, using everyone's input, and, together, we solidified what it was we had to do. We moved forward with a shared Vision and a concrete set of Values and Operating Principles, creating a Strategic Plan that laid out goals we hoped to achieve in the next 5, 10, and 15 years.

Just four years later, when I chose to leave to focus on building my consulting business outside of UTARI, we had increased research expenditures to more than $15 million per year. We were well on our way to achieving the president's goal, and the organization as a whole was set up to continue on that path, full stop, even in my absence.

The reason I mention this right up front is mostly to point out that I've learned a thing or two about how to get things done. It's also to point out that I know a thing or two about robots. And I can tell you one thing: People are not robots. Robots have no empathy. Sure, they can mimic empathy and other feelings through the trained use of certain words and deeds. But they fail to meet the very definition of the word "empathy" because they do not have "the ability to understand and share the feelings of others." They can't. They're not human.

Why is it important to point this out?

Because sometimes, certain leaders in the corporate world overlook this fact. They act like robots, and they treat their workers like robots, too.

I'm here to tell you: That's a recipe for disaster. It's an outlook that embraces mediocrity, encourages poor performance, and—at its worst—leads to long-term organizational failure.

High-Performing Organizations are made up of teams of human beings. Living, breathing, feeling human beings. And that is not a weakness. Quite the opposite. It is the ultimate mark of strength. It is our humaneness which serves at the core of what we do best—as business-people, as leaders, as brothers and sisters, and mothers and fathers, as members of our communities, and even as soldiers. The Army recognized this more than twenty years ago, when we realized that the way to create a higher-performing, more-efficient, and resilient Army was to stop treating our men and women in uniform like machines, and instead start treating them like the human beings they are. Human beings capable of incredible performance, ingenuity, resilience, and power, at the very same time they require routine assessment and mentorship, time to heal, time to be with their families, and to gather strength from having strong, human-to-human relationships with their senior officers.

From the top, we stopped talking *down* to our men and women in uniform, and instead, we started talking *with* them—which led to a whole lot of listening and learning.

Since then, even in these times of global challenges, strained budgets, and dwindling numbers of volunteer soldiers, the Army has grown stronger—because the Army started caring about its people.

And if Corporate America wants to grow stronger, too, it absolutely needs to do the same.

I've been out of the Army for twelve years now, and let me say this up front: I loved my Army career. But I've also loved the time I've spent outside of the Army, engaging with Corporate America, leading organizations, consulting with and training everyone from first-day employees to seasoned CEOs at corporations big and small for more than a decade now. Why? Because I've continued to build upon the very same passion I pursued in the military—not a passion for building robots, but a passion to build concerned, caring, compassionate, adaptive leaders across our nation.

If you've read any of my previous books, you already know that I am absolutely convinced that the solution to our nation's problems—and, candidly, the world's problems—resides in effective leadership. And what better place to continue to develop leaders, at all levels, than in the trenches of Corporate America?

Accepting the position at UTARI came on the heels of my last job in the Army: A Pentagon role, running all of the Army's installations, worldwide. That's 163 installations around the world, employing 120,000 people, only 2,000 of whom were soldiers. The rest were government employees and contract civilians. It was the equivalent of running a Fortune 100 company with a $20-billion budget, while also acting as a city manager for 163 cities, complete with transportation and waste-management issues, and everything else a city manager might encounter. During those two years, I was also tasked with overseeing a massive, *25-percent* budget cut in the middle of my tenure as "CEO." So it's not a stretch to say I was already teed up with some understanding of the sorts of issues Corporate America faces, but I'm also humble enough to acknowledge that I didn't truly understand the particular challenges Corporate America faced until I started living them firsthand these last twelve years.

I've now worked intimately across a wide range of pharmaceutical companies, distribution outfits, robotics developers, financial institutions, construction companies, consulting companies—even a grocery-store chain and a top-of-the-line hotel. They all faced challenges they had to work through, because, as I've said in every book and every speech I've given, the world is a Volatile, Uncertain, Complex, and Ambiguous place. That's VUCA in military-speak, and while the term was invented to describe certain battlefield scenarios, it most certainly applies to the corporate world today. I know, because I've seen it in every field: As soon as we think we got things figured out, something happens; some changing circumstance causes the need for effective, adaptive leadership and an adaptive workforce capable of making it over, under, and through a set of unexpected obstacles.

I feel blessed that I've been able to help watch and care for my clients—not only C Suite executives, but people at all levels—as they worked through some of these difficult issues. And now? It's time to share what I've learned.

In the military, one of our greatest strengths is found in what we call an "After-Action Review." For every event, whether it's a training event or a combat event, when it's over, we stop and say, "Okay, what happened? What can we learn from that?" And then: "How can we apply what we've learned in order to be better in the future?"

In general terms, I guess you could say that this book is an "After-Action Review" of my twelve-plus years working with Corporate America. I'll highlight the things that worked well, from my perspective, and I'll highlight the things that didn't work so well—all with the goal of letting you learn a few things, so that you can apply those lessons to your own organization, no matter how big or small. My hope is that people will take the lessons they find in this book and apply them, so that their corporations become more effective, regardless of what kinds of corporations they might be.

And that's important. Because if you're not facing uncertainties and obstacles right at this moment, you will. It's inevitable. It's also inevitable that without some training, you might feel like you can't get through whatever new challenge is placed in front of you; as if you suddenly have no choice but to reinvent the wheel and write a new chapter for your organization—and do so without a guidebook.

Well, I'm here to tell you that the wheel already exists, and the page is never blank. For every circumstance you might go through, somebody else has already gone through a similar circumstance. If you take time to learn from them, you're more likely to succeed.

I want this book to be that guide for you. That reference you can turn to. Only what I'm giving you here is even stronger than the advice or guidance you might get from an individual who went through one particular trying moment. It's an overview, a summary report, a broad After-Action Review filled with information gained from experience at more than thirty different companies. And if you can't learn something from all of that, then you probably aren't listenin'!

The power of learning from the recent past is at a peak right now, because, if you remember, starting back in the beginning of 2020, we as a nation went through the COVID-19 pandemic. If ever there was a test of Corporate America's abilities to "adapt or die" under pressure, this was it. (*Adapt or Die* also happens to be the title of my first book on adaptive leadership, and if you haven't picked up the 10th Anniversary Edition of that book, I encourage you to do so.)

During COVID, I saw clients work their way through the challenges, and I saw some of them flourish, even in difficult times. I also saw some of them collapse. The deciding factor between the two outcomes was simple: It all came down to how empathetic and human the corporate leaders were in their treatment of their employees. And in the face of that, every leader of every company in the world should be asking themselves, right now: "How can we emulate the best practices of companies that thrived during COVID, as we prepare ourselves *now* for the next pandemic or global crisis that comes along?"

My goal is to help you answer that question, not just with ideas, but with concrete steps you can take to strengthen your organization, starting right now.

Like I said, this book is all about sharing lessons learned, and one of my mentors—a guy you may have heard of, named General Colin Powell—wrote a book entitled *It Worked for Me*. In it, he captured thirteen leadership lessons that he used over and over again throughout his career, both in the Army and as a civilian leader. He wanted to break things down and make it easy to share those lessons with a larger audience, and that's what I'm aiming to do here. I'm going to work my way through several topics and several chapters, and, at the end, give you a summary list of some of the actions you can take, which I believe—scratch that, which I *know*—will translate to higher achievement and better success at any type of corporation, big or small.

I'll also amplify these observations through the use of stories. And please note: I've made a conscious point not to put any thumbprints on most of the events themselves, so you can't trace back and find out which company or which individual had the particular successes or struggles I'm talking about. I've done that out of respect for these companies and their leaders, and I hope you find that the power of the lessons of the stories themselves loses nothing in translation. After all, what I'm sharing with you doesn't come from some academic, theoretical study, poll, or statistical analysis. It all comes from real-life, on-the-ground experience.

I'll share a different kind of story to help drive home some of the larger points as well. As some of you may know, in addition to the leadership training and consulting work I've been busy with for the last twelve years, I've spent the last seven years taking folks from Corporate America on Leadership Tours to historic locations across the country and around the world. Why? Because I am absolutely convinced that we can refine our leadership skills by studying leaders from times past. Using the lens of history to teach leadership, I've taken groups from all sorts of different organizations to see the beaches at Normandy, to look at those cliffs and stand on that sand that played such a pivotal role in the outcome of World War II. I've taken folks to Gettysburg and Vicksburg; to Little Bighorn, and to Chickamauga, Georgia, just to name a few of the places where modern-day America was won and where so many of our ancestors' lives were lost. I've also taken groups to Selma, Alabama, where a different type of battle was fought. In each case, we studied what happened. More importantly, we studied the leaders to learn what they did or did not do, and to talk about how we can apply those lessons learned to what we're doing today, including to our efforts to become better leaders.

I'm planning lots of Leadership Tours to the above-mentioned sites and others in the months and years ahead, and at each site, we'll be sure to ask and answer questions such as: "During these extreme examples of war and social upheaval, what did those individual leaders do? *Why* did they do it? And what was the outcome of the actions they took?" We'll then ask, "How does this historic example apply to what we're doing in the boardroom, or the C Suite, or in everyday conversations we're having with our Sales Teams, Marketing Teams, and more?"

People sometimes argue with me about the relevance of the decisions these historic leaders made. The brave ones even raise their hands and say, "Well, Rick, what we're dealing with at our company isn't a life-or-death situation, so it's just not the same." And to that, I say, "Wrong." In whatever kind of a company you're leading or working for, you've got people's lives in your hands *every day*. If your company goes belly up, people are likely to lose their homes. Whole communities could be deeply affected by the loss of jobs. If you misjudge an upcoming quarter or don't have a plan for the inevitable ups and downs, and end up laying people off, there are whole families that will be plunged into crisis and upheaval—and don't go telling me, "It wasn't my fault." If you were the one responsible for leading those people, then all of that upheaval is on *you*! And if you cut corners, if you don't get your testing and research right, if you act less than honestly and ethically, perhaps allowing glitches in your manufacturing process or something worse, then somebody using your product, whether it's a new drug, a medical device, a car, a toy, a circuit board, an appliance, or just about anything else, could not only get hurt, but *die*. So don't tell me that what you do isn't life or death. *It is*.

So that's another part of what you're gonna get when you read this book: lessons learned from history; specific examples of things that worked in difficult circumstances, and specific examples of things that *didn't* work, too, in which lives, battles, and sometimes entire wars were lost. I know that you can absolutely learn from every one of them.

I also know this: In the dozens of keynotes I've given at corporate outings and leadership conferences since leaving the Army, I always tell my audiences, "You gain more from criticism than you do from applause." I hope you'll keep that in mind as you read this book, especially if you come across something you're doing at your organization that I happen to criticize in these pages. If I'm describing a poor practice at an organization, and it feels a bit like you're looking in the mirror, I ask you: Please, don't turn away. Instead, stand tall and look deeper. Listen up. Read that passage again. Because if all people do is continue to tell you how great you are, you'll never grow; but if you listen closely to things that you might have done better, and then work to improve them, you'll *do* better. And by doing better, by continually improving, no matter how high of a position you're in, that's a sure-fire way to get where you want to go—to the end goal of creating, maintaining, and leading truly High-Performing Organizations.

That is the overriding theme of this book: "How can your company become a High-Performing Organization?"

I know there are a lot of folks who've written about HPOs, calling them "High-*Performance* Organizations," but I think the focal point of that phrase needs to change. It should focus on a verb, not a noun or an adjective: "Performing" is an active endeavor. It shouldn't be measured on past results. It needs to be current and future oriented: How can we perform *better*? How *will* we perform better? What specific activities can you undertake that will allow us, as a corporation, and me, as an individual, to *do better*?

The surprising thing I've observed about so many corporations in this country, especially the ones that are *not* acting as High-Performing Organizations, is that they just aren't paying attention to the things I'm about to share with you. And the frustrating part about that is this: It ain't rocket science. All it takes to become an HPO is a shift in mindset, some active, engaged leadership, and enough humility to realize that no one—not even *you*—has all the answers. Especially when the going gets tough.

And it *will* get tough. I guarantee it. Some challenge you can't even see right now is waiting up ahead, and it's gonna hit your company like an IED (an Improvised Explosive Device)—when you least expect it. If that doesn't scare you, it should, because unless you're scared, chances are you're not getting prepared.

Never forget that we are a nation at risk. We've got external threats like Russia, China, North Korea, and Iran. We also have internal threats from things like a growing lack of respect for law-enforcement personnel and first responders, which, in part, originates from the massive threat of divisive people: leaders, politicians, and media personalities within our own ranks who divide us for personal gain, regardless of the consequences to our nation. We also have a very real issue with internal threats from domestic terrorism, some of which is egged on by these divisive people. Plus, who can say what new virus will emerge, or what old virus will mutate and turn into the next pandemic?

I am convinced that the solution to all these problems starts with better leadership.

And one way we can do better is by leading more effectively in the corporate world. By creating and maintaining High-Performing Organizations through Engaged Leadership. By establishing shared Vision, Values, and Operating Principles. By tackling Corporate America's severe lack of effective performance appraisals, head-on. By using routine counseling as a means to fend off our fear of letting poor performers go, while simultaneously protecting our companies against the threat of post-exit litigation. By learning not to accept mediocrity on our teams. By bolstering trust and commitment in order to foster better teamwork, which leads to innovation. We need to take the necessary steps to ensure that we create and maintain the types of nimble, adaptive, truly High-Performing Organizations that are ready to weather any storm; to pivot in new directions when the path we're on suddenly becomes impassable; and to turn even unseen obstacles into opportunities.

Now tell me: Who *doesn't* want to work for an organization like that?

How do we get there? How do we ensure that it happens?

In short, we need to remember: We're Not Robots. We must do the human work it takes to get our workers, our leaders, our teams, and our entire organizations working together, so we can all move forward—creating and maintaining the High-Performing Organizations that we want and need more of in America, right now.

That is the purpose of this book, and I hope that you enjoy reading it.

PART I

Define Your Values

CHAPTER 1

TAKE CARE OF YOUR PEOPLE

Ever since I first started working with corporate clients more than twelve years ago, there's been one overriding general trend that's become obvious to me: Organizations that truly, truly take care of their people are far more likely to be successful than those that don't.

"Take care of your people, and they will take care of you." There's a reason that phrase exists. Because it's true. It's not new. It's not some groundbreaking, novel approach to running an organization. It's a tried-and-true fact—one that, for some reason, too many leaders ignore at their own peril.

In my previous books, I talked a lot about taking care of people. My nine Leadership Principles from *Adapt or Die* (which are listed in Appendix I) were *all* about taking care of people. And almost every time I give a speech, I remind audiences of the phrase that my wife taught me and reminds me of all the time: "People don't care how much you know, until they know how much you care."

Why does it matter to the people in your organization that you and your company care about them? Because they're people. No matter how hard certain leaders (and boards) want to believe that people are just another expendable component or commodity to be used or discarded as necessary on the road to increasing revenues and shareholder value, they're not. They're not machines. They're human. And unlike robots, at those crucial moments when things go wrong—not *if* they go wrong, but *when*, because it's inevitable that things will go wrong for your company—people who feel neglected, unloved, and uncared for by their company are likely to roll over, give up, or walk out, while those who feel cared for won't. In fact, people who feel that their company and their bosses take care of them will look turmoil and challenges in the eye and do something miraculous: They'll want to work even harder. Why? Because they don't want to let their company down. They don't want to let their *leadership* down.

That's just human nature.

Coming out of the COVID pandemic, you would think that the importance of fostering an organization full of workers who actually want to work and work well in the face of tremendous challenges would be a no-brainer. But it's not. Big ideas like this too often get lost in the shuffle of the day-to-day challenges of running a business. Too many corporate leaders fail to make and take the time to think, and see, and plan in any big-picture way. Which is why you'll hear me highlight the idea of *Taking Care of People*—including *you*—time and again over the course of this book.

If we're not taking time to think, and we're acting like robots not interested in taking care of our people, then no amount of leadership training I can provide here is going to help you create and maintain a High-Performing Organization. And I know some of you are probably skeptical, thinking, "What does an Army General who led troops into combat know about taking care of people?" Or something really off, like, "Why should we take care of our people when most of our people are useless?" But I hope you'll stick with me. My whole career has been built on the idea of taking care of people first, and what I'm about to show you is that the upside of taking care of people (beyond the fact that it's just a good and decent stance to take in life) is ultimately more stability, along with ingenuity, durability, agility, endurance, profit, and, overall, more happiness and fulfillment for all involved. Even *you*, the *skeptic*.

I do believe in the basic goodness of people. I'm 69 years old as I write this, and I don't believe I've ever come across somebody who truly *wants* to do poorly. In all my years, I've never come across somebody who comes to work every day and says, "Hey, I'm gonna screw up today. And then I'll go home, and tomorrow, I'll come in and do it again and, hopefully, screw up even more!" I don't see that. Instead, what I see is the basic goodness of people who want to do well.

Some of them don't do well, of course. Some of them screw up royally. And we should always examine those folks and what's going wrong on a case-by-case basis, so we know *why* some of them do well and some of them don't, so we aren't just guessing. We'll talk about how to do this, routinely, as a regular course of doing business, in Part II. But let me give you a clue as to why, in most cases, people don't do well at their jobs right now: Candidly, it's a result of ineffective leadership.

It used to aggravate me when I'd have conversations with people, and they'd want to put all the blame for poor performance on a bad boss. But the evidence I've gathered now, after twelve full years of study, is awfully hard to refute.

I also don't believe in gross stereotypes as they tend to be laid down from the top. I can't stand it when I'm talking to a CEO or Senior VP or a whole group of top execs at a company, and they want to label an entire generation of younger people with having no work ethic, saying that they're all too entitled, or that they're lazy. I don't buy that. I've seen youngsters who have a passion to work hard and do well. I also see youngsters who just don't want to work and want somebody else to provide for them. But it has nothing to do with age or generational issues. So let's get those kinds of sweeping generalities out of our heads right now, before we get any deeper into this.

You certainly can't take care of people if you start out by (wrongly) thinking they're not worthy of your care.

Instead, as leaders, we have to start out with the goal of creating a High-Performing Organization in our minds. And in order to build an HPO, we have to believe in the people who are part of the organization itself. We have to start thinking, *What are we going to do, specifically, to get everybody in this outfit to be a valued member of our team, so that they can contribute to this HPO?*

In order to build a High-Performing Organization, you need to create an organization in which everyone contributes. *Everyone.* Which means *every person* in that organization has to feel valued and be encouraged to want to contribute to the absolute best of their abilities. And the best way to do that is to reassure them of their value from day one.

When I was in command of the Corps at Fort Hood, Texas—the largest Army installation in America—every Wednesday, my wife, Sarah, and I greeted our new arrivals to the installation personally. They'd come over to the NCO Club (the Non-Commissioned Officers Club), and we'd stand up—I'd tell them what they could expect of me and what I expected of them. And then I'd ask the audience, "Who out there is seventeen?" Because believe it or not, we've got soldiers enlisting in the Army at age seventeen, just because they *can.* They aren't allowed to deploy until after they turn eighteen, but they can enlist. And they do.

So, one of the seventeen-year-olds in the crowd would come up, and I'd have him stand right on stage next to me. I'd look at him, and I'd say, "Well, how old are you?"

They'd give me that look like my teenage kids would when I already knew the answer to the question. They'd say, "General, you already asked that. I'm seventeen."

"Well, how old do you think I am?" I'd ask, and the audience would chuckle from the safety of their seats. The smartest ones responded, "Well, General, when I look at you, I think you are about 35." That made me feel good. I was around fifty-three at the time. If they said, "Well, you look like you're in your mid-60s," I'd correct them. Then I'd ask them what our difference in age is, and it's amazing how many of them had a hard time doing the subtraction of seventeen from fifty-three when they were up on stage.

"I'll answer for you," I said. "The difference between us is thirty-six years of life. So I've had thirty-six years' more education and experience than you did. So, does that make you less important than me?"

Inevitably they would answer, "Yes, sir," thinking I was trying to trap them in some kind of a trick question, and not wanting to go toe-to-toe with the General.

But I'd look them in the eye and say, "No, son. You're as important as I am."

I would take this brand-new private and rip his rank right off his uniform. (Our rank insignia are held on by Velcro, so don't worry.) Then I'd rip my stars off of my uniform, and put his rank on me, and mine on him.

I'd have my photographer take a picture, and the audience would applaud. Then I'd send the picture to the parents and say, "Your son impressed us so much that we put him in charge for thirty seconds on his very first day."

Why did I do that every Wednesday, with all the new recruits?

I did it to demonstrate their value. To let them know they're *important*. The private is as important as the Lieutenant General, and in the corporate world, everybody is equally important, too. Some people just have experience and education that other people don't have. That doesn't make them a more-important person.

You've got to empower every member of your team to know that they're valued members of the team. Their input is important, and what they do is important. I don't care if you're the Private or the Lieutenant General. I don't care if you're the machinist or the CEO. Your input is as important as everybody else's in a High-Performing Organization. The leaders at an HPO realize that a break at any link in the chain of command still leaves you with a broken chain.

Showing empathy and taking care of your people doesn't mean you go easy on 'em. You still have to be demanding, and you *always* want to raise the bar. Everybody who ever worked with me would say, "Lynch is never satisfied." I took that as a compliment, not as criticism, because we should always be trying to do better. That's how you build a High-Performing Organization. So it's good to be demanding. Just don't be demeaning.

> A break at any link in the chain . . . still leaves you with a broken chain

I mean, have you ever worked for a demeaning boss? I have. People who would belittle you in public and doubt your contributions, scream at you—I've had all of that, and their actions certainly didn't build trust or respect. Don't do that. Leading with empathy, integrity, and care has more upside, and a lack of integrity hurts the bottom line, period.

We'll get into all of this more later in the book, but it's important to keep these things in mind from the start: Taking Care of Your People *matters*. Get that one idea into your head, and try to keep it there and to use that point of reference in every decision you make. You'll be off to a great start.

"MISSION FIRST, PEOPLE ALWAYS."

To go a little deeper into this concept, which, again, will show up in discussions throughout the rest of the book, I want to share a couple examples of what "Take Care of Your People" can look like. It doesn't *have* to look like these particular things at your organization, but it *can*. Ultimately, it's up to leaders to decide what's right for their companies and what it truly means to take care of the employees who make up their teams.

There's a well-known phrase in the military that I believe should apply to every aspect of American leadership: "Mission First, People Always."

It means that we must care for our people, no matter what our mission is, and no matter how our mission changes. Our people are at the heart of everything we do. *Always.*

I know that sounds confusing to some people when we're talking about the military. How can we go possibly go into combat—an arena in which some of our people are potentially going to get *killed*—and say we're "taking care of our people"?

In general terms, I'll say this: Sometimes the mission of keeping America safe, protecting the sovereignty of our nation and the essence of our freedom, requires great sacrifice. And accomplishing that mission means the military is doing the job of taking care of America's people at the highest, most-honorable level possible. The American people are the very reason we fight, the very reason we serve.

But on the ground, what "Mission First, People Always" meant to me was doing everything I could to take care of the people in my charge. It meant never losing sight of the fact that whether we were deploying to combat or not, every single one of my soldiers was a human being. A person. Not a robot. Not an expendable commodity. But a *person*. And more than that, a person with a family who deserved the utmost care, attention, and appreciation I could afford to give them.

On the ground in Iraq, it was not unusual for me to lend soldiers my satellite phone so they could call home and talk to their moms, or their wives, or their sons or daughters. I would get on those calls myself, just to let them know what a great job their child or spouse or parent was doing, and to thank those family members for the sacrifice *they* were making by allowing their son or daughter or mom or dad to serve their nation.

On a daily basis, I made myself available to any soldier who needed to ask a question, or just to get something off his or her chest. My door was always open.

In the evenings, I'd invite soldiers to come smoke a cigar with me. In the mornings, I'd invite soldiers to work out alongside me, or to join me for morning prayers if they were interested.

We were all in this together, and I let them know that through my actions.

Being human with your employees is something I'll talk about later in this book as well, and I know it rubs some HR directors the wrong way. We've put up a sort of "church-and-state" type wall in Corporate America, with this false idea that work is work, and life is life, and those two things should never be intertwined. That's a lousy idea, even on paper, and some business major likely came up with it as a way to justify a bunch of soulless decisions based on nothing but making money in a vacuum. But life isn't a vacuum. People are people, whether they're at work or at home, and there is no real-world separation of the two.

A LESSON FROM HISTORY

The thing is, this idea of a leader paying attention to the home lives, spouses, children, etc., of their workers isn't new or "woke." It predates the very existence of HR departments. In fact, a man who many still consider the greatest leader in American history took his subordinates' family matters into consideration all the time. I'm talking about President Abraham Lincoln. One fine example of the attention he paid came early in the Civil War, when he noticed that the stress of battle was taking a toll on one of his most promising Generals—General Ulysses S. Grant (who would later lead the entire Union Army and become President himself). As the war heated up, Lincoln got word that Grant was drinking a little too much whiskey. At first, he laughed about it, saying, "Well, what kind of whiskey is he drinking? Because we ought to give some to the rest of my Generals." But he also knew things wouldn't end well if the drinking continued unabated. We didn't have 12-step programs or rehab centers in the mid-1800s, and there was no way that Lincoln was going to relieve one of his most-promising General Officers from duty. So, as a way to help Grant cope with the strain, he called upon Grant's wife, Julia. Lincoln knew Julia the way a leader should know the spouse of any of their top commanders, and he knew that Julia would be a calming influence on her husband. So he reached out to her and asked her to join him at Grant's headquarters in the field. Not on the front line, but not hundreds of miles away, either. To be there when he came back from battle, to help him regroup and collect his thoughts without the sense of isolation that war can sometimes impose upon a General Officer.

Julia's calming influence was exactly what Grant needed, and the fact that he went on to lead the Union Army to victory, and later to become President of the United States himself, can be traced back in great part to the influence of Julia—who would later become one of our strongest First Ladies.

So don't tell me that spouses and other familial influences don't matter. In the military, we always included spouses, going so far sometimes as to *require* their attendance at major military functions. To this day, I recommend that my wife, Sarah, travel with me everywhere I go—to every speaking engagement, every consultation. Her history as a military spouse to a Three-Star General is enormously important, as she brings another perspective to the table in all matters—an important perspective. Corporate leaders who don't take advantage of that kind of knowledge and connection from the spouses of their own team members are missing out.

What we can't forget is that spousal involvement is present, whether we take advantage of it or pay attention to it or not. When it's *not* paid attention to, there are times when a spouse's influence can go too far and cause problems. For example: As a contrast to the Julia Grant story, just look to the influence of Libby Custer.

Libby Custer was the wife of General George Armstrong Custer, a Union cavalry officer who was quickly elevated during the Civil War to become the youngest-ever Brigadier General in the United States. Watching her husband's quick rise to fame and glory, Libby developed some high aspirations: She desperately wanted to see her husband become President of the United States.

There was just one hitch in her plans, though. When the war ended, Custer got reverted from Brigadier General back to Lieutenant Colonel, and that came as a big hit to his ego. It shouldn't have. Many young soldiers were called upon to take high positions in a war that killed so many of the Army's top leaders. But once the war was over, those relatively inexperienced and untrained soldiers needed to be put back into a hierarchy that made sense to the Army as a whole. But Custer was crushed, and there are all sorts of stories of him struggling from 1865 to 1876. Then, finally, he was given the opportunity to lead a large force in the Seventh Cavalry to go capture a bunch of escaped Native Americans (they called them "Indians" back then) and put them back on the reservation the U.S. government had set up for them. Libby Custer said, "Hey, George, this is your chance to get back out in the national media. To get your picture back on the front of the magazines!" As Custer was getting ready to head out for what would become the Battle of Little Bighorn, Libby had her eyes set on the Democratic National Convention, which was only one month away. She had convinced herself that he was going to do so well at this assignment of killing and capturing Indians that it would make him a public hero, which would make him the shoo-in to become the Democratic nominee for president.

One can't help but wonder: *If Libby hadn't pushed him so hard to go in there and act like a hero for the cameras, would he have spent more time nurturing and developing the soldiers who served as his backup team on the battlefield?* A backup team that didn't show up when he needed them. A backup team that failed to back him up, in what would famously become known as "Custer's Last Stand"—the battle that cost him his life.

PRIORITIES MATTER

Leadership isn't about being in charge or making yourself famous. It's about taking care of those *in* your charge. Caring about your people's families is a part of the deal if you're going to lead any High-Performing Organization.

Keeping this in mind during all of my decisions as a leader is a fairly easy thing for me to do, in part because I have a set of priorities that I keep front-of-mind every moment of every day: My relationship with God is number one; my relationship with my family is number two; and my profession is priority number three. Having those priorities in place has served me well. They're the bedrock of who I am. And having priorities in place at a corporate level is just as important.

Which means that it's important for us, as leaders who want to take care of our people, to think about making decisions for our *people*. As humans. Not as robots, and not just as cogs in a wheel, but as people. And people have spouses, partners, friends, and family whom they (hopefully) want to take care of, and who also have a strong influence on them.

In my first two books, I talked about many of these sorts of human decisions I made as a leader in the Army, and especially while I was Commander at Fort Hood. But in case you haven't read them, and as a reminder to those who *have* read them, here are a few examples: I insisted on soldiers taking mandatory family time as part of their regular work schedules. I built a Spiritual Fitness Center on base, where soldiers and their families could come for non-denominational guidance and support to deal with their troubles and express their faith as needed. I insisted that all soldiers and their superiors go home early on Thursdays to play sports, or coach Little League, or just be there for their kids. I insisted that they leave at the end of the workday instead of working late all the time. I insisted they not work weekends (unless their job called specifically for weekend work), and more. Why? Because I recognized that every one of our soldiers is a person, and the more well-balanced and happier they were as *people*, the better soldiers they would be to the Army.

I did not have a legal obligation to think that way or to take those actions. In fact, it was the opposite of the way many leaders in the Army had run things for a lot of years. But I *did* have empathy for my soldiers, and I believe that I had a moral obligation, and an ethical obligation, to bring my values to the workplace as a leader. Work-life balance, spiritual fitness, physical fitness, family connections—those things matter to me. They matter to Sarah. In my view, it would be wrong of me to pretend that those things *don't* matter to the people who were directly under my command.

We're talking about 65,000 people on that base. That's 65,000 people who had no choice but to follow my orders.

So how did that work out? Did bringing my moral and ethical values to my leadership position in the Army work against me? Did productivity, output, discipline, safety, readiness, or anything else suffer because I treated my subordinates and direct reports as the people they are? *No!* In fact, Fort Hood enjoyed measurably improved productivity and safety statistics while under my command.

The same applies in Corporate America: Taking care of your people is a profitable venture. And it's not just me saying it. Billionaire entrepreneur Richard Branson has famously stated, "Take care of your employees, and they'll take care of your business. It's as simple as that." And bestselling author and motivational speaker Simon Sinek put the onus on leaders: "Leadership is not a rank, it is a responsibility. Leadership is not about being in charge, it is about taking care of those in your charge." And I couldn't agree more.

As a leader in the Army, I commanded 25,000 soldiers in Iraq as part of the Surge. I commanded the largest installation in the free world, Fort Hood, Texas, at a time when it was 65,000 soldiers strong. I led more than 120,000 mostly civilian employees across military installations around the world during my time at the Pentagon. And I saw to it that Taking Care of my People was my #1 priority in every position I held.

I've also had the great privilege of working with some of the best companies in America since my time in the Army ended, and, without fail, the best companies are the ones who take care of their people. They do so in lots of different ways, of course, but, without fail, their actions and deeds always match their words.

The example I'm about to share could not be more personal to me and my family. It's an example that involves one of the largest privately held corporations in America—a company that I consult with, and a company that happens to employ my son, Lucas. (You may have read about this in the 10th Anniversary Edition of *Adapt or Die*.)

This company provides its employees with a fantastic health plan—not a traditional health plan, but a custom-fit, cohesive plan that is personally funded by its CEO. Yes, you read that right: The CEO personally funds the healthcare coverage offered to his employees. He doesn't even call them "employees." He calls them "partners." And that's what they are. If you work for his company, you're family. You're a part of a team. And those aren't just empty words on a corporate mission statement. That partnership is demonstrated in actions and deeds.

Just a few years ago, my son went through a major health crisis. One that required a surgery to save his life. A surgery that cost hundreds of thousands of dollars. But because he worked for a company that values taking care of people, Lucas was taken care of when he needed it. That's a simple-enough equation to understand.

My son is alive and well, and not bankrupt or suffering in debt—because his employer values him as a human being.

Reciprocally, how loyal do you think my son feels now to his employer? If Lucas ever thinks about changing careers, do you think he'll look at companies that *don't* value their employees the way this particular company does?

Companies that don't have a reputation for taking care of their people won't ever have a shot at hiring my son. *Ever.* And in a post-COVID world, more and more employees are choosing their employers with this moral imperative in mind: If they don't feel that a company cares about its people, they'll walk (or run) to work somewhere else, or they won't bother taking the job in the first place.

Leaders of companies that don't care about their people are left scratching their heads, in a constant state of turnover turbulence—turmoil that costs them time, money, and stability when they need it most.

Now, healthcare coverage is a controversial topic, and I'm not going to get into the fray on whether our government should do more, or whether corporate entities should work harder to lower healthcare costs for individuals. That's not the important point here. What is important is that, at the corporate level, a lot of our more Wall Street-minded leaders have come to the conclusion that healthcare costs are simply too high, and their response has been to do their best to spend as little on employee healthcare as possible.

On paper, for shareholder value, making those sorts of decisions might make sense—especially in the short term, when looking at quarterly share price. But the important piece that's often left out of the equation in their response to cut back is that without healthy, functioning, financially able people, you don't *have* a company, let alone a productive one.

Without healthy people, there is *no* productivity.

Putting the idea of Taking Care of People first, knowing that it leads to positive results, there is just no way that a company would want to shortchange its workforce in terms of healthcare coverage, is there?

When you stop acting like a robot, when you exhibit empathy, when you make your people your priority, it changes you. When you put your people first in every decision you make, it sets you up for success in every way: Because when the chips are down, when the obstacles come, it's your people who will get your company through. But they'll do so only if they know you've taken care of them. They'll do so only if they believe you'll do what you say you're gonna do. They'll do so only if you've shown them, time and time again, that they're valued and that all of you are committed to working as a team and moving in the same direction.

So how do you do that?

In order to take care of your people, you first need to establish a foundation and a framework. And that's what the next chapter is all about.

CHAPTER 2

VISION, VALUES, & OPERATING PRINCIPLES

As leaders, we have to ask ourselves three questions, constantly:

1. Are we doing the right things?

2. Are we doing things right?

3. What are we missing?

If we want to create High-Performing Organizations (which starts with Taking Care of People), we need to apply these questions to how we carry our values into the workplace, and to consider these questions when it comes to instilling our values in the policies we set.

I hope one thing we can agree on is that the Army is an example of a High-Performing Organization. As an organization, regardless of such massive changes in circumstance as the Great Depression, two World Wars, major terrorist attacks on our own soil, and changes in our Commander in Chief (i.e., the President) every four to eight years, the Army continues to get the job done, and done well. And the reason for that is because the Army is a values-based organization.

In the Army, every soldier is taught the importance of seven key values: Loyalty, Duty, Respect, Selfless Service, Honor, Integrity, and Personal Courage. There's even an acronym to help us remember those values: "LDRSHIP."

People always want to talk about corporate culture in the corporate world and sometimes forget that culture has to start somewhere. With a shared purpose. A vision. A well-defined mission that every member of the organization believes in and acts upon. In the Army, our "corporate culture" was clearly predicated by a shared purpose: To protect our nation's freedoms and to support and defend the Constitution of the United States against all enemies, foreign and domestic. We had that shared purpose. So we had this unified culture. We all knew what we were trying to accomplish every day. And oh, by the way, in order to accomplish that, we not only established the set of shared values that I mentioned (Loyalty, Duty, Respect, Selfless Service, Honor, Integrity, and Personal courage), but we nurtured those values throughout the organization, all the time.

Guess what? Shared purpose, well-defined values, and a unified culture are found at the very foundation of every High-Performing Organization I've had the pleasure of working with these last twelve years. It is those organizations that flourished through the challenges of the pandemic. It is those organizations that are thriving, both in private ownership and at the behest of shareholders, despite all of the changes they've faced, in technologies, economies, workforce demands—everything.

No surprise: The organizations that operate day-to-day without shared purpose and values, the organizations that give lip service to values but exemplify the opposite, by doing things differently than they said they would, are the very organizations that floundered, lost value, faced massive exoduses of their employees, and in some cases failed so miserably that their CEOs and others in C Suite positions have all been fired—leaving the companies in perilous positions that, frankly, aren't improving. Why? Because "Out with the old boss, in with the new boss" doesn't change anything if the culture isn't there, if the values aren't real, if the purpose isn't clear, and the people don't feel taken care of. Oh, and, by the way, now's a good time to remember the title of this book.

The good news? No matter what position your company is in now, you can get started moving it in the right direction, or at least in a better direction immediately. How? Get your people together, and start talking about who you are and who you want to be.

Ask yourself, as an organization, "What is our shared purpose?" Maybe start with, "Why do we exist? What is our company's raison d'être? What's our very reason for existing?"

I've tried to do this with each of my clients, and the ones who did a good job (or were already doing a good job) didn't have a problem with it. They could articulate their reason for existing in just one meeting. The pharmaceutical companies across the board came to some similar conclusions, about helping humanity and improving quality of life, or extending life duration for patients. Other companies talked about serving customers or providing service to customers and communities. Even a major construction company I worked with had a purpose: To build quality construction at reasonable cost.

> Ask yourself, as an organization, "What is our shared purpose?"

If you don't know what your purpose is, then how can you reach that goal? How can you accomplish any mission? If coming up with this is a struggle for your organization, then you've got some deep-seated problems that are gonna need addressing, and I suggest you hire R Lynch Enterprises to come in for a full 360 evaluation of everything you're doing wrong.

But, assuming you're able to articulate a purpose, then step #2 is to make sure you've established some values—clearly articulated, clearly identified, clearly enforced values. Just like we did in the Army with the "LDRSHIP" principles. The values you want to instill in your company are up to each company to define, of course. But they can't just be values that are placed on a bumper sticker and forgotten. They have to be shared. They have to be lived. In worst-case scenarios, the idea of "company values" just becomes a joke; this idea that employees and even leadership thinks, "Yeah, we say we got these values, but we clearly don't live by those values." Sadly, I saw this all the time, and it's problematic. So, a lot of work has to be done to develop the values.

One of the companies I worked with came up with these six: respect, commitment, teamwork, honesty, integrity, and innovation. And we took some time to understand, explaining why each value was important. "Every person is entitled to dignity and respect" is easy enough to understand. "We will value the skills, work ethic, and creativity of all of our employees" goes a little deeper, since a lot of organizations tend to be led by people who think those "beneath" them aren't as capable as them. That's not a good starting position. The conclusion they came to was that it would be better to start from a positive point of view, assuming that they hired good people who were capable of getting the job done, which would help support the values of teamwork and working with honesty and integrity, etc.

Having shared values leads to a better-functioning organization—one that's not constantly blocked by passive-aggressiveness, where assignments don't get followed or tasks aren't completed due to mistrust, lack of honesty, lack of respect, etc. I know you've all encountered that in the workplace. I sure have, in nearly all of the workplaces I've been involved with trying to help these last twelve years. Honestly, I see passive-aggressive people as the #1 problem in most corporate organizations, so I'll be talking about how to recognize them—and get rid of them—a whole lot in the chapters ahead.

But back to the main point here: Establishing values not only helps make sure you're all in alignment with a shared purpose, but it also gives you some criteria upon which you can evaluate your employees' performance. We'll talk a lot in Part II about employee evaluations, but it's important to mention it in context right here. Because when you do performance appraisals, you want to evaluate your people not just on their performance, but on how they lived in accordance with the organizational values. And I'll say this with the backing of experience: Nine times out of ten, those who exemplify the company values tend to show higher performance all-around. Those who don't? Nine times out of ten, they shouldn't even be there. They're the ones listening to your instructions and then rolling their eyes and ignoring them. They're the ones who are keeping the majority of your organization from thriving. And they're the ones who should be let go and encouraged to seek happiness elsewhere.

Having a list of established values gives you the ammunition you need to enforce the types of behavior you want your organization to uphold. If you don't have it, you're defenseless.

Fair warning, though: When leadership tries to dictate a new set of values from the top down, especially in a company that's been operating without any clear values for some period of time, they're unlikely to catch on. If you're gonna go and do this midstream, I suggest you bring your people into the mix and ask *them* what they think the company values should be. Chances are, you'll end up with a great list, and during the process, it'll open up a dialogue that has a very good chance of getting your people excited about the positive changes to come.

GETTING TO VVOP

While Purpose is paramount, and Values are crucial, they're really just the start. What you need in order to build a truly High-Performing Organization is VVOP, which I pronounce out loud as "Vee-Vop." It's my shorthand for Vision, Values, and Operating Principles.

We've already talked about values. Those are generally one-word definitions, and they should be fairly easy to remember. For example, my personal Values include God, Family, and Profession, in that order. I try to approach everything starting with God first, my family second, and my profession after that, and I do my best to lead by example, hoping that my family will live by that same flowchart. And whatever your company's Values are, it's important to remember that the people in your organization can't remember things that aren't taught to them. So right away, it's important to make sure you share those values with everyone in your company, old and new. They need reminders. We all need reminders. And when new hires come aboard? They need to be steeped in your purpose and values right away.

I mentioned earlier that, when I was the corps commander at Fort Hood, Texas, every Wednesday my wife and I would greet every new arrival to the installation along with their families. In addition to calling out the 17-year-olds and bringing one of them up onstage to show them how much I valued them, we used that opportunity to remind them of the "LDRSHIP" values, and told them, point blank, that we were going to hold them responsible for adherence to those values. The same thing needs to happen in Corporate America: You can't just have a poster on the wall that lists the values of the organization if nobody lives by them.

And while this may seem obvious to some people, apparently it isn't obvious to all: The essence of a High-Performing Organization is having a culture that's interested in continually improving itself. You can't be High-Performing if you're looking to sit on your laurels or rest on past results. Nobody in the outfit should be satisfied with where we are. Ever. Everybody in the outfit should want to get better when it comes to accomplishing the identified purpose. Your people need to be told that from the start, and they must be on board with that from the start. That attitude, that direction that leads you to constantly improve in the direction of your purpose, is something that needs to get codified in a mission statement.

What's a Mission Statement? In its best sense, it's a whole lot more than an empty corporate exercise, and it's a crucial matter of Strategic Planning. It's a detailed, written explanation that everyone can understand and follow: "Here's what we're trying to do." This kind of clarification gets everyone to start moving in the same direction.

The corporate leaders I worked with who did very well took the mission statement and used it to define, in great detail, their vision for the company. "Where do I see us a year from now? Where do I see us in five years?"

Some people get frustrated by this idea. They think, "How do I know what the world will look like in five years?" And here's the thing: That's all the more reason to have a well-established vision, a mission statement on where you want to go. Because the world is a volatile place, and when things go wrong (which they will), and you don't have a vision or plan in place, your chances of adapting in order to continue your mission are slim to none—because your mission was never clearly defined.

As I observed the thirty-plus different clients I've worked with, the ones who managed to survive and thrive through the unforeseeable pandemic had certain things in common. Number one is that they, the organization, had established a shared purpose, a shared reason for existence. That was helpful. The organizations who simply said, "We've got to survive the day and only deal with what's right in front of us," rarely survived the day, because when the chips were down, there *wasn't* a shared purpose. Chaos ensued.

Number two was that those organizations that thrived had established Values that ensured that people stayed focused on being the best they could be. So the organization would be the best it could, and, therefore, could accomplish its purpose, no matter the circumstances.

And number three was that the organizations that came out on top were those with Vision—the first part of VVOP—clearly in place.

Sadly, only a handful of companies I've worked with met that mark, as so many corporate executives I've encountered fall short when it comes to creating mission statements. Too many of them couldn't see past what it's going to be like in five minutes, let alone five years, and they didn't understand why the vision is so critical: Because the Mission Statement ensures that everybody has a shared vision of what we're aiming to look like in five years, which allows them to adjust and move toward that vision as necessary when the going gets tough.

You want to add ten new stores in the next ten years? You want to bring your costs down and your sales up in five? You want to bring three more drugs to market by the end of the decade? Whatever it is, a strategic leader needs to lay it out, in detail, and describe how to get there under reasonable/expectable circumstances, based on what's happening in the world and in the marketplace, right now.

Will the circumstances change in the future, in ways you can't predict? Almost certainly the answer is, "Yes!" But those changes are the reason we develop adaptive leadership. You'll be able to tackle them when they come. The Vision is what matters.

Think of it like a destination on a map. If you don't have a destination, and you just start driving with some vague intention of thinking you'll wind up somewhere, someday, who knows where you'll end up? But if you set a destination, there are usually a hundred different ways to get there. By car, bus, train, plane, hitchhiking—whichever way you choose. And if you hit roadblocks along the way, washed-out roads, planes being grounded by the FAA, it doesn't really matter. You just adjust your method of travel, or adjust the route you're taking. At least you know where you want to go. As long as you have the time, strength, money, and means to get there, you can get there.

Now, the key component for when it comes to *carrying out* the vision you have is having the resources needed to get there. You can't fly to Europe if you don't have enough money to buy a plane ticket, right? So, leaders. Please write this down: "Vision without resources is hallucination."

This statement is true in all walks of life. You can have a vision, but if you don't have the resources, that vision cannot come to pass. And in Corporate America, resources come in three categories: people, time, and money. Without them, you can't get there from here.

Vision without resources is hallucination

High-Performing Organizations have the resources to be able to accomplish the mission.

You can't keep telling your folks, "Man, we're going to take it to this level!" without providing the adequate resources to do it. Because then, you just sound silly. I mean, keep talking wild like that, and I guarantee you: Nobody is even paying attention to you. It's like you're not really paying attention to what is in the realm of possiblility, and your people all know it. So if you've got this vision, you've got to provide the resources necessary to accomplish your vision. And if you really want to convince your people that your vision makes sense, the vision has to be captured in a Strategic Plan.

I'm amazed at the number of my corporate clients who didn't have a strategic plan.

We all know that plans don't always go as planned. They *usually* don't go as planned. It does not make the planning less important.

Eisenhower said it best in preparation for the liberation of France at Normandy Beach: "It's not about the plan. It's about the planning." And we in the military always say, "The plan doesn't survive the first contact with the enemy." It's the same way in Corporate America. Corporate America is equally Volatile, Uncertain, Complex, and Ambiguous (VUCA), and if you don't bother to put together a plan, you're left just reacting, day-to-day, to whatever the event of the day might be. And that just doesn't work. Instead, you need the vision, and the Strategic Plan is an elevated Vision: It's the five-year or ten-year plan that says, "Here's what we're going to do, and here's how we're going to allocate our *resources* to be able to achieve the vision that's identified in this Strategic Plan."

Want it to be even stronger? Then develop that Strategic Plan collaboratively. To get everyone on board in a High-Performing Organization, it can't just be the senior executive going home and sitting down at his kitchen table, writing a strategic plan, and then announcing it; you gotta get the entire team to participate in building the plan, because then they're going to buy into it, because they were a part of it.

Too many times I've seen Corporate America say, "Here's the new plan," and then 90% of the people on their teams say, "Well, there's no way that can happen." So they just become passive-aggressive, which, as I've stated, is the number-one problem I see in Corporate America today: passive-aggressive individuals who don't believe anything about what's going on, but also don't voice their opinion; they simply smile and nod and go back to their respective office or cubicle and do their own thing. That just can't happen. So the strategic plan has to be developed collaboratively; it has to be documented and codified. And then? Review it every six months.

High-Performing Organizations have to keep performing. It's not about resting on laurels. It's about constantly improving. And this is where we're finding people struggling, because circumstances change, and assumptions that they made are often proved to be invalid—causing them to wring their hands with worry and get stuck.

The essence of a Strategic Plan is you articulating facts and assumptions up front. "Here are the facts that we know that are bearing on a problem. And here are the assumptions that we're making." And that's great. But the beaches at Normandy turned out to be far different in reality than Eisenhower had anticipated, and if he'd just stuck to the plan on the original assumptions—or stopped to wring his hands while our forces were slaughtered—we never would have taken that beach.

That's why, every six months, a strategic/adaptive leader will be sure to review their original assumptions and adjust as necessary.

There's a big difference between facts and assumptions. So you've got to review your strategic plan and see which of your assumptions proved to be valid and which proved to be invalid; which ones became facts, and which didn't. When you do that, you also have to develop branches and sequels for this strategic plan. You can't wait until things go wrong and knock you off your plan to come up with a new plan; you've got to have branches and sequels, or *If/Then formatted annexes* to your plan. "If this happens, then we'll do *this*. And if *that* happens, then we'll do *that*."

It's critical. If we're going to have an effective, High-Performing Organization, it's got to be based on a plan that's an *executable* plan. Not a perfect plan, but an *executable* plan, backed up with resources, and branches and sequels that anticipate the inevitable roadblocks and changes in circumstance.

NEVER LET PERFECT BE THE ENEMY OF GOOD ENOUGH

A lot of times, organizations don't publish their strategic plans because they're not perfect. Well, I've got news for you: No plan is ever gonna be perfect. So never let the perfect be the enemy of the good enough. General George S. Patton said during in World War II, "A good plan violently executed now is better than a perfect plan executed at some indefinite time in the future." In business, I like to think of that sentiment as, "A 70-percent plan executed now is better than a 100-percent plan executed too late."

Afraid that your plan isn't good enough? Great. That's the reason we need to develop the last part of VVOP: Operating Principles.

Operating Principles are critical because, as I've said more than once, things are gonna go wrong. But if you have established Operating Principles, then your team will know: "When things go wrong, this is what we do. This is how we operate within this particular company." So they've got a foundation, a touchstone if you will, to be able to continue to do what needs to be done.

The organization has to be values-based in order to pull this off, and those values have to be lived by, or none of this works. At least half my clients had values that weren't lived by (most often by senior leadership), and if your goal is to appear silly to your employees, go ahead and draw up vision statements and value statements, and then do just the opposite. *Don't* live by the values yourself, but expect *them* to live by the values. See how that goes. (Hint: It won't end well!)

So assuming you've gone ahead and established those values, your Operating Principles will be built on those values, but with more specificity.

Your Operating Principles will let everyone in your organization know that, regardless of what's happening, this is what we do in our company. They're really an extraction of the vision and values.

Here are five, easy-to-read examples of Operating Principles drawn from the principles of some of the most successful companies I've worked with. (Note: These types of OPs can be applied to almost any High-Performing Organization, including yours):

1. **Communication: Be clear and concise in all communication.**

What this dictates is that it should not matter if the market is collapsing, or the FDA just stopped trials of your new drug, or your CEO just suffered a heart attack—*all* communications, whether by email, phone, text, or press release, or even just verbally, between colleagues or managers and their direct reports, should be clear and concise. Always. When something feels urgent, even panicked, complying with this OP means taking a breath, and maybe retyping that email before you hit "Send" or thinking twice before opening your mouth and saying something confusing, which your colleagues might misconstrue in the heat of the moment.

2. **Collaboration: Always consider what is best for the team—not what is best for you.**

Once again, because it's an Operating Principle, this is something that needs to be adhered to *always*. In this organization, we aren't working for individual credit and glory; we're working as a team, for the benefit of us all. Therefore, when making a decision, handing out new assignments, accepting thanks or awards for work well done, everyone in this organization will set aside what's best for *them*, in consideration of what is best for *all*. Think about how that changes things—as long as everyone is truly on board and leading by example.

3. **Conflict Resolution: Address all conflicts head-on.**

When something is uncomfortable, we don't set it aside. We don't let it linger. We don't let it build. We address it. We do so tactfully and with the best interest of the team in mind (assuming the last OP is being followed as well), and we're not going to be demeaning or dismissive with our language (assuming we have good Values in place), and there shouldn't be any hard feelings over the need to address whatever is wrong, because we all adhere to this Operating Principle; we know it's best for our organization. It's just how we do things.

4. **Building and Restoring Trust: Trust your teammates, both their character and their competency.**

    I'll get into the nuances and importance of Trust toward the end of this book, but, in short, a company that abides by this Principle is not going to have leaders who sit around doubting what another department is telling them, or dismissing the ideas of their direct reports on how to fix a problem they're facing, or trying to do everything themselves because they don't believe that others are capable of doing it as well as they could do it themselves. When issues arise, we turn to this OP to remind ourselves that everyone here is on the same team and working toward the same Vision, with the same Values.

5. **Prioritization and Time Management: Treat time as a precious resource. Don't waste it.**

    This OP helps us put an end to unnecessary meetings, overtime, weekend work, loss of focus, and more—and allows us to keep each other in check when we feel our time is being wasted. We all know it happens, so why not address it, and change it? And do it together, as a matter of Principle, for the betterment of us all.

Operating Principles have to be realistic. They also have to be easy to understand, or they don't work. Consider phrases like, "Robust debate leads to the best decisions," or "Results matter more than activity." That's a good one. Idle activity is useless. In the Army, I always told my people,

"Don't tell me 'We're working on it.' Tell me the specific details of what you're doing." If they couldn't do that, then we had a problem. Getting busy and getting results is what matters—not *looking* busy.

Here's another great one: "We always act with honor and integrity." That's the sort of Operating Principle that can translate powerfully when the chips are down. Let's say you're having a bad week. Some number came through in a test study of one of your products that was extremely disappointing. You learn the results in a closed-door meeting, and somebody at the table says, "We shouldn't share that number with the public." Why would they say such a thing? Because it's going to hurt the company! In the short term, the company's share price is going to take a hit as soon as that news hits CNBC, right? So this Operating Principle is there to look that executive in the eye and say, "No. We have to act with *honor and integrity*." And it is not honorable, nor is it truthful, to hide a disappointing result from your shareholders. Therefore, following the OP, the results must be shared. It may cause a dip in share price in the short term, but long term? Things like honor will only serve you well, and will allow you to continue to develop the next product, and the next, without people doubting your integrity. Because God forbid you hold something back and keep it "just between us" in a closed-door C Suite meeting, only to have it leak to the press. At that point, you're dead. Your company's gone. Or, at the very least, *you're* gone, and a lot of people are gonna suffer for breaking two basic values that should exist at the core of *any* High-Performing Organization: Honor and Integrity.

Again, while Values tend to be one-word pronouncements, your Operating Principles are more like a set of instructions: "When things go wrong, how do we do business? What do we do? We *always* do this." And they should be generic enough so that they apply to whatever the situation is. "We treat everybody with dignity and respect" is a strong Operating Principle, and when someone is guilty of not following that principle, it's pretty easy to call 'em out on it.

What's sometimes a little more difficult is making sure the OPs apply to every aspect of your organization, including the language we use to define roles.

WHAT'S IN A NAME?

In various corporations, some people are called "Employees." Some people are called "Partners." Some people are called "Associates." And guess what? The terminology is important. In the more-successful organizations I've found, they don't refer to their people as "employees," because it's taken by most workers to mean they're just there to do the minimal task and go home. The successful ones call their people "partners" or "associates," which lets them know: "If we're successful as a company, you'll be successful as an individual."

Of course, those same companies also live by their word. They don't just *call* them partners. They *treat* them like partners. It's not just semantics. It's not just a word to make them feel better about what they're doing. The partners are actually participating, via bonuses, or profit sharing, or stock plans or stock options, or some non-monetary measure of reward as growth and productivity increases, etc.

In companies full of "employees," most people I encounter feel like it doesn't matter how hard they work. As long as they show up and do the minimum, they'll get the same paycheck; so they wind up working less than the "partners" or "associates," who realize their compensation improves based on the company's performance; that the work associated with their position is actually important. The partners and associates feel as if they're collaborating, as if they're all there with a shared interest to accomplish a shared purpose.

So the word is important. It serves as a testament to the truth of your values and the core idea that your company cares about its people.

I recently got into a big debate with a CEO about why he shouldn't call his people "employees," and I used the story of my own dad to help make my point. My dad was an employee at a paper company. He operated a paper cutter. For thirty years, he went in for eight hours, did his job, and came home. He couldn't have cared less what happened to the company because it didn't affect him. His paycheck was the same at the end of the two-week period, regardless.

Back then, that paycheck and the promise of a pension someday was enough to command his loyalty, because companies tended to be loyal to employees as long as they didn't make trouble or give their bosses some flagrant reason to fire them. Today? Comparatively? How many people do you know who stay at a company for thirty years? Pensions went the way of the Dodo Bird, actual robots have taken over a lot of the strictly factory-type work, and there's hardly a handful of Americans left who don't believe that most publicly traded companies would lay them off at the blip of a bad quarter without a second thought. It's only at High-Performing Organizations that loyalty still exists. And that's because most of those organizations have found a way to make their people feel like *partners* rather than *robots*.

It all starts with establishing a Vision, Values, and Operating Principles, in service to a Purpose. It's a must-do at every HPO. And how do we stay there, once we get there? We ask ourselves, again and again: "Are we doing the right things? Are we doing things right?" and "What are we missing?"

Because that's what great leaders do.

CHAPTER 3

THE QUALITIES OF GREAT LEADERS

In the military, early on, I aspired to be a Battalion Commander. A Battalion Commander is normally a Lieutenant Colonel with a workforce of about 500 people. That was my aspiration, and I achieved that after having been in the Army for 16 years.

How did I get there?

Mostly, I just paid attention. I wanted to be a Battalion Commander, so I started taking notes in a notebook titled, "Thoughts on Battalion Command." When I saw a Battalion-level Commander do something that worked, I wrote it down, and I committed to do the same thing if I had the opportunity to command a Battalion. If I saw a Battalion Commander do something that *didn't* work, I wrote that down in my notebook as well and made a commitment *not* to do those things. As a result of that, when my opportunity came to lead, it allowed me to be a relatively effective Battalion Commander.

That's what I'm hoping this book does for you: Provide a shortcut to get you thinking, "These are the things that have worked for others and *may* work for me; and then these are the things that *didn't* work for others, so I might not want to go there. I may want to avoid that technique altogether, because it probably won't work for me."

On the organizational level, I'm presenting a series of traits that I've observed over the last twelve years that allow organizations to be successful. And post-pandemic, I realized that it's all about five skill sets: communication, collaboration, conflict resolution, building and restoring trust, and prioritization and time management. I talked about those five principles at length in the new "Part V" of the 10th Anniversary Special Edition of *Adapt or Die*.

But I've also seen some things that I know are essential to being an effective leader and which allow organizations to do even better. And those are traits in the areas of humility, vulnerability, delegation, commitment, and teamwork—all of which will get discussed at length over the course of the following chapters.

And yet, for those who haven't read my previous books, or maybe those who just need a reminder, I think it's important that we stop here and look inward for a second. It's important to recognize that we're all leaders, in our own way.

I often make a practice out of standing in front of my audiences and asking, "Who here is a leader?" And normally, less than 10% of the audience raises their hand, because they don't have any direct reports. So I say, "No, that's wrong." I say, "Everybody in this audience is a leader, either in their corporation or in their family, or in their community or in their congregation. You're all leaders." I then tell them to put their hands down, and I say, "Now raise your hand if you're a *good* leader," and a lot of them raise their hands. I find that to be interesting, because

I, personally, am still a work in progress. I am trying to become a better leader. I'm trying to work through my shortfalls in terms of anger management and listening skills, so I can become a better leader and, candidly, a better human being.

So the first thing on the road to individual improvement is to be self-aware.

And then, if we're going to apply the principles in this book in a strategic way, in the interest of building High-Performing Organizations, then it's important to remind ourselves of what it takes to be a Strategic Leader.

Strategic Leaders have four specific characteristics.

The first is that we observe and seek trends. In the military, we describe this quality pretty simply. We say, "Stand back from the map," or "Don't get so close to the map," which means: "You're looking at tactical-level issues, only. Now stand back from the map and look at strategic-level issues."

If you want your organization to truly be high performing, you've got to stand back from the map, and observe and seek trends. In real-world terms, this means that you've got to be well-read. You've got to attend conferences. You've got to collaborate with other senior executives. You've got to observe and seek trends on platforms like LinkedIn, and while you're attending conferences and reading books about the subject, you're not so enamored with how *you're* doing business that you forget to look around to see how *everybody else* is doing it, too.

Strategic Leaders spend more time looking at the bigger picture in order to make their organizations more effective, instead of being consumed with today's problems—and the most effective leaders I've encountered in Corporate America do exactly that. But I gotta tell you, about 75 percent of the senior leaders I encounter don't do it at all. They're so consumed with today's problems that they never stand back from the map, ever, and as a result, they just wind up dealing with more problems all the time.

If you want to become a Strategic Leader, step back from the day-to-day, and observe and seek trends. It's truly Step 1.

The second thing a Strategic Leader does is *sound* strategic. You can't just laze around with your communication skills and act and talk like everyone else all the time. You need to think about what you say and relay the things you've learned. Every time you open up your mouth, people should want to pick up a pen—because they know you're gonna say something important. You're gonna sound strategic. Questions and solutions are gonna be elucidated just by listening to you, because you're gonna say something at a level that they need to understand. Don't just ask more questions. Bring clarity to the table—because you've done the work. You've stepped back from the day-to-day. You're aware of what's happening all around you, both within and outside of your organization, in your industry. Say so! *"Let your conversation be seasoned with salt so that you may know how to answer everyone."*—Colossians 4:6

The third one is to ask the hard questions, and this is where many of my corporate leaders are struggling. They feel uncomfortable asking the hard questions, because they don't want to make their subordinates feel intimidated. Well, first of all, in Corporate America, you probably don't want to call your partners your "subordinates." I struggle with that one, because it's a military term, and it just makes sense in the military hierarchy. But beyond that, when asking questions as a Strategic Leader, you have to make it clear that you're asking the hard questions for a good reason: so we can *all* learn. You're not asking hard questions in order to make your people feel bad. You're not here playing Stump the Chump. The intention of asking difficult questions has to be clear. So we can all learn. So we can all grow. So we can keep improving as an organization, which should be a continuation of your values, your purpose, and your Operating Principles, too.

And then the fourth characteristic that I'd say two-thirds of the corporate executives I deal with did not do well is *make time to think*. I talk about this extensively in the *Adapt or Die* 10th Anniversary Special Edition, and I encourage you to pick up a copy. But, in short, time management and prioritization are the key to strong Strategic Leadership. Without it, you're in a constant state of being overwhelmed—and that ain't a good look. I'm not the first person to talk about time management and prioritization, of course. There are plenty of writers in the business world who've referred back to the Eisenhower Box of Prioritization, and there's a reason we all bring it up: Because it works. (Google it!)

Senior leaders have to make time to think. And then? In the same way they have to learn to ask the hard questions, they have to learn to embrace conflict. They have to create situations where people disagree: They disagree with the senior leader, they disagree with each other. When you embrace conflict, you embrace the openness to hearing different points of view. When you allow people to have those conversations, and you listen, you open yourself up to new possibilities—for solutions and circumstances you may never have imagined if all you embraced were the opinions of a bunch of yes-men.

Then, at the appropriate time, it's up to the Strategic Leader to make the call, to come to a decision and say, "Now it's time to shut up and color." That phrase comes from dealing with children, of course, but it means that the discussion is now over. It's time to do what we need to get done. There's no more talk. There's doing. And of course, we're allocating the time, the resources, the personnel—whatever it takes to get it done. Because once you *say* you're gonna do something, you need to *do it*.

DEEDS, NOT WORDS

I tell everybody in my leadership training, "The higher you go up the corporate ladder, the more your rear-end shows." I sometimes use more colorful language than that, but I say it because it's true: The higher your position, the more people are watching and scrutinizing every little thing you do.

You can go through this whole process of developing a Vision and Values and Operating Principles; you can develop a Strategic Plan—you can do all that stuff. But if the VVOP is just there in principle but it's not being followed, then it's nothing but wasted paper. And the people who have the biggest obligation to follow the principles you've laid out are the senior executives.

If you say, "we do everything with honesty and integrity," but a senior executive is anything but honest and true to her word, your company loses all credibility. During evaluations and assessments, I cannot tell you how many employees I would talk to about these matters, and they would say to me, "Why do I have to do that if this *executive* isn't doing it?"

As a Strategic Leader, you have to recognize that the higher you go, the more important it is for you to live your company values as a matter of lifestyle evangelism. If you say it's important, you've got to *show* it's important. If not, you lose all credibility.

And, by the way, don't believe that anything is happening behind closed doors. There is no such thing as "behind closed doors" in Corporate America. No such thing at all.

In twelve years of doing this, I have yet to see one instance of an executive saying, "Okay, we're gonna keep this to ourselves," when, no less than ten seconds after the doors are opened, somebody goes and tells somebody else, and whatever the big secret was gets permeated throughout the organization.

It's not necessarily a malicious thing, but it's true. In every instance, some executive would walk out of those meetings, even though we all agreed that this was just amongst ourselves, and they would pull someone aside and say, "Okay, let me tell you what we just talked about—but don't tell anybody." And then that person would pull somebody aside and say, "This is what they just told me, but don't tell anybody." And before you know it, the whole company knew.

That's consistent across all the companies I've worked with.

In the military, we called this phenomenon "The Power of Two," and instead of letting it cause problems, we used it, effectively, to share information across our organization. The basic principle is that, whenever we had something important to share, we made it a point to tell two people, because we knew that those two people would then tell two people, and those people would tell two people, and before we knew it, a thousand people had heard what we had to say. It was a positive, effective way to spread the word about what was happening in the military, and I would encourage corporate leaders to think about this when they're trying to get the word out—in a positive way. Because sitting around believing that people don't talk to each other is naïve. (We're not robots!)

It's also naïve to believe that people don't know what you're up to, and that certainly applies to issues of compensation. People say, "Well, everybody's compensation package is just between them and HR," and it's not true. Everybody knows what everybody's making these days, and where it becomes most contentious is in end-of-year bonus allocations. Like, when the company is struggling, so we don't pay bonuses to the employees, but the leaders still get their bonuses? Yeah. Everybody knows. And that causes animosity and a huge loss of trust.

On the other hand, I did have executives over the last twelve years who, in times of financial duress, would pass on their bonuses and give them to their employees instead. Talk about showing empathy. I had one, specifically, who always wanted her people to have enough money to make their house payment. That was her measure, no matter how bad things got, or how stretched thin the resources were. Guess how much trust and loyalty there was for that particular leader later on, when the chips were down in a different way?

So, just to reiterate, if you don't have a mission statement, values, etc., you can't move on. You have to define your purpose. You have to frame your company culture. But then? You have to live by your values. You can't just put them on the wall. Remember: Deeds, Not Words.

Remember: Deeds, Not Words

VALUE YOUR TIME

This should be obvious, but I've found that it's not: Living by your values actually comes down to time management. It really does.

I say this all the time, but the number-one difference between a great leader and a marginal leader is time management, and here's why: If you manage your time correctly, you'll find that you've got plenty of time to take care of your people. You've got time to leave your office, to go talk to people. You've got time to go have a cup of coffee with people. You've got time to do what Colin Powell called MBWA: "Manage by Walking Around." You've got time to do all the kind of stuff that robots can't do.

How does one accomplish this? By developing trust, and by delegating, deleting, and deferring—all of which we'll get to later in the book. But it really comes down to one phrase, which I learned from one of my mentors when I moved from running a division of 25,000 soldiers to taking over a corps of 65,000 at Fort Hood. Three days into the job, I was completely overwhelmed. There was so much coming at me, so much to do, that I couldn't seem to get a handle on any of it. And that's when my mentor told me:

"Only do those things that only you can do."

Ah. Bingo. I got it. Being a Strategic Leader means you have to *strategize*. You can't do *all* the things. You have people for that. Instead, you focus on what you do best and what only you can do from the position you're in. Once I embraced that phrase, I got to work on efficiency and streamlining, and making life at Fort Hood better than ever, doing all the things that would eventually earn me another nickname—that of "The Family-First General."

It all came down to time management.

Of course, part of time management is making sure you have time to develop yourself, too, and to make sure that other leaders in your organization are developing themselves as well.

When it comes to my observations of clients who are failing, each and every one of them is failing to invest in leader development. "We don't have *time* to develop leaders," they say. Well, guess what? As a result of that failure to invest in their own people, everything else struggles. It's obvious, even to the casual observer. But, for some reason, it's not obvious to them.

> **If you don't invest in leadership development, you're not going to be a High-Performing Organization**

If you don't invest in leadership development, you're not going to be a High-Performing Organization. You're just not.

And that's why it's so important to focus on Engaged Leadership.

ENGAGED LEADERSHIP

At West Point, we were always taught to look for what's missing.

Whether we're deep in the weeds of war or stuck in the microcosm of inner-office politics at a struggling company, chances are we're missing *something*. And often, the things that we're missing are more obvious to outside observers than they are to those in the thick of it.

The West Point way around that is to step back from whatever mess you're in and ask, "What is intuitively obvious to the casual observer?"

45

Now that I've been a casual (and not-so-casual) observer of civilian workplaces for so long, I've made more than a few observations of my own. One is that, whenever I'm giving a speech at a successful company, when I talk about "empathy" or the idea of "taking care of people," the executive leadership tends to perk up and get really excited. They recognize just how important these topics are to the long-term success of their company. And two is that, when I'm talking to companies that are struggling or to companies that have hit a wall in terms of growth, their executives get plenty excited when I mention "earnings per share" or "increased profits," but their eyes glaze over the moment I mention the word *empathy* at all.

What's ironic is that some of these struggling companies I've visited have mission statements with sweeping words about employees being their strongest assets, and yet, it is intuitively obvious to any observer—and especially to the employees themselves—that the executives in charge have no interest in paying attention to the "people" part of their own mission.

It's sometimes a long road to turn those executives around, but as long as they stick with me, once they do, they tend to see a tangible turnaround in workplace morale, which *often* helps lead them to an uptick in earnings per share and *always* leads to a turnaround in their personal job satisfaction, not to mention their life satisfaction.

I've seen this happen, even with a few executives who seemed hopeless at the outset.

When talking about soldiers and employees in my speeches, I often say things like, "You ought to love your people the way you love your own children." What do I mean by "love" in this context? What I mean is you should feel connected and engaged with them. Leaders should exhibit empathy, and ask themselves, "Am I connected and engaged with my people?" I say it because I truly believe it. And yet, I've had more than one executive come up to me after listening to one of my speeches and say, "Man, I don't even know the names of my employees' kids. Hell, I've got no idea how many kids they've got!"

How can you take care of your people if you don't know who they are?

And how can you expect your people to take care of your company's mission if they're not inspired by you as a leader?

You can't.

There may have been a time when dictating from the top down and not caring about your employees was effective, but that time has long since passed. Even in the Army, an organization where orders *have* to be followed, we let go of old-fashioned dictator-style leadership two decades ago. Why? Because it wasn't working.

Soldiers aren't robots. They're people.

Employees are people, too.

People have needs and wants and emotions, and all of those things have a direct impact on their effectiveness on the battlefield as much as they do in the workplace.

Does the Army still believe in a hierarchy? That those at the top have the experience and knowledge that's required in order to lead, and that those who are just starting out in the Army (as well as those who are still on their way up) should follow the lead of their superiors? Yes. Of course.

But the difference comes back to that phrase my wife reminds me of all the time, which is actually a quote from Theodore Roosevelt: "People don't care about how much you know until they know how much you care."

That is why the Army has been preaching and practicing Engaged Leadership for a long time now.

In the Army, in order to be effectively "engaged," leaders must get to know their soldiers, be effective communicators to those soldiers (when it comes to explaining mission expectations, etc.), and be directly involved with their subordinates, rather than dictating orders from behind closed doors in some far-off place.

The same thing goes for Engaged Leadership in Corporate America and in small businesses, in government organizations, and in community organizations. It's no different.

In fact, I think the only difference between military and private-sector leadership comes in the way we communicate.

Communication is the foundation of any mission. If people don't understand what your mission is, how on Earth can they be expected to carry it out? Clarity about your mission needs to be communicated to all, and understood by all. In the Army, that means soldiers need to know what needs to get done, and they need to understand exactly what your expectations are. That's it. After that, they just have to follow orders.

But in the corporate world? The business world? The civilian world? Workers want to know something more: They want to know *why*. Why are we doing this? Why are we making this change? Why are we starting this new initiative that's going to take up so much of my time? Why can't we just keep doing things the way we've been doing them?

And here's the catch: When they don't know why, they often just don't do it. When leaders forget to give their employees the "why," some of those workers will just ignore whatever's been ordered and keep doing things the way they've always been done. It's a quiet, passive-aggressive rebellion that stifles initiatives again and again.

I don't know why that is. It's just a fact. I've observed this behavior in nearly every organization I've consulted with since I left the Army, and I'm guessing you know exactly what I'm talking about because you've seen it happen in your organization, too.

So what's the solution?

Be the type of leader who realizes it's important to tell our people why we fight. What's in it for them? Go ahead and tell them how a change will make life better for all of us, because it's going to make the organization stronger than it is right now, or because it's going to bring our costs down, or it's going to increase sales, or make things easier in the long run.

And then? Repeat. Strategic Communication is about sharing consistent themes and messages delivered at high frequency over multiple media. Share your "why" in person, via text, via email, at corporate gatherings, in the cafeteria . . . you get the point.

As a senior leader, you cannot repeat yourself too much when it's a message that's worth repeating.

And frankly, if you can't give your people a good reason why they should do what you're telling them to do, then maybe it's not the best decision. Maybe you ought to rethink whatever initiative it is you're taking. Because when you have good reason, when you have a higher, wider purpose, and you're able to communicate that position strategically and effectively, there's power in that sort of communication.

It's important, especially for today's workforce, to show them that you are a leader who is engaged and empathetic. To let them know that you care about them and that you're thinking about them. You're not making decisions just to give them extra work and make their lives miserable. You're making decisions that matter and that are truly going to lift your whole company, or branch, or division.

So how do you show people you care, besides communicating your mission clearly and explaining the "why" repeatedly?

I talked a lot about the idea of "Leading by Walking Around" in *Adapt or Die.* Get out from behind your desk. Go talk to people who work for you. Ask how they're doing, and actually listen to their answers. You just might learn something!

But let's take it one step further:

How do you know if you're embodying the characteristics of a great leader?

You ask. And that's what this next chapter is all about.

CHAPTER 4

THE POWER OF
360 ASSESSMENTS

I can hardly put into words just how powerful it is to take the time, organizationally, to do a 360-degree assessment of the people on your team. What I mean by that is to create a survey that's handed out to everyone—peers, bosses, and subordinates alike—to assess the competency and effectiveness of how everyone is doing. An honest, anonymous survey of everyone an individual interacts with, aimed at assessing that person's effectiveness in the workplace.

Truly, it's the only way you can really know how somebody is doing, because let's face it: Everybody can do something to make their boss think that they're doing something *well* when they're really not. So what 360 Assessments do is allow the leader to get the pulse of the person that you're assessing. And when you do this, it gives you a better perspective on what an individual is doing day to day.

The most important person to start with? You!

Self-awareness and self-development are keys to strong leadership, and 360s are an important key to assessing the health of any organization.

At R Lynch Enterprises, we've developed a 360 tool with Lt. Gen. (Ret.) Walt Ulmer that we call "Perceptions of Individual Behavior," and generally what we've done is identified the 15 skills that we think people ought to be evaluated on—not just by their boss, but also by their peers and subordinates.

I encourage every senior leader I work with to go ahead and hand out this survey to all of the people they interact with on a daily basis.

You'd be surprised how many of them push back and don't want to do it.

I was surprised, that's for sure. These people are supposed to be leaders, dedicated to improvement, and operating at a high level of command.

It's obvious to me, and I think to most people, that you can't improve if you're not self-aware. And you can't just look at your reflection in the mirror to determine how you're doing, because we're never as good as we think we are. Never. So I was surprised with the number of people who would push back and say, "No, I don't want to do that."

If you want to be a leader in a High-Performing Organization, you *have* to do it. As uncomfortable as it may be for you, you've got to drop the ego and find out how you're doing—from other people's point of view.

So I encourage you to bring us in and put together a 360 Assessment for you, or, at the very least, take what we've done and come up with a 360 survey of your own.

In each of the categories, we give survey takers a chance to assess the exhibited leadership trait as something with which they strongly agree, agree, slightly disagree, disagree, or strongly disagree. And again, the caveat is *you can't just share it with your fan club.* You can't just share with people who *like you.* You've got to be open enough to share it with people at all levels: peers, direct reports, bosses—even people outside of your organization you work with, so you can get good, conscious feedback.

When it's all done, what we do at R Lynch Enterprises is to collect all the feedback, scrub it of any personal info (to help keep it anonymous), and then draw up a report for the individual in question. I then send a one-pager back to the individual to say, "Here's what your peers, your bosses, and your workforce think of you."

If I see a trend line where lots of people (generally more than half) said they only slightly agree, or disagree, or strongly disagree that the individual is exhibiting one or more of the important leadership traits, that's when we have a conversation.

Sadly, when I do my leader-development individual sessions, an important trend that I've noticed with corporate executives is that many of them don't want to hear it. They went through the 360 Assessment only because their boss said they had to, but then every time I'd raise a point, they would say, "No. I don't do that."

Listen: If more than half the people around you are feeling like you're failing to lead well in one area or another, and you don't believe it? You don't want to hear it? You don't want to address it in any way? Then you're not going to make it. Your workforce, at some point, is going to give you the dreaded eye roll and just passive-aggressively fail to do what you need them to do—and you're the one who's gonna pay the price for their inaction. It's a fact. It's inevitable. And I feel bad for you for being so stubborn.

Half the reason I'm writing this book is so whoever picks it up doesn't have to learn the hard way. Instead, they can learn something right here in these pages that will make their life easier, and their job better, and their company more functional and high-performing than it's ever been. And one way I'm gonna do that is by sharing the 15 blocks of the 360 Assessment tool right here, along with a brief explanation of the importance and intent of each item. I ask you to read them, to think about how you *think* people might answer, and then (hopefully) to find a way to share it so you can get some honest feedback on yourself—before you go and try to get feedback on anyone else.

So "Here goes":

Number One: "Makes goals and priorities clear."

Does this person make it a point to communicate to the team what the goals and priorities are? And if those goals and priorities change, does this person go back and say, "Okay, there's been a modification. This is the priority now, and these are the goals"? We all know that if everything is a priority, nothing is a priority. So that's critical.

Number Two: "Is consistent and predictable in behavior."

There is nothing worse, candidly, than having an individual in a leadership position who is just so unpredictable that they cause their workforce to be constantly deterred. They'll say and do one thing one day, and they'll say and do something else on a different day, so the folks who work with them and around them have no idea who they're dealing with on any given day. Predictability is important. A Dr. Jekyll and Mr. Hyde situation is a disaster.

Number Three: "Encourages new ideas and new approaches to getting the job done."

The individual that you're trying to appraise can't believe that they're the smartest person in the room. They can't believe that, since they know everything, they don't need any new ideas or new approaches to getting the job done. They have to be willing to say, "Okay, how are we doing? And what should we be doing different?" I mentioned earlier that strong leaders need to be asking, "Are we doing the right things?" and "Are we doing things right?" But there's a third component to what strong leaders need to ask, and that's "What are we missing?" An individual who encourages new ideas and new approaches to getting the job done is addressing that number three. In the Army, everyone around me knew that, when I asked a question, answering me with "Because we've always done it that way" wouldn't fly. It was always the wrong answer, because what I wanted to hear was fresh ideas and solutions.

Number Four: "Stays current with relevant technical and professional content."

All of us have to grow. I mean, at the age of 69, I'm continuing to grow. I continue to read. I continue to study. I continue to research because I want to stay current with what's going on. If I just continue to talk about things the way they were before, I've lost the focus on the way it is now, and (more importantly) where it *could be*.

Number Five: "Offers suggestions for improvement of work processes or outcomes."

Does the individual take the time to truly listen, to truly observe, and then make recommendations for improvement of work processes or outcomes? I mean, the four elements of being a Strategic Leader have to be evaluated routinely. Number one: do they observe and seek trends? No one is an island. Candidly, if you're doing something, somebody else is probably doing something similar. Why don't you study that? Why don't you look closely and see what to do, and see what the trend line might be? Observe and seek trends. Number two, a Strategic Leader has to keep asking: "How can we do what we're doing *better*?" and then offer those answers up to your team.

Number Six: "Keeps promises or explains why they can't be kept."

As a leader, people have an expectation that you'll keep your promises. Remember, Deeds, not Words. People also realize that things are constantly changing, and as a result of that, sometimes when you promise something, those promises can't be fulfilled. But—and this is huge—there's also an expectation that if you can't keep your promise, you at least explain why that promise couldn't be kept.

Number Seven: "Shares information and contributes to the outcomes of the whole team."

This comes down to, "Is this person an effective communicator? Are they asking good questions? Are they listening actively? Are they contributing to the outcome for the entire team?" Or, "Are they just sitting in their own little rice bowl, if you will, just worried about themselves—keeping important information close to the vest, and maybe taking credit for others' work?"

Number Eight: "Is fair, unbiased, and considerate; doesn't play favorites."

A strong leader cannot be deferential to one individual or one team. They've got to be fair, unbiased, and considerate. Cronyism is a killer of trust and integrity. Just recently, I encountered a senior executive who is completely useless. They never contribute anything to the team, at all. And yet this executive who is a buddy of the CEO keeps getting promotions and keeps getting away with not doing the work that others are scrutinized for. There's no faster way to kill morale and drive quiet animosity in the workplace.

Number Nine: "Is approachable and can handle bad news without shooting the messenger."

This is a major issue I see across Corporate America: a lot of times folks are afraid to give their candid observations because they think they're going to be shut down when they do. A leader must be approachable, with good news and bad. Too many times in Corporate America, what I've seen is individuals just hiding bad news, because they don't want the repercussions of *sharing* bad news. That is problematic, because it only gets worse over time.

Number Ten: "Accepts diverse viewpoints; distinguishes between disagreement and disloyalty."

A leader must surround himself by people with different thoughts and ideas. In the military, general officers would establish what we call "Strategic Initiative Groups" or SIGs. And they'd help Generals think through complex issues. When I formed my SIGs, I intentionally put diverse people in the mix. I had them all take Myers-Briggs Type Indicator personality assessments, so I had some introverts and some extroverts, some feelers and some judgers, some sensors, and on and on. I intentionally looked at age, gender, and race to make sure that my SIGs were, indeed, diverse. As a result of that, I always got diverse viewpoints when I asked them to study something for me and make recommendations. And oh, by the way, you've got to be so approachable that people are willing to bring you different thoughts and ideas.

Number Eleven: "Would point out to others any negative ethical implications of their behavior."

At West Point, they taught us, "A cadet will not lie, cheat or steal, *or tolerate those that do.*" The same should be taught in any organization. It's absolutely essential. In Corporate America, leaders should be fostering an environment where any negative ethical thing that's taking place is immediately brought to the attention of the leaders.

Number Twelve: "Sets a high standard for personal behavior; exemplifies the company values."

I see this sometimes working fine in Corporate America, and other times not working fine at all. You can't say one thing and then do something else. You can't hold people to a standard that you're not willing to hold yourself to. Leaders must be lifestyle evangelists—the people who most exemplify the company values and set high standards of personal behavior.

Number Thirteen: "Makes decisions on time and explains them to all concerned."

Routinely, I get this concern with my clients, that people are hesitant to make a decision; as a result, that decision is not made in a timely fashion. Then, in some cases, when the decision is made, they don't take the time to explain to everybody involved *why* they made that decision. Explaining decisions to people who are affected by those decisions is critical.

Number Fourteen: "Is candid and tells it like it is."

On the surface, this one is simple. But underneath the surface, what it's really about is: "Is this person just a sycophant? Are they simply telling you what they think you need to hear?" Which means that their input is known to be less than useful.

Number Fifteen: "Is a prisoner of electronic devices."

This last one is really a killer in the modern workplace, because what it's really asking is, "Does this individual take time to deal directly with people? Or is he sitting in his cubicle, sending out emails or texts and not actually communicating?" What people really want in a leader is exactly the opposite. Leadership is a contact sport. You've got to be out there.

These fifteen traits can be adjusted a bit to fit a particular organization's needs, of course, but all those things that we put in the 360 Assessment are critical input to a performance appraisal and should be routinely addressed. I advocate that, at least once a year, people take a tool like our "Perceptions of Individual Behavior" or any of the other

360 surveys that are out there, and get feedback from peers and subordinates as to how somebody is doing to be able to truly have an effective performance appraisal, period.

But there's one more step in this process that often gets overlooked: The all-important After-Action Review. A 360 needs to be assessed and addressed. It can't just sit there, with no result. The review must be followed up with a concrete plan to address the findings, in the interest of improving performance and perception alike.

I cannot tell you how disappointing it is when we go through this process, and make this effort, only to have the recipient of the 360 throw it away and not change their behavior one bit. Leaders and others who aren't willing to take an honest look in the mirror and make changes to improve themselves are dead in the water, as far as I'm concerned. They have little chance of leading a High-Performing Organization, because they aren't willing to walk the walk of self-development and a commitment to always be improving. And if they're not leading in those two areas, then why should anyone follow them?

After a 360, the most Strategic and Engaged Leaders we work with always put a plan in place to respond to what they discover. They ask their own people (including those not in their fan club) what they think they should do in order to improve. They set a follow-up review in 90 days just to see how they're doing. They make concrete changes and take steps to improve in the areas where they're falling short. And they never fail to do another 360 the following year, to make sure they've stayed on track.

Being self-aware is critical. If you're stuck behind a desk, not walking around, not listening to what your own people are telling you, how can you possibly know what kind of a job you're actually doing? Even if you don't have an outgoing personality, even if you're resistant to the formality of the 360 review, you've still got to get some honest feedback. Once a week, or once a month, take a cue from Ed Koch, the former mayor of New York City from 1978 to 1989, who used to ride the subway to work every day and ask people directly, "How am I doing?" You can bet a bunch of New Yorkers crammed into a crowded subway car didn't hold back with how they were feeling. Find some way to get that sort of direct feedback and honesty from your people, and you're only going to improve yourself and your organization, from bottom to top.

To me, 360s are the best way to do that. And trust me: The results might be hard to swallow, but they are very important.

UNCOVERING WEAK LINKS IN THE CHAIN

I believe that 360s are essential, not only to each individual, but in order to assess what's really going on in your company at any given time. Why? Because without doing 360s, there's a very real chance that you're overlooking weak links in your organization that might be costing you, big time.

In recent years, I worked with a company that tended to do most things right. Their VVOP was top-notch. They truly cared about their people and showed them all the time—in deeds, not words. Their workforce was loyal and dedicated in return, which helped them weather the pandemic with relative ease (in an industry that was hurt more directly than many others when quarantines swept the nation). But for some reason, they were experiencing a disturbing trend: Some 35% of their new associates were leaving within their first year of employment.

That number should give any good leader chills. You can't spend all this time and money recruiting people and onboarding them only to have them leave within the first year. It's just not feasible. That much turnover eats at your resources (especially time and money) too quick, to the point it will start affecting everything else you're trying to accomplish.

I suspected the problem could be rooted out pretty easily through the 360-Assessment process for one reason: In my experience, about

99% of the time, when people leave within their first year, it's because they've been placed under a terrible leader.

This particular business was in a tizzy, holding special meetings to try to figure out how to solve this problem, doing a lot of handwringing and saying, "Woe is me." They finally brought me into a board meeting, and I said, "Okay, show me, specifically, who was the leader that last new hire worked for when that person left the company?" They looked it up, and I said, "How much do you want to bet that the problem is with that one leader?" It was someone who'd been at the company for a long while, so they sort of hemmed and hawed and doubted my quick assessment. So I asked them to do a 360 on him and on some others who were employed at his level (so it wasn't obvious that we were targeting anyone; also, just to get a fair assessment, in case there were others involved in the breakdown). And from the assessments, the trend was just obvious to every observer: The problem really *was* with this one leader. Someone who'd lost his way, was too harsh on the newbies, and wasn't living up to the company values—even though he *had* lived up to those values and those 15 strong-leader traits in the past.

It was time for that leader to get a talking to, and, it turns out, time for him to go.

Turnover problem solved.

No more handwringing.

I can't tell you how often a set of "disturbing trends" comes down to a single area, one place where things are going wrong, which often turns out to be just one person's fault.

One bad apple really can spoil the bunch. And 360s will help you see that.

And remember, just because someone is failing to live up to the traits every strong or effective leader should have doesn't mean they're a bad person. It just means that maybe they're in the wrong position. Or maybe they're facing a set of circumstances outside of work that are negatively affecting their performance at the moment, and they ought to be moved into a different position—at least for the time being.

I saw this at one of my clients just recently. We'd discovered a weak link in the chain, and once it became apparent (after the 360s), the guy's boss fessed up that he knew what was going on. "Well, the problem he's got is his wife just left him, and he's having significant medical issues," he told me. His circumstances were tough. That's not a reason to fire the guy, right? But a leader also can't sit idly by and let one poor performer cause a ripple effect of problems throughout the organization. So we came up with a plan to move this individual, temporarily, to a position that didn't call for so much responsibility over others. As long as a leader knows what's going on, they can act accordingly. And the fact that sometimes people aren't doing well in a place because of unfortunate circumstances isn't anything to sweep under the rug or be ashamed of or afraid of. Because guess what? If you change the circumstances, then they just might flourish. And I can say with great authority that a large number of times when people were moved, in situations just like the above, they came back later and said, "Thank you for moving me." They didn't come forward up front to say, "I gotta be moved," because that's just human nature, right? We always want others to perceive that we're doing well. So it's up to effective leaders to step in and assess what's really going on. And in case after case, when someone *was* moved, they were *thankful* that they got moved.

> **As long as a leader knows what's going on, they can act accordingly**

If you act like a robot, if you don't care about your people, if you're not paying attention to what's going on in their lives, and you're not doing regular assessments, you're never going to be able to make these kinds of decisions—and, therefore, your company will have a next-to-zero chance of becoming a High-Performing Organization.

Of the corporate leaders I've worked with who were consistently getting things right, and whose companies were thriving quarter after quarter and year after year, each one of them realized that they really didn't know as much about themselves as they thought. In every conversation we had, they were looking for feedback. Honest, candid feedback. Not "You're a great boss! I love you!" but honest, candid feedback on things that they could do better. And in the course of our sessions, I could tell that they were absorbing all the feedback, because they were writing it down, taking copious notes. Not recording it so they could listen to it later, or have it transcribed by some secretary or AI assistant (which we all know is a shortcut to never looking at something, ever again), but engaging with, discussing, and writing down information, which is scientifically proven to help solidify and make memorable all sorts of input, in students and adults alike.

I've had other leaders go through the 360 process and not write one thing down. I've stopped my sessions with some, right in the middle, to ask, "Hey, do you care or not? Because you're not writin' down anything that I'm saying, which is reflecting to me that I'm just wasting my time." Those leaders? Their companies are struggling. Constantly.

I'll let you draw the appropriate conclusion about which type of leader you ought to be.

Actually, scratch that. There's only one right answer here. So let me introduce you to the next chapter.

CHAPTER 5

FIND STRENGTH
IN HUMILITY

In November of 1862, President Abraham Lincoln looked at the
beleaguered state of his Union forces and knew that something had
to change—otherwise, the Union could face defeat in what had become
America's Civil War.

As the President, Mr. Lincoln was known for gathering opinions
from the experts around him, and he did so in this case, too, in order
to put together a vision of what had to happen in order to turn things
around. He didn't know *how* it was gonna happen, but that wasn't
his job. It was the job of his General Officers in the field to figure out
how to accomplish their various missions, and in this case, the crucial
task of accomplishing Lincoln's vision fell on the shoulders of Ulysses
S. Grant: the 40-year-old Major General in charge of a Union force

that was then referred to as the Army of the Tennessee. (A more-accurate term might have been The Army of West Tennessee, since most soldiers in Tennessee, and the state itself, seceded to fight with the Confederacy. But Grant's force of approximately 30,000 soldiers were decidedly Union.)

Lincoln took a look at the map, and what he told General Grant was that he needed to take the city of Vicksburg, Mississippi. "That's the key," he said, explaining that taking Vicksburg would divide the Confederacy in half, cutting off Texas, Arkansas, and Missouri from contributing to the ongoing war effort.

So Grant got started. He tried, and failed, and tried, and failed again. The Confederacy had dug in their heels at Vicksburg. They knew how important it was, too. And the more effort the Union forces made to invade the city, the farther in the Confederates dug. As the months went on, the majority of the city's residents and soldiers alike were all living in bunkers and caves underground, which made it nearly impossible for the Union to gain any ground or take any advantage.

Things got so bad that at one point, Grant tried to have his men dig a canal to bypass the city of Vicksburg in its entirety. I'm not sure if you've ever seen the size of the Mississippi River, but that would have been one heck of a big canal!

General Grant wasn't the type to come up with these ideas in isolation. He was humble enough to realize that he didn't have all the answers. So whenever he had a task to fulfill, he gathered his best people around him. He took their advice and listened to their counsel before acting. Yet, when plan after plan failed to produce the needed result, he took the blame entirely upon himself.

Six months into the Vicksburg Campaign, General Grant and his advisors had taken just about enough. So he marched the majority of his Army of Tennessee about 200 miles, through seven separate battles, to get to the edge of Vicksburg. And on the 19th of May 1863, he launched a full-scale, frontal assault on the city—failing to so much as breach the impenetrable fortifications the Confederacy had built at the perimeter.

After retreating and regathering their strength, the Army of the Tennessee made a frontal assault on Vicksburg *again* on May 22, 1863—and that failed, too, with Grant's forces suffering unbelievably high casualties in its effort.

That's when Grant famously said, "My failures have been errors in judgment, not intent." He took the losses on his shoulders, and he turned to one of his commanding officers—General Sherman, who had expressed doubts about every plan Grant had put into place since receiving the orders from Lincoln—and conceded that he had been wrong.

Once again, he asked for help and advice from those around him, intent on coming up with a new, innovative, untried solution, and together they decided to do something that had never been done before: To combine the joint forces of Grant's Army with the forces of the Navy's gunboats on the Mississippi; to enact a relentless bombardment of the city from outside of Vicksburg's walls, essentially trapping the Confederacy inside the very fortress they had built, and never letting up. (As we point out during our Leadership Tours of Vicksburg, there are modern-day parallels that can be drawn to this scenario, which have been carried out in various wars ever since.)

Finally, on July 4, 1863—the very same day the Union achieved a massive victory at Gettysburg, hundreds of miles away, in Pennsylvania—the Confederate forces at Vicksburg, who had been cut off and left battered and hungry by the never-ending bombardment, surrendered.

The victory accomplished what Lincoln wanted, and while the war would stretch on for many more months, the Union had finally turned the tide. The confederacy was split in two.

Ulysses S. Grant was promoted to "Commander in Chief," the first-ever Three-Star General of the Union Army, and who just under two years later would be responsible for accepting General Robert E.

Lee's surrender of the Confederacy itself, which would bring the Civil War to a close. Four years later, he would become our 18th President of the United States, where instead of continuing to punish the former states of the Confederacy, he would work to implement Congressional Reconstruction, and to remove the vestiges of slavery.

Throughout it all, Grant's humility is what stood out—and what made him such a strong leader.

Even as he knew his life was coming to an end, he refused to write his memoirs, thinking it was too self-centered a thing to do. It wasn't until the great American writer Mark Twain himself spoke to him that Grant finally took to the task of putting pen to paper; after Twain convinced him that his memoirs were as important to share as a part of American history as they were to provide some income to his family.

He died three days after his book was completed. And ever since, his legacy as one of the greatest leaders in American history has stood the test of time.

Humility in leadership is no small thing.

The humility expressed in Grant's memoirs is a big part of what makes it my favorite book of all time. (And I've read a lot of books!)

In my second book, *Work Hard, Pray Hard: The Power of Faith in Action*, I talk a lot about the importance of humility in the context of faith. I note that humility is addressed forty-three times in the Bible, and I do believe that we, as leaders, have been given a directive to be humble:

"Be completely humble and gentle; be patient, bearing with one another in love."

—Ephesians 4:2.

My favorite country & western song is Tim McGraw's "Humble and Kind," and I have long believed that it's critical that leaders, *effective* leaders, be humble, too.

So it should come as no surprise when I say that humility has been top of mind as I've observed and participated in the corporate world for these last twelve years. And here's what I've found: If you've got a leader who is arrogant, who is convinced that he's the smartest person in the room, who believes he's the best of the best and doesn't need anybody's input, that organization is pretty much doomed to fail when things go wrong.

On the other hand, if you have a leader who accepts some level of humility, a leader who says, "Hey, guys, I've made some mistakes. I've learned from these mistakes I made in the past" or "I'm struggling just like you're struggling," then the organization will survive, grow, and perhaps even thrive when the chips are down. Why? Because everybody's gonna pony up and want to be a more effective member of that leader's team. They'll give their best and do whatever they can, time and time again, because they won't want to let their leader down. And the reason is simple: Because their leader is *humble*.

A good friend of mine wrote a book about the subject of vulnerability, and he and I both agree that, every now and then, the leader's just got to open his kimono, if you will, and share with the group that he's got problems as well. He's got anxieties as well. He's got weaknesses as well, and he needs some help. I tell people all the time: "If you want to be successful, whether it's in the military or in Corporate America, surround yourself with competent people, and delegate." And in order to surround yourself with competent people and delegate, you've got to know your limitations.

As tough as he is, the infamous character Dirty Harry, played by one of my favorite actors, Clint Eastwood, in the movie *Magnum Force*, talks about the fact that "a man's got to know his limitations." And I know mine. I've got lots of limitations. Over the course of my military career and my corporate career, I've surrounded myself with people who are smarter than me, who can compensate for my weaknesses and my shortfalls, because I decided to acknowledge that I have them.

Without that vulnerability and humility, you wind up placing the whole world on your shoulders. And I'm telling you right now, there is not one of us who is capable of carrying that much weight.

Even if there was, it would make no sense for that person to carry it all unless they want to stand alone. In organizations, we don't stand alone. Ever.

If you want to have a High-Performing Organization, the leaders at the top need to be humble, so the folks at the bottom realize that they've got a contribution to make; that there are opportunities to add value and not just do whatever the senior leader tells them to do, as if they're some kind of robots.

Trust me: Good things happen to those who are humble. I touched on story after story illuminating this fact in *Work Hard, Pray Hard*, and even though some people find it odd to see scripture in a business-oriented book, I cannot help but to quote this particular passage from the Bible. In 2 Chronicles 7:14, God tells us:

"If my people who are called by my name, will humble themselves, and seek my face, and turn from their wicked ways, then I will hear them from heaven, and I will heal their land."

I personally believe that this passage applies across our nation, around the world, and, candidly, all across Corporate America—because if our leaders would humble themselves, then God would heal them from all of their trials and tribulations.

I swear, half the trials and tribulations we go through is because certain leaders can't see this. They just can't get out of their own way in order to let their people shine.

The number-one issue with lack of humility in Corporate America is when the senior leaders think that they're the smartest person in the room and that, based on their years of education and experience, there's nothing anybody can tell them. Their arrogance leads them to announce things, rather than to communicate effectively: "We're gonna do it my way, and if you don't like it my way, then you can leave. My way or the highway."

In the last twelve years, I've seen so many instances where that announcement comes, and after which, everybody just shuts down—because their senior leader is not listening to input, ideas, recommendations, or suggestions. Because in his mind or her mind, they already know everything. "I've been down this road before," they say. And I feel like telling them, "No, man! You haven't. It's a different world now. Things are not the same." But unless they exhibit some sense of humility, chances are, they just won't listen.

How many times have we all heard some corporate executive say, "Well, we did this ten years ago, and I know how it went. So we're gonna do it exactly the same now, ten years later." That's just silly, because so many things have changed over those ten years. Let's not forget that the world is indeed VUCA (Volatile, Uncertain, Complex, and Ambiguous), and this is a perfect example of why leaders need to stay humble and be receptive.

Ten years ago, we hadn't gone through a pandemic. Working from home was almost unheard of in most companies. Cell phones and social media had far less influence than they do today. The economy was different. Shipping methods were different. Laws were different. The media was different. The list goes on and on. A whole new generation of customers, clients, and potential employees has come into adulthood since then, and they don't see the world the way you did when you were growing up. If you aren't humble enough to listen to them, you're gonna lose them. And is that really your goal? To lose customers, clients, and employees?

Of course not. But in order not to come across to everyone as if that is your goal, you have to let them know that you're still a work in progress. You're willing to listen. And learn.

Because you, like them, are human.

Bad things happen to leaders who think they're better than others—to those who aren't humble—and I'd like to share one example from history that makes this point to the extreme.

This particular story involves one disastrous moment the Union Army endured during the battle at Gettysburg (which, along with the simultaneous surrender at Vicksburg, marked the turning point in the Civil War, which led to the eventual surrender of the South.) This particular disaster was entirely the result of one arrogant man: General Daniel Sickles, an egomaniac who got his whole Corps wiped out before his superior, General George Meade, even had a chance to put his plan of attack into motion. You see, Sickles wanted to be a hero. He wanted to be remembered. So on the second day of fighting, rather than wait for Meade's orders, he pushed his Corps forward—and his whole Corps got wiped out while he stood safely in the back, watching. All because of his personal desire to be known as the guy who won the battle.

Who was George Sickles? He wasn't a passionate volunteer, fighting for the cause. He wasn't a professional soldier, either. He was a political appointee from a wealthy family in New York City. He was given his position as a favor. Somebody made him Corps Commander, and as a result, people died.

Just to give more of an indication of what kind of a guy Sickles was: Before the war was over, Sickle got injured, and when his leg was amputated, he donated it to the museum at the Army Medical College in Washington, D.C.—where he went to visit it, annually, on the anniversary of his wounding. But before the Civil War, before his military appointment was made, he served as a state legislator and U.S. Congressman. And in 1859, when he found out his wife was having an affair, he went and killed the guy. He wound up being the first person in American history to use a defense of "temporary insanity" in the courtroom—and he was acquitted. Not because he didn't do the crime, but because he was "temporarily insane" when he did it. (By the way, his wife's lover, the man he murdered, was the son of Francis Scott Key—the poet who wrote "The Star-Spangled Banner." Which goes to show: Anyone who thinks history is dull, is wrong!)

Why on Earth a guy like George Sickles was put into a position of military power is beyond me. It was a dangerous appointment. It cost lives. And I would hope more of our leaders in Washington would learn from history and put some deep thought into such things before they go appointing their rich buddies and inexperienced family members to various leadership roles as well.

When people in positions of power aren't aligned with the sorts of values and integrity upon which America was built, people die. And when people in positions of power in Corporate America aren't in line with the sorts of values and integrity a company needs to uphold (in order to take care of its people), companies fail.

Now, while George Sickles represents an extreme negative example, there's another example of the importance of humility to be found in the big picture of how the two top Generals on either side of the fight led their armies in the Battle at Gettysburg.

On the Union side, the man in charge was General George Meade.

Meade, a career Army officer who graduated from West Point, had just been appointed to the position of Commander of the Army of the Potomac by President Lincoln three days before Gen. Robert E. Lee's Confederate Army showed up at his doorstep in Pennsylvania. And one of the first things Meade did when faced with this potential crisis was to gather all of his commanders around him for advice and information. He gathered them all in one room, at his headquarters, on a nightly basis, and listened to what they had to say.

In those meetings, his people shared intelligence about what they knew about the size of the Confederate forces, and their whereabouts; they shared thoughts on the best way to defend themselves from the onslaught; they shared knowledge about the surrounding terrain, and the readiness of the Union forces they had at hand. His communication with all of his "managers," as it were, was direct, face-to-face, and done as a unit. He actually went around to each one of them at the end of each day and asked, "What do you think we should do?" And he listened to and considered their answers before making decisions.

Meade acted as an Engaged Leader, getting a solid idea of his subordinates' styles of leadership, their readiness, their intentions; he was able to communicate with them directly about his intentions and get feedback on the best way to get the job done.

It's interesting to note that Meade and Ulysses S. Grant had such leadership styles in common, and both emerged victorious on July 4, 1863—the crucial turning point in the war.

But, to the point: Meade was a humble guy who listened to other people's input.

Lee wasn't.

General Robert E. Lee graduated from West Point, too, and had a brilliant career up until this point. Maybe too brilliant. Because he was victorious in Chancellorsville and at two prior battles against the Union forces just before this, historians generally agree that Lee was convinced he knew all the right answers. And that, I think, led to one of the great failures in history. Sure, he talked one-on-one with some of his commanders, but, for the most part, he dictated orders and sent and received messages to and from his people in the field through intermediaries. Sometimes bits of those messages were lost in translation. There were instances during those three days when he wasn't receiving accurate intelligence about where the enemy stood and how many of them there were. Maybe it was Lee's lack of direct engagement with his subordinates that caused one of his subordinates, named James Longstreet, to completely ignore an order and fail to attack the Union flank in a timely manner—which caused major suffering. I don't know for certain, because I wasn't there.

What we don't want to do is to be Monday-morning quarterbacks when it comes to history. There are so many factors that go into every decision, and the human factors definitely play a part. Many people don't know that General Lee suffered a heart attack not long before the Battle of Gettysburg. Maybe his body and mind were in a weaker condition than he let on. Maybe he didn't prioritize his own health and wellness before getting back into the fight, and maybe that hurt his decision-making abilities. A more-humble man might have stepped down because of that. But Lee didn't. Why? Even in the case of this highly studied turning point in American history, none of us truly knows every factor that went into General Lee's decision-making and communication, because none of us can get inside that man's head at that exact moment in time.

But from the outside, what we *do* know about those three fateful days is that General Meade exhibited some of the strongest traits of humble, engaged leadership, in ways that Lee didn't—and, given the outcome, a casual observer might find it intuitively obvious that being a humble, engaged leader made all the difference.

JOB TITLES

Stepping away from the historical/military analogy and back into the corporate sphere, I want to talk for a moment about job titles. I don't understand, twelve years into this, the criticality of job titles in Corporate America, but I do know it's the coin of the realm. People aspire to positions of increased responsibility and authority, and as a result of that, they get new job titles—and some people tend to wave them around and use them, like weapons or shields.

In Corporate America, you've got directors and senior directors, vice presidents, senior vice presidents, and executive vice presidents; you have C Suite executives, including the Chief Financial Officer and the

Chief Commercial Officer; then you've got the CEO and the board, and directors on the board, and a chairman of the board. And all those things are important. I acknowledge that people have their own roles. I just worry about the number of times I see people relying on their job title as a façade as to what they really do or have control over. "Look at me! I'm an executive vice president!" or "I'm a senior vice president!" which would then allow the listener to believe that these people have a lot more duties and responsibilities than they really do. It's not humble, and it's not healthy to the organization. So I coach the executives I work with in Corporate America to be very sensitive to over-amplifying their job titles.

Job titles are important. But they have to be carefully used.

And oh, by the way, we should never assume that a person has a lot of throw weight or opportunities to make decisions within the company just because they're a "senior vice president." I get a lot of senior vice presidents I deal with who really have no decision-making authority at all. So that's something to be sensitive to.

Plus, I don't care what your title is—you're still just a human. I don't care how much money you make; I don't care how established you are, how invested you are—you're still just a human. And I think that senior leaders must demonstrate their humanness.

How do we do that? First off, we have to learn the difference between coming across as confident and coming across as arrogant. And here's how:

It's okay to remind your folks that you've been down this road before and that you learned from the experience. In the military, we always talk about the importance of the After-Action Review, taking the time to highlight lessons learned, and, candidly, not just learned, but also put into practice. That's critical. So it's okay to be confident and remind people that you've done something similar before. But you then have to acknowledge that this is different, because every *circumstance* is different. If you come across as arrogant, saying, "I've got this figured out," everybody's just gonna stop listening and then just do what they're told (if you're lucky), which probably gives you about a 50-percent solution, as opposed to if you actually solicited their input and let your people give you a 100-percent solution through their thoughts and ideas.

Another way to demonstrate humanness is to admit mistakes. I always make it a point to tell people of the things that I've done wrong *and* the mistakes that I have made, because that opens the aperture for a good conversation.

Nobody's perfect.

Going back to the Bible and some of what I speak about in *Work Hard, Pray Hard* again, in the book of Romans, Paul says, *"We all sin and fall short of the glory of God."* In the same book, Paul questions God about his state of sinning: *"Why do I do what I know I'm not supposed to do?"* The answer's pretty simple: We're humans! We make mistakes, some large and some not so large. So it's more than okay for senior leaders in Corporate America to demonstrate humanness and be humble by admitting mistakes. That doesn't mean a leader has to lay out all the dirty laundry of all the things they've ever done wrong in times past. But for sure, by acknowledging that mistakes have been made, a leader can connect with and better gain the trust of the workforce.

Along the same lines, as my friend wrote about in his book, it's important for a leader to practice vulnerability. Not continuously, of course. A leader also needs to show strength and conviction. But it's absolutely okay, and sometimes critical, for a leader to say, "I'm not sure what we should do here. I don't have all the answers, and I need your input, so that, indeed, we can have the product be the best product."

Vulnerability can be a bit of a slippery slope. If you're a corporate executive, and you walk around all the time appearing vulnerable, then your folks might develop less confidence in you. "If that person has all those problems, and all those issues, why in the world do we rely on him for our health and well-being?" So don't take it too far. But if you're never saying, "I'm not sure what we should do here, and I need your input," chances are, you're not getting the best out of your employees.

A bit earlier, I mentioned that, throughout my time as a General Officer, I created Strategic Initiatives Groups (or SIGs)—a group of people who helped me think. I picked eight to ten people based on a detailed analysis of what they could contribute. And it wasn't just on-the-job experience. It was all things: it was age, it was gender, it was race, it was religious beliefs. I wanted a group of people who were *different* from me, so when I laid the problem out for them, they all approached the problem with different perspectives.

Creating a SIG is an example of practicing vulnerability and humility.

On a regular basis, I would put my SIGs in a room and say, "Okay, here's what I'm dealing with. Here are the issues at hand, and here are the circumstances. And here's the decision that needs to be made. I need your help." Then I'd go away. I wouldn't direct the conversation. I wouldn't be the person in the room that people were trying to impress. I'd just go away, and I'd come back three days later and say, "Okay, what did you come up with? What did you collectively, as a group, come up with in terms of recommendations on how I ought to proceed and what decisions I should make?"

I also do that with all my clients in Corporate America: I recommend that they put together a group to help them come up with new ideas and share different perspectives and opinions. And that group can't just be full of C Suite executives. I do see that a lot. Some CEO will say, "Well, I already meet with my executives once a week. I already table issues and ask for their input." What I have to remind them is to be a bit more humble than that and to remember that those C Suite executives aren't necessarily the smartest people in the room, either.

In fact, I always advocate that the most important person in an organization is the newest arrival. It's the person who just got there. It's not the CEO with 30 years of experience—it's that new arrival, because they're bringing something brand new to the table. Whether they're straight out of college or straight from another company, they have contributions to make, and you've got to make it a point to listen to them.

Your people have something to say. They want to contribute. Always. No matter who they are. And I got a funny reminder of this not long after I moved my family to a ranch in Central Texas in 2015.

As a lifestyle evangelist, I practice what I preach, not only in the workplace but in my home life. So we were sitting around on the ranch one day as a family, and I went around to all the adults in the room and asked them to speak out loud what their goals were for the coming year. As each one of us spoke, I put those goals on paper, and when we'd all had a turn, I put my pen down. We thought we were finished, until suddenly my five-year-old grandson, J.W., spoke up and said, "Hey! I got goals." We all laughed, but he was serious. He didn't want to be left out. So I picked up my pen and listened to what he had to say, and wrote down his goals, too. They were typical five-year-old goals, along the lines of wanting to play on the playground and spend more time in the pool. But to him, they were important. And I share that story as a reminder that everybody's got goals and ambitions. Everybody. We're all human.

THE HUMILITY OF TIME

One of the major issues I see with corporate leaders when it comes to the allocation of time, believe it or not, has to do with a lack of humility, too—which has a direct effect on the long-term health of any company.

As senior leaders, we're supposed to be building the bench. We're supposed to find people out there who are ready, or *will* be ready, willing, and able to take our position if something were to happen to us. But too many executives seem to operate under the assumption that they have all the time in the world. As if they're going to be there, leading the company, forever. And that's just foolish. There's no guarantee that you're going to be here *tomorrow*. All any of us has is the present. And that's why it's called "the present." The only gift that God has given you is today. You could have a traffic accident on the way home, God forbid; you could have a major issue with your health, God forbid; somebody will have to be ready to step up to the plate. So part of humility is acknowledging that you're not gonna be around forever and that you want to teach, coach, and mentor people to allow them to be prepared to assume the mantle of authority and responsibility, if indeed required.

I don't see that much in Corporate America. I don't see people allocating time just to teach, coach, and mentor. And this gets back to time management: The more senior you get, candidly, the more time you ought to spend out of your office, out and about, talking to people. In my own career, I did find that the higher I got on the totem pole, the less I really knew about what was going on. Why? Because my direct reports would feed me, in many cases, what they thought I needed to hear and not what was really going on. So you've got to get out and about, to walk around, in order to understand what's really happening in your organization, and then take the time to teach, coach, and mentor while you're there.

I also see some confusion as to what it means to coach and to mentor. Coaching and mentoring isn't about dictating and announcing or telling people what to do. It's not about demanding perfection, either. Seeking perfection has a way of stifling creativity, ingenuity, profits, and, most of all, people.

So as you're out and about teaching, coaching, and mentoring, you have to allow people to do things without expecting that everything they do will come back perfect. Instead, keep asking, "Is it good enough?" If you spend your time needling every aspect of your associates' recommendations, they're gonna give up and shut down. Instead, just accept what they want to try (within reason). "Okay. If you think it'll work, then let's do that." Go in thinking, "That's good enough," and then see what happens.

I do believe in giving your people freedom to fail. You've got to give people the opportunity to succeed, of course, but sometimes they're going to fail, and you have to acknowledge that. That's all part of being humble: admitting mistakes, highlighting the number of times that you made mistakes or were given the opportunity to do something, and you failed in that, whether it's professional or personal.

Humility and humanness go a long way in building trust, which is crucial to any High-Performing Organization.

WHAT'S IN A NAME?

Going back to the over-emphasis placed on job titles for a moment, I want to make one last point—one that gets beyond just the position and straight to the humanity of how we deal with each other at work.

How you introduce yourself matters.

I've worked for senior leaders, both in Corporate America and in the military, who made it a point in their introduction to talk to me about their title, as a means to stress to me how important they are. And that just sets the stage for the rest of the conversation.

I left the Army with three stars on my shoulder. I commanded our Third Infantry, of 25,000 troops, during the Surge in Iraq; commanded 65,000 solders at Fort Hood; commanded 120,000 soldiers and civilian employees as the head of all Army Installations, globally, at the Pentagon . . . and I spend a lot of time today telling folks, "Hey, call me 'Rick.'"

There are a lot of people out there who seem to want to call me "General," and I think it's because they don't know a lot of Generals. Maybe they think it's pretty cool that they know a General, and they can refer to me that way: "The General wants this, and the General wants that," and I acknowledge that. But I don't introduce myself as "the General." I don't say, "I'm General Rick Lynch," unless that's the appropriate introduction, based on the audience. I normally just say, "I'm Rick." And when people ask me, "How do you want to be referred to?" I say, "Rick."

An interesting story with my name: My legal name is Ricky Lynch, because, in 1955, when I was born, my mom turned to my grandmother and said, "Go ahead and name the boy." And her favorite character at the time was Ricky Ricardo on "I Love Lucy," so they named me Ricky, after Ricky Ricardo. And that's my legal name. In fact, these days, because my aide-de-camp gave me a gmail account with the name "Ricky" in it when I was leaving the military, a lot of people think, as a result of that, they should call me "Ricky."

No one who knows me well calls me "Ricky." I mean, there's very few people who know me well who still call me "Ricky," because they've heard the Ricky Ricardo story, and some people think it's kind of cute. So they like to refer to me as "Ricky." But I introduce myself as "Rick," and I do this knowing there was a long line of very strong, influential senior leaders before me who asked others to call them by their first name, too. Even though they were senior political appointees, senior leaders in the military, Admirals, and Generals, they would introduce themselves by their first name. And at the end of their emails to me, rather than say, "This is Admiral so and so," they'd say, "This is 'Mike' or 'Bob' or "John,'" whatever it might be, just to get their humanness across.

I first learned this from Admiral Mike Mullen, the Admiral who ended up being the 17th chairman of the Joint Chiefs of Staff. When I was a Two-Star in Italy, he was the commander—a Four-Star General. And he would send me emails that ended with "Mike." He wouldn't say "Admiral Mullen." He'd say "Mike," which allowed me to think, "Hey, I think we've got a pretty good connection here."

That simple difference worked. It was part of what made me want to work hard and do the right thing by Mike, always. That simple difference mattered to me. So I do the same thing in all my correspondence.

I say, "I'm Rick," and as a result of that, people realize that I'm not that big a deal. As I talk about a whole lot in *Work Hard, Pray Hard*, even those of us in the loftiest positions are just human. And the strongest leaders throughout history are those who demonstrate humanness, admit their mistakes, practice vulnerability, don't get the big head, who act with confidence, not arrogance, and the list goes on.

If we want to be the strongest leaders we can be at all levels in Corporate America, we ought to do the same—and prove to our teams that we're not robots. More so, we ought to act with humility to create SIGs; to surround ourselves with people smarter than us. Don't be thin skinned. Don't try to defend your position just because you're already the executive. You don't need to do that. What we need to do is to ensure that we maintain a High-Performing Organization by instilling trust and integrity in our employees (or, better yet, our "partners" or "associates"—because, yes, there is a difference in the titles we assign to our people). We ought to be self-aware and incentivize ourselves to keep doing better. We ought never think we're the smartest person in the room—instead, we should get focused on listening and growing.

Lastly, we ought to develop our employees and incentivize *them* to self-assess and grow with humility as well. And that is what Part II of this book is all about.

PART II

Develop Your Employees

CHAPTER 6

THE MISSING LINK: JOB DESCRIPTIONS

What's in a name? I asked this question in relation to job titles and hierarchy in the last chapter, and the conclusion was basically: Not much. What's much more important than any title you have is what you do and how you act.

"Deeds, Not Words." "Deeds, Not Words." "Deeds, Not Words."

That phrase can't get repeated enough.

But there's another aspect to job titles that's plaguing Corporate America on every level, and it cuts to the infuriating feeling that seems to pervade the entire corporate landscape: This idea that no one is ever held accountable, for almost anything. Whenever something isn't working or something goes wrong, it's always somebody else's fault. Somebody else is to blame. And that causes all kinds of issues that dig deeply into the bottom line.

So here's my blunt assessment, after twelve years of observation and frustration: What's causing people not to be held accountable is a lack of distinct, finite, well-worded job *descriptions* to go with people's job *titles*.

See, I can't hold you responsible for something I didn't tell you was your job. I can't do that. And if I do, and you get fired, chances are, you're going to sue me for wrongful termination—and that is an issue that has turned into an epidemic of wasted time and resources in Corporate America today.

It should be fairly simple to understand: If a job description says do X, and the employee doesn't do X, then they have no case for a wrongful-termination suit. On the other hand, if a job description says do X, and the company was making me do Y, and I wasn't doing Y well because I wasn't supposed to be doing it in the first place, and I wasn't trained and equipped to do Y, then I might have a wrongful-termination suit. If there is no job description at all, then it's all left up to whim and chance, isn't it? How is a company supposed to defend against a wrongful-termination suit when there's no clear, definitive answer as to how or why the employee failed to do a job that wasn't described in the first place? To me it's just common sense. But, as I often said during my Army career, "If common sense were truly common, more people would have it."

Unfortunately, I've had little to no effect in twelve years of getting people to see the importance of job descriptions, and making them well worded, finite, and very descriptive. Why? Because corporate leaders don't seem to want to be "constrained" by anyone's job description. They want the freedom to tell their employees to do, basically, whatever they want. And the result is the mess so many companies find themselves in now, in a litigious society full of very demanding workers.

What's strange is that, in the military, where subordinates have no choice but to follow orders, and have little to no recourse to do anything in terms of suing a leader or the Army itself if they feel they've been wronged, there was never a single job I had that didn't include a very well-detailed job description. Every evaluation I had listed that job description at the top, and my performance was then based how well I performed the duties laid out in that job description.

Here's one example, copied from an annual evaluation of my performance that was handed to me on the 28th of June 1988.

Principal duty title (i.e., job title): Robotics Project Officer.

Job Description: *Oversee robotics activities for USAARMC, as well as for TRADOC Close Combat Heavy forces. Duties include staff-interface responsibility with TRADOC, AMC, DA Staff, and DOD agencies, as well as with Allied countries. Act as a member of joint work groups at all levels planning robotics activities. Plan, coordinate and implement all RDT&E and FDT&E activities for robotic materiel systems for the Close Combat Heavy Force. Supervise other programs/activities as appropriate.*

Putting together a job description isn't difficult. In fact, most corporations go about creating similar descriptions all the time—when seeking candidates to fill positions. Companies regularly create detailed descriptions for the job postings they put up on LinkedIn, or Indeed, or whatever jobs boards might be out there at the time. So, I don't understand why there's such a hesitation to include detailed job descriptions as a part of every employee's files once they're hired.

As you can see in the example above (even if you don't understand all the acronyms), my job was well-defined, and it required me to supervise "other programs/activities as appropriate." So my duties weren't strictly limited. The scope of "as appropriate" could be wide at times—and was. But at least I had something to look at, to remind me (and my supervisors) what I was supposed to be doing on a daily basis.

The reason to do something similar in Corporate America? Again, it's mostly to protect yourself when something goes wrong, in order to allow you to course-correct quickly, and, hopefully, to learn from any mistakes. And I'm just not seeing that in Corporate America, at all.

Without well-thought-out, detailed, refined job descriptions, you can't do RACI, which means that you can't pick out who you hold Responsible, who's Accountable, who needs to be Consulted, and who needs to be Informed.

And FYI, putting such job descriptions in place for every position doesn't restrict you from anything. If you ask the person to do something that's not in their job description, you just need to modify their job description to include that thing. Done. Covered. Easy. But most of the senior executives I've dealt with don't want to take the time to get into it, because—they say—they want to have more flexibility.

I understand their initial thoughts on this. For many of my clients, especially post-COVID, there is a shortage of resources. A shortage of people, time, and money are causing people to do multiple jobs. On some regular basis, the bosses are saying, "Okay. You've got to do this, which is what I hired you for. But in addition to that, you gotta do *this*, because I can't afford to hire another person." So people end up doing their job as well as somebody else's job. And the leaders don't want to put the truth of that situation into the job description, because as a result of that, they'll probably be forced to do something to properly compensate the person that they're working to death.

If any of that sounds familiar to you, especially if you've been on the receiving end of it, you know how frustrating it is. And if you've been on the other end—doling out the extra work without proper compensation—chances are, you know you're guilty of it. You may not care, or maybe you feel guilty about it but don't see any way around it. It doesn't matter. The end result of this type of leadership is a loss of integrity, a loss of trust, and, ultimately, the loss of the overworked employees—some of whom you might have to let go (because they're not able to do all the jobs you've told them to do) and some of whom just may sue you on their way out the door. Which means this practice is costing you time and money, and hurting your bottom line regardless. So why not do something about it? Why not get out in front of the problem and stop it before it goes any further?

Detailed job descriptions do more than protect your company from lawsuits. They provide an easy way for your company to evaluate performance. They provide an easy way for employees themselves to measure their own performance (remember the importance of self-awareness) against a tangible, visible standard to which they're expected to adhere. They allow you to hire appropriately, evaluating the skill set for a given job rather than some vague, ever-evolving set of expectations that a new hire may not be able to fill—which will cost you when they leave after a short period of time, and you have to start the hiring process all over again. But mostly, they bring peace of mind to all involved.

And a little peace goes a long way.

The most important thing to remember is that we're dealing with humans. So a job description doesn't have to be a program, in the sense that we might have to program a robot to handle each step of a particular task.

One time, in Fort Worth, while I was in charge of UTARI, I was asked to be keynote speaker at a large function. So I turned to my research scientist and said, "Develop a program where this robot we're working on will wheel itself down to the head table at this function. Have it ask the guests, 'Would you like red wine, or white wine?' listen for the answer, and then pour the appropriate wine into the guest's glass." That was a pretty high-risk thing to do. This was a formal gathering. There were women in white gowns ordering red wine from our robot. But the research scientist came through, and the robot performed beautifully (thankfully!)

Robots need programs to work, otherwise, they're just expensive boxes. Humans are intelligent. They can pick up cues, learn from what others are doing, etc., and often manage to get by without a job description. But why would we want our employees to just "get by"? In any High-Performing Organization, we want our employees to be the best they can be, from day one, if possible. There's no need to let them waste time and energy trying to figure out what they're supposed to be doing. Just tell them! It can be as simple as a clear directive for an achievable task, and, if they're a strong thinker, they'll get to the goal themselves, without all sorts of detailed or micromanaged "programming." Remember how Ulysses S. Grant handled the job description he was handed by President Lincoln: Go take Vicksburg. Or later, in World War II, when General Eisenhower was given a "job description" from the Combined Chiefs of Staff to invade Germany. In this case, it was a little more detailed than the instructions that Grant was given. Eisenhower was told to go through England, cross the European Continent, and, in conjunction with other allied nations, undertake operations aimed at the heart of Germany and the destruction of their armed forces. It would be up to him how to figure out how to accomplish all of that, but the directive was clear. The job description was clear. He knew what had to be done and what he was responsible for. He was not responsible for handling public relations, or public perception of how things were going. He was not responsible for leading the allied-nations' forces, but rather to work in conjunction with them. It's a big example, and a little bit of a stretch, I realize, compared to what a company might hand to a research assistant or a computer analyst. But I hope you get the point.

The thing is, in addition to lawsuits, I've found that the lack of clear job descriptions causes other types of friction in companies, too. I watched a worst-case scenario happen with one of my clients, in which two of the senior executives didn't get along. So, one of the executives hired a direct report to work for his team, and only his team, and he did so without providing a job description. He then sent this direct report off to do various tasks, which he was very good at, but which were inevitably stepping on the toes of the *other* leader's team members. This caused all kinds of problems and friction within the company, and the poor direct report had nothing to back up what he was doing except to say, "Well, my boss told me to do that." He didn't have a job description to point to, to let others know that he was now assigned to take over those tasks. I tried to sit these two leaders down and talk to them about what was happening, to try to resolve the friction, but neither of them was willing to sit across a table from the other, and neither one of them wanted to change their ways—especially when it came to clarifying roles and defining which team members were handling which tasks. They were so territorial that it hurt the whole place.

If either of them had been given clear job descriptions themselves, perhaps they wouldn't have come to blows the way they did, let alone gone and messed up other people's careers while they did it.

When you all know what's expected, there are far fewer misunderstandings, which means there are fewer problems in the workplace. Fewer mistakes. Fewer slowdowns and bottlenecks. Instead? There's more productivity and a higher chance of getting jobs done.

Improving job descriptions is just one link in the chain of changes you can make to help move any organization toward the goal of becoming High-Performing. But it's an important one, and a strong one: a link that will help hold the whole chain together when the inevitable forces of our VUCA world try to pull it apart.

> **When you all know what's expected, there are fewer problems in the workplace.**

CHAPTER 7

THE POWER OF
PERFORMANCE APPRAISALS

The lack of detailed job descriptions isn't the only major missing link I see causing Corporate America's overall failure to create High-Performing Organizations. The other is a disturbing trend that I want to talk about in detail here: the lack of effective performance counseling.

How are people supposed to know how they're doing if they're never evaluated and told how they're doing? And how in the name of anything that makes any sense is a company supposed to know how its people are doing if they never take the time to find out?

As I would tell my commanders in the Army, "Anything that is not inspected is neglected."

Yet, I've got clients who, candidly, don't talk to their people at all during the course of the year. The only performance counseling, if any, takes place at the end of the year, with the requirement to do an annual appraisal. And oh, by the way, since we didn't counsel them during the course of the year, the annual appraisal at the end of the year tends to be overinflated and all focused on the positive—because bonuses are determined based on that annual appraisal.

What's especially problematic to me is that one of the only reasons there's no counseling during the year is because so many leaders in Corporate America are unwilling to have uncomfortable conversations with their people. Out of fear or uncertainty—and, in some cases, a misplaced sense of politeness—leaders are just plain hesitant to set somebody down and say, "Hey, you're good, but not *that* good. There are things that we need to work on, so that you can improve and be a better contributor to the team."

Everyone who ever worked for me, from the time I graduated from West Point in 1977 to this day, gets counseled once a month—in writing. Once a month, I set my direct reports down and I say, "Okay, let's talk about how the last 30 days went."

First, I highlight strengths: What went well over the course of the previous 30 days? You want to start every conversation upbeat and positive. Highlight what went well, and *then* talk about areas for improvement. I don't ever say, "These are the weaknesses that I've observed," because (as I learned the hard way, early on) your people will just shut down. You can see their demeanor change as they sit there thinking, *Who do you think you are telling me I've got **weaknesses**?* So instead, I highlight the fact that there are areas that we need to work on to improve, and how we can work on those things *together*.

Did you notice I said, "We"—the first-person-plural pronoun? After all these years, I'm absolutely convinced that leaders should never, ever use the second-person-singular pronoun ("You"). They should always talk in the collective pronoun "we." What can *we* do together? Not specifically what do *you* need to be doing or what I did. And once you do that, then you find yourself able to have a conversation that highlights both good things and bad things.

Once that discussion has happened, then we move on to the last part of the evaluation: My direct reports and I agree on the objectives for the following month. "What are we going to get done in the next 30 days?" And we agree on those objectives. Then I sign the document, and they sign the document. They take a copy; I keep a copy. Thirty days later, we pull it out, and we start at the bottom of the paper: "What were the objectives that we agreed on? What did we say we were gonna get done in the thirty days? And what did we actually accomplish?" That starts the whole process over again: areas for improvement, strengths that have been observed—that kind of stuff.

I can honestly say that if I had a military career that was successful, at all, it was because I did that. I talked to my people. My people knew where they stood. Nobody who worked for Lynch has ever said, "I didn't know what he was thinking," because I told them. I told them once a month, and I did it in a professional manner.

There's a lot of folks who say, "Well, I don't do that." Instead, they do what we in the military called "footlocker counseling," where they talk to their people "all the time." Of course, we all know that "all the time" is usually an exaggeration. But even if they're doing it often, the point is it's not formalized, it's not rigid, and it's not scheduled. And that's fine. I'll never argue that footlocker counseling isn't important. It's super important. Those conversations are helpful conversations, and I'll spend the next chapter about the importance of routine counseling. But they're not the same as a formalized evaluation, which offers consistency and takes the fear away from both parties. This isn't an either-or situation: You can do plenty of footlocker counseling, but that doesn't negate the need for more formalized appraisals.

I saw it in action, and I learned it firsthand: If you want high-performance, if you want consistency, if you want to keep track of what's going on with your people (and to have them keep track of what's going on with you), then, once in a while, you've got to sit 'em down and have a detailed conversation, so that, at the end of the conversation, they leave knowing exactly where they stand and what it is they need to do. And that makes this entire process of performance appraisals unbelievably easy.

Oh, and, by the way, at the end of every performance-counseling session, it's the perfect time to ask, "How am *I* doing?" Give your direct reports a chance, then and there, to share a little assessment of your own performance in the interest of self-awareness. It's a simple ask, and as long as you're listening, actively, and acting on what they tell you, it's an ask that helps to build camaraderie and trust between you and your direct report.

I'll talk more about this a little later in this chapter, but it's a good thing to keep in mind as we go along: You continuously ought to be interested in getting feedback on yourself, even as you're giving feedback to others.

As stated in the Bible, in Philippians 2:3: *"Do nothing out of selfish ambition or vain conceit. Rather, in humility value others above yourselves, not looking to your own interests but each of you to the interests of the others."*

THE NUMBERS

Now, obviously, you can't keep track of all your people if you've got too many people to deal with. You can't be spending an hour on each of them if you've got 40-plus people under your watch—you'd never do anything else. Time management is such a big part of all this, and in twelve years of trying to teach various corporations about this, it's the time issue where I get the biggest pushback.

So let's talk about structure and the issue of how many direct reports fall under the leadership of any one person. In the military, we would limit the number of direct reports any one of us had to between five and seven. As a result of that, we had a limited number of people we were dealing with, and we could effectively do the performance appraisals and routine counseling required in a High-Performing Organization (which, as I think we agreed early on, the Army most certainly is.)

Unfortunately, in Corporate America, I see a lot of folks who have fifteen to twenty direct reports in their care, and, as we say in Texas, "That dog don't hunt." No empathetic human being can effectively teach, coach, and mentor twenty separate individuals. It ought to be limited to five to seven.

If you limit yourself to five to seven, and you spend one hour a month counseling each one of them, that's seven hours. Now, when I'm preparing to counsel and counsel effectively, that's another seven hours I spend just getting ready for those one-on-ones. So that's fourteen hours of time well spent.

"Fourteen hours!" some folks complain. "How can I possibly find fourteen hours a month?"

The *how*—which is all about time management—is up to you, so let me explain the *why*. This isn't about fourteen hours of meetings. It's not fourteen hours of people talking garbage. It's fourteen hours of *development*. It's one hour per direct report, face to face. To do this effectively, that means one hour per person, no distractions, no devices. No secretary walking in saying you got a call. (I'll get deeper into this in the next chapter as well.)

What's happening now, unfortunately, with most of my clients, is they say they're too busy doing other stuff. So they put off their Performance Appraisals until November, to get ready for bonus time, and then, "Ooops! Somebody wasn't up to par and had to be let go. And we had no written record from the first ten months of the year to show any bad performance from that person, which means that the person who got fired turned around and sued us. Oh, no! Better settle."

Come on, people. We've got to do better.

Of the thirty-plus clients I've worked with, only five do performance appraisals effectively. And guess what? Those five are the most-successful companies I work with, by far. Coincidence? Don't fool yourself. High-Performing Organizations take care of their people. And a gigantic part of taking care of your people is letting them know where they stand and listening to where they want to go.

The numbers are tricky. Time is stretched, especially in organizations whose resources are stretched. So a little bit of adaptation may be necessary (*Adapt or Die*, right?). Maybe you can't get it done once a month. But in my mind, and in my experience, you have to do it at least once a quarter to have any impact. I always advocate once a month. But once a quarter is reasonable—and the majority of businesses don't do even that. Even when they do, it's often some generic performance appraisal or something too bureaucratic, which isn't effective and yields little to no outcome.

With a proper performance appraisal—i.e., once you've done all your preparation, you've got all your information, you've filled out all the appropriate forms, and you've brought the person in—you actually make it enjoyable. I've seen so many times where people just dread the performance appraisal. "Oh, my God, that's gonna be miserable"—and that's both the person who's being appraised *and* the person who's doing the appraisal talking.

When you think about it, the reason we even do performance appraisals is, number one, to have an accurate and actionable evaluation of the performance of the individual. I mean, that's critical to talk about. It's got to be accurate, which means that, over the course of the reporting period, you had to have taken detailed notes; you had to have kept a folder, if you will, on each individual, noting when things occurred, good and bad. You keep a note in that folder (either paper or electronic), so when it's time to do the performance appraisal, it's an accurate reflection of performance and an actionable evaluation.

The second reason we do performance appraisals is to encourage improvement—improvement in individuals, so that the organization itself improves.

That's critical. An organization cannot improve if its people aren't improving.

Heck, even robots need to receive new programming if we want them to do new things or do things differently. It shouldn't come as a surprise that people need a boost and some education now and then, too.

> An organization cannot improve if its people aren't improving

In the military, we spend a whole lot of time developing people. I mean, I left West Point in 1977 as a Second Lieutenant, and I left the Army in January 2012 as a Lieutenant General. And over those 35 years, there were amazing opportunities for me to grow and learn.

The same should apply in Corporate America—and it does in High-Performing Organizations.

In the military, we say you grow and learn in three different ways.

1. You grow and learn based on **institutional development**. So the army sent me to West Point, they sent me to the Command General Staff College, and they sent me to the Army War College. Spending time in those institutions allowed me time to improve, pause, reflect, study, research—all those things.

2. The second aspect is **organizational development**: Put folks in a position that they're prepared to execute well, and let them work there and learn as they go. In many cases, I've seen it both in the military and Corporate America: you give individuals what's called "on-the-job training." You put them in something outside their

comfort zone, so they can learn. I remember vividly when I was selected to be an Assistant Division Commander. Within Army Divisions, there are two Assistant Division Commanders, one for maneuver and operations, and one for support. And when I was selected to be an Assistant Division Commander, I thought for sure that the Division Commander was gonna make me the Assistant Division Commander for Operations and Maneuver, because that's what I had done for my whole career. Instead, he said, "No, I'm making you the Assistant Division Commander for Support, because I want you to learn that side of the Division." Let me tell you: That was invaluable. That was organizational development via on-the-job training.

Another time, as a One-Star General, I was sent into the Balkans to become the Chief of Staff for the Kosovo Force, even though I didn't know anything about peace support operations, or multinational operations, or life in the Balkans. The Chief of Staff of the Army said, "You gotta learn, so we're gonna send you there, and you can learn." That's organizational development, and I do occasionally see that in Corporate America as well, where we give people the opportunity to grow and learn by giving them different jobs within an organization.

3. And the last pillar of development is **self-development**. There is an obligation for individuals who want to grow to learn to develop themselves. So what we did in the military, and what I advocate for Corporate America, are things like: Have a reading list. Distribute a list of books that are professionally rewarding, and ask your folks to read those books and then discuss them with you over time. There are just so many things available online now in terms of webinars. There is no way to argue that, if your people take some time to develop themselves, they're going to

be better people and, therefore, help to improve the overall performance of your division, and your organization.

So that's why these performance appraisals are so critical: Because they help us develop our people in all three areas. And, in simple terms, it's how we tell folks how they're doing. It's our chance to answer: "Are they indeed doing the job in a professional manner—and to which they were assigned?" and then identify those things that we need to work on and want to work on—so that the individual *and* the company can continue to grow. Together.

In this context, I hope you can see why I dedicated the previous chapter to job descriptions: You have to tell people what they're responsible for, and what they're accountable for before you hold them to some standard for a particular job. Writing down, in detail, precisely what the individual is responsible for makes the task of doing the performance appraisal easy. You evaluate performance against those skills that are identified as a requirement in the job description. I know there are fluid areas. I know there's lots of moving parts. I know a lot of times you expect people to do stuff separate from their own jobs, because it needs to get done, especially in small organizations. But you've got to take the time to do detailed job descriptions, or you can't have an effective performance-appraisal process.

And this is all part of the whole performance-appraisal rubric. You have to evaluate people on their actions. You have to evaluate people on their adherence to values. You have to evaluate your people on their potential to perform other jobs. You got to identify specifically those skill sets that need to be strengthened and come up with a plan on how to do that.

ENDING THE DREAD

So let's talk specifically about how better to address the whole performance-appraisal process. Candidly, if you study this as I have these last twelve years, there is, without question, an overall dissatisfaction in the process. Senior leaders, CEOs, and C Suite executives don't think the performance appraisals are helpful in identifying the top performers. When it comes to the people being appraised, when it's not done well, I've found that fewer than one out of five are motivated by the process. So it becomes a process that everybody dreads. "Nobody wants to do it, but we have to do it, so let's do it once a year and get it over with." No! That's the opposite of what it should be about, which is to create and identify an accurate and actionable evaluation of employee performance, so that, at the very least, they can develop skills (as necessary) to do what's in their job description.

I do have clients who do it well. They acknowledge that they gotta have a process to do annual performance appraisals, but they also have a requirement for monthly touchpoints that is monitored by the senior leaders in the company, to make sure it's happening. And that monthly touchpoint is not just, "Hi, how you doing?" It isn't about checking the box. It's a detailed discussion of performance on a monthly basis. And all that feeds into the annual performance appraisal. These are High-Performing Organizations that recognize it's critical. It has to be done.

As I already mentioned, it's amazing to me how resistant so many corporate leaders are to performance appraisals, just because people are averse to having uncomfortable conversations. That's why I try to coach leaders to start every conversation in a positive fashion. Ask them how their family's doing. Then go in order, every time. Start by talking about what they did well over the reporting period, and then talk about areas where there's room for improvement. "What can we improve on?" Take some ownership that it's not going as well as we would like—meaning, "I'm part of the problem. And you're a part of the problem. So what can we do to improve?" Then you can start into the objectives you can both agree on.

Finding it difficult to have uncomfortable conversations isn't anything you need to be ashamed of. In all these years, I've found that *most* people are uncomfortable telling somebody else that they're not living up to the established standard. My own wife, Sarah, has a hard time telling anybody when they're not doing well, even if it's clear as day to everyone around us. My son, Lucas, finds it difficult to confront poor performers in his role, too. My daughter, Susan? She's more like me in that regard. She just confronts people when they need confronting, and she's learned from me that it takes some finesse, so that the person she's confronting doesn't shut down.

You can learn this stuff, just as I learned it, by taking it on one step at a time and seeking out resources to help you accomplish your goal. I have a book I go back to time and again, called *Crucial Conversations*. That book helped me, and I'm sure there are other books that address this topic as well. The main thing I want to get across here is that it has to happen, or your organization will inevitably falter.

One last thing about the Performance Appraisal meetings themselves: Toward the end of the meeting, it's important to put your pen down and ask whoever you're counseling, "How am *I* doing?" which gives the other person the opportunity to give you some feedback. The first time you do that, they'll probably say (as they did to me), "Oh, you're doing great. I love working for you!" and it's up to you to be the humble, active, listening leader and say, "Unacceptable. Now go away and come back for our next meeting with a list of three things I need to work on. Thanks!"

At the next meeting, and the next, the conversation will get easier—and more productive—for both of you. I promise.

STEPPING BACK FROM THE MAP

Now that you've heard some up-close advice about what to do in the room during the actual Performance Appraisal, I think it's important to step back from the map for a moment and observe a few other trends I've seen across thirty companies in twelve years.

The fear of having uncomfortable conversations gets in the way of accomplishing forward movement in other areas as well—especially in meetings.

One thing I did for a lot of my clients was to monitor their executive-team meetings, not so much listening to the substance of the conversations but instead watching body language and responsiveness. Many times, executives would call me after one of those meetings and say, "I should have said this." So I'd ask them, "Why didn't you say it?" And they would say, "Well, I know you're gonna talk to the CEO anyway, so I'm hoping *you* can tell him what the point is."

Rather than directly confront the CEO, they would ask *me* to confront the CEO for them!

Come on, folks. We're all adults. We can do better.

Worse still? The same thing often came from the CEO. I had CEOs telling me, on multiple occasions, "You know, Rick, this particular person isn't toeing the line. Would you tell them that they need to do a better job with that?"

Seriously. This is happening across all sorts of corporations. My answer was always, "Well, why don't you tell them, Mr. or Ms. CEO? It's important for *you* to have that uncomfortable conversation yourself."

Honestly, this sort of fear of confrontation is the rule, not the exception. So, now that the cat's out of the bag, how about we change things? How about we stop looking at honest conversation as "confrontation" and instead start talking to each other, like grown-ups?

Like leaders.

Just remember: This isn't gonna work if you're not an engaged leader from the start, if you don't have established values on display and visible through your actions, and if you're not talking to each other on a regular basis and carrying out performance appraisals as a regular part of doing business.

AN EXAMPLE FROM HISTORY

I get into all these sorts of issues during my Leadership Tours, just to give a broader perspective of how important these same issues have always been, in all sorts of organizations. I often find that C Suite leaders who've been resistant to changing their minds on performance appraisals and the importance of engaged leadership change their minds once they've stood on Civil War battlefields, or the beaches at Normandy, and compared their daily activities to the weight of what happened on those hallowed grounds.

As I try to make my points about why performance appraisals matter, and why having difficult conversations matter, I often turn to the lens of history to remind people that sometimes even the best leaders step out of line and need to be kept in check for the good of the organization.

There is perhaps no clearer case of this to be found than in the relationship between President Dwight D. Eisenhower and General George S. Patton toward the end of World War II. Patton and Eisenhower both went to West Point, with Patton graduating in 1909 and Eisenhower graduating in 1913. They both served as early participants in the Army Tank Corps (a path I would also follow in my early Army career), and Patton served in combat in World War I before rising to the high position of leading our Third Army in World War II.

The two men crossed paths along the way and became friends—but they always had a tumultuous relationship. They would argue over things, even screaming at each other at times. Yet they always came back to the friendship, which grew out of the huge respect they had for each other and the skills they each brought to the table. One time, they worked together to disassemble an entire tank, down to the last bolt, and then rebuilt it themselves, just for the sake of being sure they knew everything about the equipment they were preparing to take into battle. Talk about dedication.

In the end, even though Eisenhower was younger, he became Patton's superior when he was appointed Supreme Commander, Allied Forces Europe (and later when he became the Commander in Chief, as President)—and, at that point, when referring to their friendship, Eisenhower was once described as "a nice man who owns a pit bull." When Pitbull Patton got out of line, Eisenhower had the task of reprimanding him. He couldn't let friendship or anything else get in the way.

Things really came to a head in 1942, when Patton was visiting a hospital, and he met a patient who was suffering from shell shock (which is akin to what we now refer to as PTSD). For whatever reason, Patton felt it was appropriate to slap the man—and the media was right there watching when he did it. It was out of line, and Eisenhower gave him a talking-to. It was such a scandal at the time that Eisenhower had no choice but to remove Patton from command. He also made him go apologize to the whole Third Army. (There's a great presentation of this in the movie *Patton*. It's worth a watch.) He then explained that he expected Patton would change his behavior going forward, "because fundamentally, he is so avid for recognition as a great military commander, that he will ruthlessly suppress any habit of his that will tend to jeopardize it."

Eisenhower was right, and Patton was on his best behavior for a while. Plus, he truly was the best man for the job. There's no arguing the fact that we won the War, and Patton's leadership represented a large part of our ability to do so. Of course, Patton was who he was, and in 1945, he caused problems again when he was speaking to a group of women and publicly disparaged the denazification process. He basically said we should go fight the Russians, then and there, since we would have to deal with them eventually. And while his words were prophetic, they were not in line with what America stood for at the end of that war, and Eisenhower, once again, had to remove him from duty. Even after all of that, when Eisenhower was asked in 1945 to rank all of the American Generals in Europe, he ranked Bradley and Army-Air Force

General Carl Spaatz number one; Walter Bedell Smith, his chief of staff, number two; and Patton as number three. So even after he relieved him twice, he still ranked him as the third most capable General in the United States Army.

Treating Patton appropriately through Performance Appraisals was a necessary part of getting the job done—in this case, the job of defeating a global enemy.

In a 1946 review of the book *Patton's Third Army*, Eisenhower wrote, "George Patton was the most brilliant commander of an army in the open field that our or any other service produced. But his army was part of the whole organization and its operations part of a great campaign."

Patton and Eisenhower remained friends from WWI through the end of WWII, 'til the day Patton passed away in a tragic accident. It could not have been easy for Eisenhower to step in and reprimand him and relieve him, twice. But it was necessary for the good of the whole. And it just goes to show you that, as a leader, sometimes you've got to make the hard call.

Now tell me: What situation does a C Suite executive face that's more dire and important than what Eisenhower was facing with Patton? I can't think of one. Anyone who commands the attention of shareholders from quarter to quarter, directing thousands, millions, even billions of dollars in value and resources should certainly have enough gall to stand up for an uncomfortable conversation whenever it's needed. Even if they have to have that difficult discussion with a friend.

It's not that hard.

I'm happy to say I've batted better than .500 in terms of getting my clients to change their approach in order to be at least somewhat more effective with performance appraisals in these last twelve years. And it's made a tremendous, positive difference in each of those companies. The people the executives were working with tended to become more responsive and more receptive, because they were convinced that their bosses truly cared about them. They stopped dreading performance reviews and started to embrace them instead, for the simple fact that they started to believe that their bosses were trying to help them be better.

And that's the whole key, right there: People want to know that you *care*.

I already mentioned the three aspects of development: self-development, institutional development, and organizational development. And when the CEO or another top executive comes across as the guy or gal who truly wants to help you improve, then everyone else tends to be more receptive, too.

A CORPORATE EXAMPLE OF SUCCESS

I do have a client who, in my opinion, has perfected the art of performance appraisals. Not only do they perform annual performance appraisals at bonus time, but they've initiated monthly check-ins that are automated. This particular company requires every supervisor to sit down with their people on a monthly basis and highlight good and bad things from the performance of the previous month. And it works at all levels: with managers who are evaluated by directors, directors who are evaluated by senior directors, senior directors who are evaluated by vice presidents, vice presidents who are evaluated by senior vice presidents, senior vice presidents who are evaluated by executive vice presidents, and executive vice presidents who are evaluated by C Suite executives. In order to make sure that it's not overly cumbersome, this particular company automated the entire process, so it could be done relatively easily. It forced the leaders to think through: "What did I observe in the performance of my direct report? Over the course of the last 30 days, what went well? What should be amplified, highlighted, and congratulated? What *didn't* go so well?"

I'm happy to say that, over an extended period of time stretching back many years, this company has done extremely well—including through COVID and after—at weathering storms and adapting to rapidly changing forces in their particular marketplace. Why? If you ask them (and I have, again and again), almost everyone at the company agrees: It's because everyone in the company knows where they stand. Always.

This particular company even took it a step further: In addition to standard performance appraisals, this company put together a collective meeting, once a year, with all of the appropriate leaders, in which they review the cross-functional performance of the subordinate leaders in the company. Why? Because what they found after putting in all of this effort is that, often, though an individual may do well in his or her particular chain, they might do a lousy job cross-functionally. And there's not a client out there that doesn't have a whole series of stovepipes, whether it's sales and marketing, finance, production, or whatever it might be. And often, people may be doing well in their respective silos, but they don't do well between the silos.

So this particular client gathers all the leaders together on an annual basis and does what they call "calibration." They gather the appropriate leaders in a room, and they tee up a name. Then, collectively, they talk about that individual. And when they come across an individual who may be doing well in his stovepipe but is doing a lousy job helping the company cross-functionally, they recommend and take appropriate action to deal with it: teaching, coaching, mentoring, re-assigning, or whatever it might be. That all comes out of the annual calibration.

So that's a real, bright, and shining star with performance appraisals—and the company's quarterly results reflect the consistent efforts they make.

Unfortunately, across my thirty-plus clients, that client was an anomaly. Even in some cases where the company policy mandated quarterly or semi-annual appraisals, they just weren't happening; and in some cases, the senior leaders didn't mandate it because they didn't do it themselves. It wasn't uncommon to see people go the entire year without anybody sitting down and saying, "Here's how you're doing." Other times, these clients *would* have performance appraisals, but because they didn't have adequate job descriptions in place, the appraisals weren't based on any type of metrics. They were way too subjective. There was nothing that people were being measured against, and, as a result, it was difficult to tell them how they were doing.

Finally, in some cases, even if there were some metrics to measure the job by, the company had failed to establish refined goals—the important aspects of establishing a foundation that I talked about in Part I. (I hope by now it's clear that corporations ought to have corporate goals that everybody's being held accountable for, and then individual goals as well.) A number of my clients never went through the gyration to establish goals, be they individual *or* corporate. So the performance appraisals weren't specific in terms of either. They weren't direct. They weren't focused on a specific topic. Which left their people feeling directionless, even after a sit-down with the boss.

The worst part is that every one of those companies that failed to improve in these areas suffered financially because of it. Maybe it didn't happen in one quarter or another. But at some point, every one of them took a tumble, which left their boards sitting there, wringing their hands, wondering what went wrong—when the obvious answer was right there in front of them the whole time.

If you want your company to do well, quarter-to-quarter, you need to stay on top of how your company is doing. Not just on paper, but in the deepest corners of your organization. You have to know that the people working for you are actually working *for you*. And in order to do that, you need to spend time and resources developing your employees—and assessing how those employees are doing—at every turn.

CHAPTER 8

THE GIFT OF ROUTINE COUNSELING

Performance appraisals are one thing. But they still don't dig all the way down to the heart of what turns an organization into a truly High-Performing Organization.

As I've mentioned in all my previous books and in the intro to this book, the most important thing that we can do as leaders is take care of our people. Our people are the most precious resource we have, which is why, in the military, we have a saying: "Mission first, people always." In Corporate America, it's the same: If you take care of your people, they will take care of you.

These phrases exist because they're *true.*

As I mentioned in the last chapter, I truly believe that the one thing that made me relatively successful in the United States military and beyond is the fact that I talk to people routinely about their performance. I counsel my people, all the time.

It's sad to me that in both the military and in Corporate America, that phrase tends to be taken negatively: When people think about "counseling," they think, "You only get counseled when you do something wrong."

That's not right.

What's right is: You get counseled by people who *care about you*. You can trust that those people who care about you will tell you about how great you are and what you're *doing* great, and also tell you what we need to work on, and what we all ought to agree upon as objectives for the following period of time. So I'm going to spend a lot of time in this chapter digging deeper into the importance of routine counseling.

Just to reiterate: Since I left West Point in 1977, everybody who's ever worked for me has been counseled once a month—in writing. Now, when I was in charge of IMCOM at the Pentagon, that was 120,000 people I oversaw. Clearly, I didn't counsel 120,000 people one-on-one. But I *did* counsel my direct reports, and they counseled their direct reports, and on and on throughout the entire chain of command. And if you work the simple math, you know the counseling period that I'm going to describe to you lasts about an hour; and it takes about an hour per counseling period to prepare. So it's two hours per counseling period total. And if you've got five to seven direct reports, and you counsel them once a month, even in a worst-case scenario, you're spending 14 hours of the month either preparing for or conducting routine counseling.

There's a reason I'm repeating this information, and the reason is simple: This routine counseling is the best money that you can spend in terms of time management—because the rewards and return on investment are so great.

FACE IT, FACE TO FACE

If you've read a thing or two about leadership, then you already know that leadership is a contact sport. And that description most certainly applies to this: You can't do counseling effectively unless it's face to face. When people say to me, "Well, that just can't happen, General, because we've got people nationwide," I say, "Well, there are such things as trains, planes, and automobiles." But I understand what they're saying, and, if you truly can't do it face to face once a month, you ought to do it at least *virtually* once a month. It's the connecting with people, seeing them, talking eye to eye that matters most, and technology allows us to Zoom right into people's living rooms, wherever they are. That's important: To see their face, see their attire, see their expressions, see their environment. So if that's the best you can do, that's adequate, but not nearly as good as in person.

Always remember, leadership is a contact sport. And if you want to be an effective communicator, you've really got to do things by hand and in person. There is no substitute. Especially in times of crisis or difficulty.

I mentioned in the last chapter that some of the C Suite executives I've counseled have learned to embrace difficult conversations and performance appraisals after standing on battlefields during my Leadership Tours. Well, the same applies to Routine Counseling. I've seen more than one of my clients decide to get tougher about dealing with their own people after a trip to Gettysburg, that's for sure—especially after they learn about what happened between Gen. Robert E. Lee and one of his most-trusted subordinates, Jeb Stuart.

Stuart was a cadet when Lee was the Superintendent of West Point, and the two of them bonded early on. Stuart regularly went to Lee's house for dinner. He was practically a member of Lee's family long before he became a magnificent cavalry officer for the Confederacy during the Civil War.

As Lee was going into Gettysburg, he needed Stuart to be his eyes and ears. But Stuart, who'd just got his butt kicked in another battle, let his ego get in the way. Instead of checking with Lee first and following orders to move north into Pennsylvania and scope out the scene, Stuart tried to regain his fame by doing an end-run around the Union forces and attacking our nation's capital—without telling General Lee. So not only did Lee not know what was going on, but he was left blind as to how many forces the Union had near Gettysburg, because Stuart got tied up in Washington rather than going ahead into Pennsylvania as he'd been ordered to do.

Stuart's misguided excursion ended up being a big reason the Confederates lost so many soldiers—and so much momentum—at Gettysburg.

A leader can't lead when one of his subordinates leaves him flying blind. Stuart needed to be reminded of that—via some pointed routine counseling, in real time.

This particular scene plays out in the movie *Gettysburg*, which is required viewing and a big topic of discussion for this particular Leadership Tour of mine, and I encourage anyone with even a slight interest in American History to watch that movie if you get the chance.

Even though they had been close, like family, for years, when the appropriate time came, General Lee called Jeb Stuart in and asked his aide to leave the room. He then stood there, in his full-dress uniform, and was very direct with his counseling—telling him exactly what he did wrong, and why his actions were unacceptable. They were actions that cost hundreds of lives!

At that point, Stuart was ashamed. He offered to resign.

Lee's response? "We have no time for that." He needed Stuart in the fight—but he needed him to get back in line and improve his performance.

"Any questions?"

"No questions," Stuart said with his head bowed.

"You're dismissed."

It's a poignant example of the importance of routine counseling—in this case, after lives were lost, and the strength of the Confederacy itself was put at risk because of the inappropriate actions of Lee's young, trusted friend and confidant.

As I've talked about in previous books, 70 percent of communication is in the hands of the listener. In the case of Lee and Stuart, Lee was left with no doubt that Stuart had heard every word he said. He could see it in his demeanor. And that knowledge was crucial. If Stuart hadn't been paying attention, didn't care, or seemed to have his mind elsewhere, perhaps Lee would have had no choice but to relieve him of his command. But because he could read Stuart's body language and because he knew him so well, Lee had full confidence that Stuart wouldn't try anything like that again in the days ahead.

READING THE ROOM

An engaged leader needs to know that his words have been heard.

What I find today, when using virtual technology, is that it's difficult to determine whether the person that you're talking to is truly listening, just based on watching for active-listening signals. So I think this *all* ought to be done face to face whenever possible, even if it means traveling to do so; and that's how I'm going to describe how I teach my executives and others to hold their monthly one-on-ones.

Just so you know, all of these techniques have now been used by various clients of mine, all with good effect.

First off, the format for your one-on-one counseling sessions ought to be very, very comfortable. And while it might be awkward to start this from scratch, ultimately, the people you're talking to ought to look forward every month to coming in and having a conversation with their boss. So you've got to make it a safe environment. They've got to feel like you truly care. They've got to know that you care about their concerns, and that you care about *them*. So it's just really got to be a comfortable environment: Your personal, closed-door office, if possible, or a private conference room or other area of some sort where no one has to worry about being overheard.

I've said this before, too, but you ought to start off every session with a question, like, "How's your family?" I mean, that shows them that you care right away, but at the same time, it sets the stage for the rest of the conversation, because it recognizes that you see them as human, and not just a cog in the wheel. (Also remember: An engaged leader doesn't ever ask a question that they don't want to hear the answer to. So if they tell you, "I'm glad you asked; you know, my family is struggling with these things, or we're dealing with these issues," then you have to spend some time—not in this counseling session, but at a later time—trying to help them wrestle with the issues that they've got from a family perspective.)

And, oh, by the way: don't forget to tell them about *your* family. Tell them about the people that you care about. What are your kids doing? What's your wife up to? How are your parents doing? What plans do you have for an upcoming vacation? When are you gonna take some vacation? Where are you going to go? If you've got an hour together for a formal counseling session, I recommend that you spend nearly fifteen minutes just kind of setting the stage, to make it a warm environment. An environment where they want to be. Where they can recognize that you sincerely, truly care.

I have been disappointed over the course of the last twelve years with some corporate leaders who have no idea about the personal dynamics of their people. They know about what they're required to do at work, they know how to manage a person at work, but when I ask them, "Tell me about their families, tell me about their kids, tell me about their likes and dislikes, tell me about their hobbies," they can't answer. They don't want to know their people, and that's problematic. It's naïve to think you can separate work from home. I mean, there are folks who believe that those are two isolated islands, if you will: what the person does at home, and what the person does at work. And I just don't believe that's the truth. Anything that's going on at home, good or bad, affects the person at work, and vice versa. I'm living, walking proof. There were numerous occasions in my military career when I was so disgruntled that I came home in a bad mood and took it out on Sarah and the kids, and I regret that. So, just know you can't separate work from home. Asking your people about what's going on in their home life is as important at work as it was to me on the battlefield. (And believe me, it was as important there as it could possibly be, as detailed in my first book, *Adapt or Die*.)

Here come the HR reps, right? "Well, General, you can't do that. Because, you know, there are lines of privacy that you don't want to cross." I get all of that. I'm not telling you that you should have your employees bring their checkbook so you can monitor their expenditures. I'm not telling you that they ought to bring in their doctors' reports so you can read what the doctors say. What I'm saying is that you've got to demonstrate that you truly care by asking some probative questions. If they look like they're not doing well, if they look like they're not sleeping well, if they look like they're troubled about something, I'll ask them what's going on, and nobody can tell me it's an inappropriate thing to do.

As an aside, I did actively participate in suicide-prevention programs in the Army while I was on active duty. And a major issue was that people don't ask hard questions when it comes to somebody who looks like they're struggling. If somebody is going through all these personal and professional issues, and they look like they're struggling, they may be having suicidal ideations, and that's one big reason why it's important for us, as leaders, to address the issues we see—that we talk to them and see what's going on with them. It's critical.

This is yet another reason why we want to make sure that the environment itself, where the counseling takes place, is formatted for a good, casual conversation. It's amazing to me when I see corporate leaders sit behind a desk and address people, while their people sit on the other side of this big, wooden object between them. Don't ever sit behind your desk when you're conducting routine counseling. Get out. Have a couple of chairs that face each other, have a coffee table in the middle, have a cup of coffee, or a glass of water there. Make it so that there are no barriers to communication between you and the individual.

I also think it's important to have your office or wherever you're doing the counseling neat and orderly. It's amazing to me when I walk into a corporate executive office, and it looks like a hand-grenade exploded and paper went everywhere. It just sets the stage for the employee to think, *Well, this person is so disorganized, we're probably not going to have any kind of productive conversation here.* So clear off your desk, you know? I learned at West Point that there are really two kinds of people: pilers and filers. Pilers are those people who keep everything on their desk because they want to see it. Just stacks of paper on every flat surface in the office. And candidly, that sets the wrong impression. It looks like you're disorganized. I tend to be a filer. I tend to put things in their proper place. And, oh, by the way, sometimes I just clear off my desk and throw stuff into a drawer, just because I don't want it to *appear* like I'm disorganized, even though I may be at that time.

I'd also recommend that you have this conversation in the place where you've got lots of family photos. I am still amazed that, in Corporate America, I find offices of senior executives where there are no family photos. It's like they don't want anybody to know they have a life outside the office. Again, in these routine counseling sessions, it's critical for the hour that you spend to be a *good* hour. It's critical to make that hour something that your direct reports look forward to every month, so they can't wait to get back in to talk about how they're doing with a boss they know truly cares.

One last critical element for the setting: Don't be distracted. I'm still amazed when I see corporate executives with a pen in one hand and a cell phone the other hand, and they're having a conversation with somebody, and they get a text, and they immediately divert their attention to the device as opposed to paying attention to the human being that they're talking to. You can't have any devices in the room where you're doing a counseling session. There can't be active phones, there can't be computers that are dinging, there can't be anything that would cause a distraction. You've got to make this an active conversation, to make sure that they know that you're listening *and* that you value their input.

GETTING IT DOWN ON PAPER

As you get down to the nitty-gritty of talking about their strengths over the past thirty days, their areas that may call for improvement, and your shared goals for the *next* thirty days, it's important to capture the nature of it all on paper. But it's also important to keep it simple, not cumbersome, so both you and your counselee can walk away with clarity.

In the interest of accomplishing that, I came up with a simple form that I'll share with you on the next page. As you'll see, there's a space for their name at the top, and down at the bottom, there's two places for signatures: one for me to sign, and one for them to sign, once the meeting is over. The body of the paper is then broken into the three areas of discussion:

1. The top third is for strengths. "What did this person do that's just wonderful?" You'll find those things by talking together in the session, but also, if you're an engaged leader who's been managing by walking around, you'll have a few of them tucked away in their folder already, ready to pull out and talk about. So

that's three pluses. And, by the way: make sure to identify different strengths each month, so the process isn't overly redundant. Encouraging your people is important. It's even talked about in the Bible:

"Therefore, encourage one another and build each other up, just as in the fact you are doing."

—1 Thessalonians 5:11

2. The middle third of the paper is designated for areas for improvement. And it's here that we want to find three things to work on. This is critical. As I mentioned earlier, in my process of doing this back in the late '70s, I had that middle third identified as "weaknesses." And I realize now that when I called them "weaknesses," the person I was talking to just shut down. So I now recommend that every one of my corporate clients refer to these as "areas for improvement." What can we do better? Lots of times you'll find that these three come down to communication: sharing thoughts and ideas, sharing reports, sharing what's going on. But there's always something in that thirty-day period that didn't go right, and it's important to concentrate on that, as an After-Action Review: What happened? Why did it happen? What did we learn from that, and what can we do better?

3. The bottom third of this piece of paper is three arrows, which represent objectives: What are we going to accomplish together in the next thirty days? Remember, leaders should never use the first-person pronoun. I hate it when I hear a corporate leader say, "I did this, and I did that." That's just not true. Your *people* did that. *We* did that, *collectively*. So that bottom third is, "What are our objectives for the next thirty days? What are *we*, together, going to accomplish?" The next month, the first thing we talk

Routine Counseling Form

Name:_____

STRENGTHS
+
+
+

AREAS FOR IMPROVEMENT
—
—
—

OBJECTIVES
→
→
→

_____   _____
Counselor   Counselee

about when the counseling starts is, "How'd we do with those objectives we had?" And that sets the stage for the next session.

I spend a lot of time in my third book highlighting the importance of active listening, and that is definitely something to keep in mind as you conduct these sessions. (I acknowledge that active listening is one of my weaknesses, and I'm working on it.) In the counseling session, you shouldn't be the only one talking. You've got to solicit feedback by saying things like, "Here's what I'm seeing. What are *you* seeing?"

One technique that I use that works well is to have them come into the session with a blank form already filled out: What did *they* think their strengths were over the last thirty days? What did *they* think the areas for improvement were? What do *they* think the objectives ought to be? That's a great way to start the conversation. That way, it isn't just *your* views. It isn't just me talking, but an active exchange of thoughts and ideas.

And when it's all done, when the form's been filled out, at about the fifty-five-minute mark (and please, always make sure you're conscious of the time, so it doesn't drag on so long that the person coming in dreads the next time), you say, "Here. Sign it." They sign it, then you sign it, you give them a copy, and you keep a copy—not only for yourself to reference in future reviews, but for HR purposes.

Trust me, none of this is a waste of your time. If the person is doing great, that ought to be retained and then reflected in their annual performance appraisal. If the person is not doing great, it ought to be retained and reflected in their annual performance appraisal, too. And when that negative stuff shows up and they say, "Well, I didn't know that's what you thought," you can pull out the paperwork and say, "Well, whose signature is this at the bottom of the sheet?"

So they can't say they didn't know.

And here's the way to maintain fairness, the way I always have with these counseling sheets: If there's an area of improvement that goes away over time, it never needs to show up in the annual report card. If it shows up in multiple months and *doesn't* improve, then it shows up in the report card for sure. And I might as well go ahead and say this now: When areas for improvement are never improved, and it's a constant struggle with one thing or another, there are some people who simply ought not to be on your team anymore. I do believe that one bad apple can spoil the whole bunch, so there are going to be people who need to go seek happiness elsewhere. And you can tell them to do that in good conscience, if every month you've sat them down and talked about their performance. (This aspect of the counseling/appraisals is crucial, so there'll be more on this in the upcoming chapters.)

Once the signatures are in and the session is essentially over (with a few minutes to spare), that's when I always put my pen down and say, "So, how am *I* doing?" And if you've followed my advice from the last chapter, hopefully they've thought about it and are ready and willing to share a few areas where they'd like to see improvement from you. And you're happy to listen, because you're a humble, active-listening leader.

As my personal experience has shown over the course of my entire career, and as I've seen it put into action at roughly half of the organizations I've worked with in the last twelve years, following the above steps leads to a very productive one-hour session, where both parties involved get an honest feel for how they're doing. And that is absolutely critical.

BEYOND JUST WORK

Thinking about the things that come up in routine counseling, it's important not to lose sight of the fact that what happens at work—and what trickles down from the top—carries over into people's lives.

I am proud of the fact that I was called "The Family-First General" on active duty. I am the guy who believed that people need to be home with their families. I am the guy who, when I commanded the Corps of

65,000 people, demanded everybody be home for dinner by six o'clock, that they don't work on weekends without my personal approval, that they leave work early on Thursdays at three o'clock in the afternoon to have some time with their families, be it at basketball practice, or whatever it might be, and more. And I do tell my audiences these days that most of the problems we're having as a nation can be solved around the dinner table, a space where people sit down with their families, with no devices, no distractions, and talk about, "Hey, how'd the day go?" If there are kids, it's "How did it go at school today? What problems are you having at school?" With a spouse, "What happened in your life today? Here's what happened in mine." Like a routine counseling session, your dinner conversation should be a viable conversation, where the family comes together and coalesces, and becomes a more effective family unit, if you will.

Of the thirty-five years I was in the Army, I was away from my family for thirteen of those years, either on deployments or training exercises, whatever it might be. But when I was home, I was *involved*. I was a coach for my kids' sports. I helped them with their homework. Sarah and I together met with their teachers, and hand in glove, worked through the education of our children. It's still amazing to me when a kid does not do well on a test, how everybody wants to blame the teacher. The teacher has the kid for only a short portion of the day. The parents have 'em the rest of the 24 hours a day, 7 days a week. Parents have to be more involved. If we take the techniques we're talking about in routine counseling for direct reports and use those at home, it will probably have a good effect.

PAYING ATTENTION

The next thing I want to make sure that you think about during the course of your routine counseling is whether or not you're watching for triggers. Body language is important. I spend a lot of time doing leadership training for senior executives, and I can tell pretty much at the beginning of the conversation, whether it's in person or via Zoom or Microsoft Teams, if that person is engaged and wants to be there—if they want to be part of this conversation or are simply going through the motions. If they're easily distracted, if they're looking around, if they're checking their phone, if they're looking at their watch, I know for a fact they're not there. And I've been known just to stop the session and say, "Okay, you clearly have something else on your mind. You're clearly thinking about something besides what we're doing right now. So let's just terminate this because I'm wasting my time and your time. Feel free to come back when you're more ready to be involved in the conversation."

So watching for body language is critical. And it's amazing to me the lack of note-taking that I see in Corporate America. I'm a very deliberate note-taker. Almost everywhere I go, I carry a pen and paper with me. And as conversations take place, I just make it a point to write down the important things, so I don't forget them. That way, those important points stay with me, even though the conversation might be over. I'd say that, 60 percent of the time I'm dealing with Corporate America leaders, they're not taking notes. They're not writing anything down. So I just confront them. I say, "Either you don't care about what I'm talking about, or you have a photographic memory—and I doubt that you have a photographic memory. So let's just think about this. Why is it that you're not taking any notes?" And so often the response is, "Well, I remember all the key points. And that's all I need." And that's just not true. You know, I did go to MIT. I did study robotics. I did run a large research institute tasked with building robots. And I can build a robot that *can* remember everything. But a human can't. And using a voice-recorder, even with the latest AI-driven transcription technology, doesn't guarantee that you'll be able to recover the most-crucial parts of a conversation later on. In most cases, I find people never go back and look at or listen to notes taken by a machine. Ever. And even if they do, nothing is underlined, highlighted, circled, or starred—it's just a bunch of black words on white paper that the brain has a hard time discerning. At this point in time, technology doesn't come close to replacing the centuries-old methods of putting pencil or pen to paper and writing down important phrases, words, touchpoints, etc., as you're listening. There's even science to back up the fact that most people, when taking notes, burn the important information into their brains in a much-more effective manner than those who listen without taking notes.

So I look for note-taking, whether I'm speaking to a group of ROTC students getting ready to finish their college courses, or I'm sitting with the CEO of a billion-dollar corporation. And you should, too. If someone's not taking a note during the course of your routine counseling session, then you got to stop 'em and say, "You really ought to be writing this down."

Funny story: I did have a group of corporate executives one time complain to me that I didn't provide a pen and paper for them to take notes on, which I just find to be ridiculous. As if, somehow, I've got to be the clerical supervisor and give them something to write with. But, being the active listener I am, I made it a point from that day forward to have pens and paper available for that group.

Whatever you can do to make it easy, memorable, even fun—go ahead and do it. Because what you'll find is it's so worthwhile to have people checking in and just making it a routine thing. So it's not a big deal. It's not a big nerve-racking thing. It's just part of what we do.

Great organizations do routine things routinely.

Trust me, once everyone's on-board, your entire organization will look at the implementation of routine counseling as a gift. And a big part of that is because, finally, everyone, from top to bottom, will feel more heard—and everyone will know that the people around them are being held accountable for the jobs they're supposed to be doing.

Which brings me back to the acronym, RACI: who is Responsible, who's Accountable, who needs to be Consulted, and who simply needs to be Informed? Routine Counseling and Performance Appraisals, when done and done well, automatically help to clarify the RACI during any given situation. And when the RACI is clear, the High-Performing Organization is able to weed out the bad apples, stamp out mediocrity, and more—all of which we'll dig into in the following chapters.

Great organizations do routine things routinely

CHAPTER 9

ONE BAD APPLE: DEALING WITH POOR PERFORMERS

I am amazed, as I work with my corporate clients, how many folks they have on their teams who aren't pulling their weight. They're not doing the job for which they've been hired, and, candidly, they're not earning their paycheck.

Why is anyone letting those people stick around? What good does it do—for the organization, or even for those people themselves?

I spent a lot of time studying Jack Welch, the former CEO of General Electric and the author of a number of bestselling books on business and leadership. I know there are some people today who think the Jack Welch style of leadership feels a bit dated in the modern world (he was chair of General Electric from 1981 to 2001), and, of course, times have changed. We can't just do what people did in the past and expect the same results in a changed world. But without a doubt, one thing Jack Welch did a great job with was analyzing his people based on performance and potential.

Every year, he would require ratings of all of his people, using a three-by-three matrix that he developed. (I discuss this at length in the 10th Anniversary Edition of *Adapt or Die*.) Basically, at one end of the spectrum, you have your high performers with high potential, and, at the other end, you've got your low performers, who also exhibit low potential. What Welch advocated was that organizations should "cull the herd" (for lack of a better phrase) by 10 percent, annually. So if you've got a company of a hundred people, let ten of them go seek happiness elsewhere, because they're draining the team. They aren't doing what they're supposed to do, but they're still there drawing a paycheck, and that's not good for anyone.

There are other studies that highlight the fact that, in general, 15 percent of each organization's workforce aren't pulling their weight, and unfortunately, I see people tolerating that on a regular basis. They're just allowing that to continue to happen. And it's draining *everybody*.

THE IMPACT OF POOR PERFORMERS

The impact of tolerating poor performers is drastic. It affects the team dynamics, how well folks are working with each other, how much they want to continue to inspire each other to work harder, and much more.

One major way tolerating poor performers gets reflected, which many leaders don't seem to consider, is in talent retention. Think about it: If you're a talented individual, working to your very best, all the time, and the guy next to you is doing a lousy job, all the time, and you're both collecting the same paycheck, it's going to cause you to want to go work elsewhere. And I've seen it happen, time and time again, where a leader's failure to let the poor performer go leads to the talented person leaving, while the poor performer stays. How does that serve your organization? It affects the company culture. It brings everything down. If people aren't working their hardest to do their best for the good of the company, it's like letting air out of a balloon. It affects the financial stability of the company as well as the credibility of the leaders.

I mean, if you're a leader, and you're allowing poor performers to stay on your team, everybody *knows that*. It's not a secret. Believe me, everybody is aware of who's pulling their weight and who's not pulling their weight, and if you're the leader who allows that person to stay on your team, it affects not only your credibility but also the corporation's growth prospects: Nobody wants to come join a team that's full of a bunch of poor performers.

So we've got to quit fooling ourselves and thinking that it's okay to tolerate poor performance, because it's not. There's significant impact, and tolerating poor performance erodes the ability of Corporate America to get the job done, let alone get it done well.

Why are corporate leaders so unwilling to address this issue?

One thing that seems to be reaching epidemic proportions (which I touched on in the last two chapters as well) is this ballooning concern that firing somebody will automatically draw a lawsuit. And here's why it's become an epidemic: If there's litigation involved, and the leader has not taken the time to annotate that employee's performance, good and bad, over a period of time, then the lawsuit is gonna lean in favor of the fired employee. And that's problematic. The majority of those litigations get settled out of court because it's easier for the corporation simply to pay a severance package and not involve themselves in detailed, drawn-out lawsuits that may cost more than the compensation package itself.

Guess what? All of your employees see that when it happens. They learn from it, and therefore prepare themselves to pursue the same type of litigation before you have a chance to let them go—and the epidemic ensues.

This is why it is crucial to adhere to a regular schedule of routine counseling and performance appraisals. You must be honest and thorough in those appraisals and counseling forms, and use them as a record. With that record in hand, the reasons for any firing will be clear and documented—which tips any potential litigation back in the company's favor and will serve as an effective vaccination against the plague of post-exit litigation.

Renowned poet and philosopher Ralph Waldo Emerson famously said, "Do the thing, and you shall have the power."

I promise you, do this *one thing* right—routine counseling—and your company will have the power to stop tolerating poor performers.

TALKERS VS. DOERS

I want to take a moment here to talk about the difference between talkers and doers. There are plenty of talkers in the world, people who complain, people who see the bad in things, and wish someone would fix them. Talkers basically spend all their time *not fixing problems*.

Doers, on the other hand, are people who get things done. They're the ones who see a problem or maybe hear about a problem from one of those talkers, and actually does something about it. They might not have the ability to change the world, but they change what they can. They contribute where they can.

My advice? Be a doer, not a talker.

Now I know what some of you are thinking, because I hear it all the time: "But, sir, I don't have the power to fix the problems I see. I'm just the low man on the totem pole." And frankly, I don't tolerate that response. Don't tell me you can't affect things positively from whatever position you're in. It doesn't matter where you are in the corporate hierarchy.

Sure, it would be great if everybody at the top would be doers, fixing our problems and making things better for the rest of us all the time. But the fact is, there are a lot more people located from the middle of the hierarchy on down, especially in the corporate world. If everybody at the bottom did their part, we'd have a lot fewer problems at the top. In fact, I think it's safe to say that, if everybody did their part to fix things, even in the tiniest amount, rather than just talk about things, most of our problems would go away.

This applies not only in Corporate America, but in the rest of America, too.

As I mentioned in the last chapter, I truly believe that leadership starts around the dinner table. It is there where we can start teaching our children how to be doers, rather than just talkers.

Now, people want to argue this point with me because a good portion of America's youth are being raised by single parents, and it seems problematic to put so much weight on a single parent's shoulders. But I do know that, if we take time to truly listen to our children and grandchildren, to provide them input and set the example, and if we show them what right looks like when it comes to working hard and what the results of that can be, it'll make a big difference.

I remember vividly going to see my dad at the age of thirteen and saying, "Hey, Dad, I want to buy this." And he replied, "Great, Rick. Go get a job, earn the money, and buy it yourself!" That's why I went out and found my first job at the age of thirteen and have never stopped working for what I wanted a day since.

As I look back and study my time with my parents, it's striking to me that, even though my dad only had a seventh-grade education, and my mom had an eleventh-grade education, and they both worked at a paper factory, they managed to instill a strong work ethic in me and my brother. They instilled values in us that allowed us to move forward, with faith, believing that the harder we worked, the luckier we would become. That attitude is what led me to where I am today. And I believe that's what we have to do as leaders for America, across the board: We have to continue to work with our people. They're our most important resource, and it's up to us, not only as parents but as leaders in all walks of life, to teach our people to be doers—to be productive, to be effective workers, to be of high moral values, etc., so that they feel good not only about what our companies are doing but also about where they're headed in their lives.

Remember: people aren't robots. People have feelings. We need to let them know that we *want* them to do well, just as much as they want to do well themselves.

Once we do that, once we create more doers than talkers, then we as a nation will do better. Almost automatically.

By the way: This doesn't mean I'm letting those at the top off easy. One time, I was at a dinner with one of the boards I serve on, and the whole night this big group of rich and influential people kept complaining about the state of our nation. Finally, the CEO turned to me and said, "General, you've been awfully quiet. What do you have to say on the subject?" And I said, "I'm tired of you all complaining all the time." They all quieted down pretty quick. "Sorry to be so cut-and-dry, but all you're doing is talking about the problems. What are you doing to fix the problems? You are wealthy, you have influence, you have lots of opportunities to address these issues, but instead you're just talking about the problems."

I hope some of them took that to heart. The fact is, you can be a part of the problem, or you can be a part of the solution. And if you walk by a problem without doing something about it, then you're definitely not part of the solution.

THE ROOT CAUSE

Now, tolerating poor performance in the workplace is one thing. If you want to lead a High-Performing Organization, it can't happen.

That should be clear. But let's stop to take a look at why and how poor performers develop, too—because these are the sorts of things that can't happen in *any* High-Performing Organization. And sometimes, what looks like "poor performance" is really the result of a larger problem.

For example, one of the major issues of "poor performance" is actually a lack of resources. As I've said before, "Vision without resources is hallucination," and that's true. You can take a superstar employee and tell them, "I want you to do these things," but if you don't give them the resources, i.e., the people, time, and money to accomplish the assigned task, it's not gonna happen. And then it's going to look like the person himself isn't doing a good job, when in fact, he or she is doing the best they can. That's not their fault, it's yours! And that's a major issue. Allocate time, allocate money, allocate people that help get the task done if you want it done in accordance with your vision.

The next one is Corporate America's ongoing inability to have uncomfortable conversations. I talked about this in the previous chapter, but the lack of routine counseling, the lack of effective performance appraisals, allows ineffective people to stay on the team ineffectively. With routine counseling, someone who's struggling in one area or another can be counseled to set goals, to develop, to take courses or find a mentor to help improve their poor performance, which means they won't have to be let go at all.

Those conversations shouldn't be difficult. They should be routine. They should be expected. They should be thought of as positive conversations between a caring boss and a dedicated employee—or, better yet, *partner*.

But senior executives should also be having certain "uncomfortable conversations" among themselves. Together, they have to decide to initiate, mandate, and support effective performance appraisals and routine counseling, as I highlighted in the previous chapters;

and then, if, indeed 10 percent of the people should be let go every year, you'll be able to sit down and easily conclude which 10 percent it should be.

I'm amazed at how many times I sit down with corporate executives and say, "Okay, let's take this nine-box based on performance and potential, and figure out who's in each box." I'll leave the room and leave them to it, and when I come back, they've gone and put everybody on their team in the top right box—as if everybody is a high performer showing high potential—and that just can't be. It can't. Somebody in that box has to occupy the low-potential/low-performer profile, and those are the folks you ought to be looking at, to see if you can improve them, or if they just need to go work somewhere else.

By the way, letting someone go isn't always something awful. Sometimes it's a gift.

And let's not forget: Firing somebody isn't your only option.

I often tell this story, which highlights what I'm talking about in a major way.

Back when I was a battalion commander, one of my company commanders came to me and complained, "This young private is useless. He's not performing well. He's not doing what he needs to do, and he just needs to go."

In the Army, back in the '90s, we had this thing called the Expeditious Discharge Program, where a Battalion-level Commander could quickly discharge a soldier with a general discharge—not an honorable discharge but a general discharge. And the process took only about five days. So this company commander was coming to me, saying, "Hey, we need to discharge this young man." So I brought the person in, and I talked to him, and I pretty quickly concluded that he seemed like a good guy who was just in the wrong place. I sensed that he was being a poor performer because of the situation that he was in, the environment that he was in, and the people around him. So instead of discharging him from the

Army, I just moved him from one company to another company. And guess what? He not only improved his performance—he flourished.

At the end of the year, out of all 25,000 soldiers in the division, this private was identified as Soldier of the Year. He had risen from, "let's discharge this youngster," to being the best soldier in a 25,000-person division, all because I had the sense that maybe his "poor performance" was a product of his environment and not a direct reflection on him as an individual.

As stated in the Bible, in James 2:13:

"Because judgment without mercy will be shown to anyone who has not been merciful. Mercy triumphs over judgment."

I often find that people flourish when you move them out of their current situation. They may be a poor performer in one environment but not in other environments. So we've got to be empathetic leaders and always be conscious of that.

And clearly, if you want to create and sustain a High-Performing Organization, then sitting idly by and tolerating poor performance is never an option. You've got to do *something*.

SOME LESSONS FROM HISTORY

While we're spending time looking at poor performers in this chapter—both how to spot them and how to get rid of them—it's important to remember that there are exceptionally strong performers in any organization and that those good performers ought to be recognized and promoted accordingly, whenever possible. (Another benefit of Routine Counseling and Performance Appraisals is being able to spot your best performers early on, before they feel neglected or ignored and have a chance to get snapped up and go serve one of your competitors.)

In the Army, promotions are generally given based on time and service. But if you're an exceptional performer, sometimes you get selected for promotion early. How does the Army know who to promote early? Performance Appraisals and Routine Counseling. I'm proud to say that every one of my promotions in my Army career was an early promotion, and were it not for the consistency of my performance as reflected on my Performance Appraisals, I may well have been overlooked or passed by at any stage of my career. I had bosses I didn't get along with, the same way someone in Corporate America might when they change positions or move to a new office. If there weren't a concrete system in place for the Army to be on the lookout for strong performers—a system that was bigger than any one individual—then perhaps I never would have made it to the rank of Lieutenant General. And this is exactly why it's important to put strong practices and programs in place in your organization: Not only so you weed out the poor performers but to ensure that your best performers don't get left behind.

My wife, Sarah, comes from a long line of seasoned military leaders. Her great-grandfather fought in the Civil War, her grandfather fought in World War I, her father fought in World War II and Korea—and I thank God that all of them were good performers, and that all of them made it through those wars.

Her great-grandfather, First Lieutenant David Roush, fought in the Battle of Chickamauga, Georgia, in 1863, and he did so well that his name stands on one of the monuments on that hallowed ground. It's emotional for Sarah and, frankly, for me, to see it every time we visit on one of our Leadership Tours. He served in the First Ohio Cavalry, and he was identified as a good soldier early on and promoted accordingly. The thing we found in the military is that we cannot afford to have lousy leaders or poor performers in our senior ranks, because when it happens, people die unnecessarily. And in that time of Civil War, when vacancies opened up in the senior ranks because of casualties, the Army promoted its best soldiers quickly. David Roush was promoted from private, when he joined the First Cavalry in 1861, at the age of 23, to First Sergeant, to Second Lieutenant, and then First Lieutenant in just two years. He was actually a Company Level Commander during the Battle of Chickamauga. And it's just so strange to think about, but had he not been promoted to that level, and had he not survived that battle, he may never have gone on to marry, at the age of 42. He may never have had six children, one of whom would become Sarah's grandfather.

If no one was paying attention to how good a soldier David Roush was, he may never have made it, and perhaps the whole outcome of the Battle of Chickamauga might have been different as well. Paying attention and making the right promotions matters. It affects people's lives—not just in the moment, but generationally.

On the other end of the spectrum, I mentioned General George Custer earlier in this book. Most of you, even if you're not a military-history buff, have probably heard of Custer. You've heard of "Custer's Last Stand" at the Little Bighorn battlefield, and you've probably seen paintings of him, sitting on a horse, with his long ponytail of golden hair. (Later in life, he shaved his head. But he still had his portraits done with the hair as part of the image he tried to project.)

A guy you probably *haven't* heard of is Captain Frederick Benteen. Why haven't you heard of him? Because Benteen was a poor performer and well-known drunkard—whom Custer kept around, and who ultimately sealed his fate. Why would Custer keep a poor-performing soldier around and, in fact, promote him along the way? Because Benteen's cousin owned a newspaper, and Custer wanted to use the Benteen family connection to make sure he got lots of good press (in part of because of his wife's ambitions to see him get elected President).

Little did Custer know that Benteen would turn out to be one of those passive-aggressive type of people I've mentioned; the type who tend to hurt their own companies—particularly their bosses—out of spite.

To be fair, Benteen certainly had an axe to grind with Custer, which was established long before they reached the battlefield where Custer would meet his fate. During an earlier battle, the Battle of Washita, Custer ordered the massacre of a large number of Native American "enemies," including a large number of women and children. During that campaign, one of Benteen's best friends, Major Joel Elliott, and seven of his men had broken off from the rest of the Seventh Cavalry to pursue Custer's goals. But when the battle wrapped up and the Cavalry came back together, Elliott and his men were nowhere to be found—and Custer decided that he wasn't going to risk his forces in order to go looking for them.

Today in the military, we have a solid, honor-based tradition that no soldier is ever left behind. Custer was not at the forefront of establishing that rule.

Elliott and his men were later found slaughtered, and Benteen never forgot it. So at the battle of Little Bighorn, when Custer was in trouble and sent for reinforcements, Benteen received the message. He was far off, safe on a hill; sitting in charge of nearly half of Custer's men. He could have swept in and easily helped Custer escape from the relatively small band of Native Americans who had decided to enact their revenge on Custer. But he didn't. He received Custer's call for help, and then sat there—for 90 minutes—doing nothing. He waited until Custer was killed before bringing his troops down to a battle that had already been lost.

Remember the oft-repeated phrase, "Take care of your people, and they'll take care of you"? Custer exemplified the opposite of that phrase in action. It wasn't just with Benteen and his friend Joel Elliott. His soldiers were poorly trained, and poorly equipped. They were malnourished, as he kept them in the field too long without replenishing supplies. And he visibly ate well when they didn't. So no one really fought Benteen's passive-aggressive behavior when it happened—not even the other commanders who were serving at Benteen's level. They all just sat around and let it happen.

One bad apple with a grudge turned out to be the passive-aggressive "employee" who was willing to sit on his hands when the chips were down and let his leader die.

If that doesn't give every uncaring senior leader a cold chill up the spine, I don't know what will.

BEWARE OF BROAD IMPACTS

Just to continue to emphasize the major impact of tolerating poor performance and what one bad apple can do, let's remember the common phrase: One bad apple can spoil *the bunch*.

I do believe that poor performers *reproduce*.

When I was a leader in the Army, whenever a new soldier came to me, I did my best to remember that they still had not been formed. They were basically like playdough. They'd been through basic training. They'd acquired some basic skills, but they were still impressionable. And whether it was an enlisted soldier or noncommissioned officer didn't matter: I intentionally took that new soldier and aligned them with a great soldier. I partnered them up and put them in close proximity to each other based not only on their job but also on things like where they lived and who they liked to hang out with. (I truly got to know my soldiers, or this wouldn't have been possible.) And I found that when I did this, the new soldier would become a good soldier, too, based wholly on who he associated with.

The converse applies as well. If you take a new soldier and you allow him to operate next to and hang out with a poor performer or a bad soldier, they'll tend to take on the traits of that poor performer themselves. So then I'd wind up with two bad soldiers. And I see this happening in the corporate world all the time.

We spend a lot of time and money during the hiring and onboarding process. Why on earth would we waste that investment by then allowing our new hires to align with poor performers? It makes no sense.

First off, we should go through all of the steps above and make sure we have no poor performers on our teams, period. But if we don't? If that isn't happening, for whatever reason, what's gonna happen is this: Whenever you allow poor performers to stay on your team, and they sit in a cubicle adjacent to another person who's tasked with doing the same job and drawing the same pay, it is inevitable that an otherwise good performer will wind up looking over the cubicle and seeing the poor performer working at about half speed and spending most of the day not focusing on the job at hand. That's de-motivating. And it won't be long before that otherwise-good performer is going to realize, *Hey, I can work about half speed, spend more time with my family, spend more time in the gym, spend more time at lunch, come in later, leave earlier, and still draw the same paycheck!* That's just what's gonna happen.

It's human nature.

So let's put an end to that. Right now.

Of course, "poor performers" can be measured beyond productivity as well.

I am very concerned with people in corporations who tolerate unethical behavior. I've spent more than a dozen years now advising clients on how to develop vision, values and operating principles. That involves articulating the company's purpose, since people naturally want to have a purpose in order to thrive in life. (Rick Warren's book *A Purpose-Driven Life* articulates this issue well.) And it all comes down to a set of values, which should be agreed to and lived out, every day.

Well, too many times in Corporate America, I see somebody knowingly and clearly violating the company's values, and yet, they are still allowed to stay on the team. That just brings everybody down. I mean, why would people want to work harder to live by the company's values, if they're being shown by example that you *don't* have to live by the values, and you can continue to stay employed at that position? Lifestyle evangelism figures in here, as the leaders not only have to live the values but then demand that the people who work for them live by those values as well. And the minute they don't, then they need to be taught, coached, or mentored into doing better, and, if they *still* don't change their behavior, then they need to go seek happiness elsewhere.

The companies that don't do this inevitably suffer all kinds of turbulence, which affects their stock price and everything else. But still, I find that leaders are afraid to let people go—if not for fear of lawsuits, then for fear that they won't be able to replace them once they're gone. Certain leaders get lulled into thinking that having a poor performer on the team is better than having no one, and that's just not true. I mean, if I didn't make it clear in the examples above, let me reiterate it in one sentence right here: If you keep the poor performer on your team, you're gonna have other poor performers pop up over time, and it'll keep happening until the entire organization goes down. This whole idea of growth prospects and financial stability go right out the window, because the old saying is true: One bad apple can absolutely spoil the bunch.

Don't be the leader who decides to keep a bad performer around based on today's environment, in which it's hard to hire people. Trust me, because I've seen it in action: That decision is going to hurt you. Oh, and, by the way, I don't buy the fact that you can't hire somebody else. Maybe that's true if you solemnly swear to stick by the principles of the mediocre-to-poor-performing organization you're struggling with right now. But if you create an environment that everybody *wants* to join and be a part of, then great hires are gonna make it a point to join your team. They just are.

When we make the environment and the culture at the company so important as to prove to even casual observers that you care about your people, then really great people are going to want to join the team, and your best people are gonna want to *stay* on your team.

GETTING AHEAD OF POOR PERFORMANCE

I hope it's clear from previous chapters that the number-one way to avoid the toleration of poor performers is to take up routine counseling and use it, accurately, to develop your performance appraisals. And one of the reasons that works so well is that it ensures that the person is made aware that they're falling short of the mark.

A lot of times, people are not self-aware. As I mentioned in Part I, I spend a lot of time with senior leaders doing 360 Assessments, because without them, the only assessment they get is either from looking in the mirror or listening to their bosses (most of whom are afraid to have the honest, uncomfortable conversations). So it's important not only to the individual to hear how they're assessed, but also to the organization— because it *is* possible in Corporate America to fool your boss. You can look like you're doing great work when you're really *not* doing great work. Your boss has got a lot of irons in the fire, and he or she may miss it. So the key to avoiding these sorts of oversights is to have a detailed system in place to do 360 Assessments and to expand those 360 Assessments to all levels. Make it a part of your performance counseling by asking peers, colleagues, direct reports, and others how *they* think the person is doing. That can't be done monthly, of course, but it can be done annually. I guarantee it will give your organization more clarity when it comes to weeding out those who aren't up to snuff and who have no interest in improving themselves or their behavior. However, it *will* also shine a light on those who might deserve to be promoted and give those individuals who want to do better more opportunity to do just that.

Remember, it's critical to remind ourselves that we can develop people three ways.

We develop people by sending them off to school. I went to many leadership courses over the course of my military career, which allowed me to be introspective, reflect on being a better leader, and talk to other leaders. So institutional development is important.

Organizational Development is important, too, and, clearly, we bring about a lot of growth in Corporate America by taking a person who's destined for greatness out of their comfort zone and putting them in a role they're not comfortable in. That's how they grow. That's how they develop. And, oh, by the way, when you put them in that new role, it's even more important to teach, coach, and mentor them, to surround them with good people, and to continuously tell them how they're doing and give them encouragement.

And the last piece is self-development. I wish it were true that every human being out there wanted to be the best human being they can be. I wish that were true, but it's not. Some people are just happy doing the minimum, and I'm going to talk about how mediocrity is a problem in the next chapter. But no matter what a person's stance is, it's helpful to give them direction on how to self-develop—give them requirements to read books, for example, or take webinars, or attend conferences so they can get better at what they're doing.

I mentioned earlier that, as a Battalion Commander, I required each of my officers to read a book a month. What I didn't mention is that we shared what we learned with that book at the end of each month, and everybody learned something because of it. Everybody got a little better at whatever was talked about in those books.

There was some resistance, at first, just as there might be in corporate circles. It's not uncommon for folks to say, "I don't have time to read"—and that's just silly. I spent a lot of time in my earlier books talking about time management, and how my days are broken into segments of "15, 7, and 2." That's fifteen hours, seven hours, and two hours. I spend two hours a day doing fitness, both spiritual and physical, I spend seven hours a day sleeping, and that leaves me with fifteen hours a day to do what I want to do. If you follow a similar schedule, even if you're working ten-hour days, you still have five hours a day to do what needs to be done or what you want to do—and that should include reading. That should include self-development. It's absolutely critical.

Along these same lines, one way to help avoid poor performance is to get your people into good associations.

Associations come in two forms. One is to make sure to take the individual that you want to grow and allow them to work with other individuals in your organization who have already grown, who have already achieved a level of performance that you think is appropriate. And the other is to have them join professional associations filled with people who are doing what they're doing. If they're in the finance world, or the marketing world, or whatever it might be, have them join some affiliated associations. That way, they get together routinely and talk about best practices and new or best ways of doing business. In the military, we call it a discussion of tactics, techniques, and procedures, and anyone who belongs to an association, where they're surrounded by others, has a chance to absorb new information and grow.

Another thing you can do as you try to weed out poor performers and—more importantly—build good performers, is to be careful with praise.

I cannot tell you how many times during the past twelve-plus years I've had a C Suite executive complain to me that "so-and-so isn't doing their job," and yet, at a meeting or some public forum, that same executive would praise that person for the good job they're doing. That just sends conflicting signals, because guess what? Everybody on the team knows who's doing well and who's *not* doing well, and the minute you praise a person who everyone knows in reality is *not* doing well, you create an environment and a culture that leaves people saying, "If *that's* all you've got to do to get praise, I'm just going to ratchet back and do much less, too!" And that's a major issue.

THE UPSIDE

If you haven't figured it out by now, tolerating poor performance has to end in any organization that wants to make itself better. And let me tell you, the benefits of not tolerating poor performers are amazing.

For one thing, I see too many leaders spending only 10 percent of their time with their best people, because they're forced to spend 90 percent of their time dealing with their poor performers. So what I'm about to say should be a no-brainer: If you get rid of your poor performers, then you can spend *all* your time with your good people. Imagine how great that feels! What a breath of fresh air, especially after being dragged down and smothered by a handful of poor performers for years.

To not let go of your poor performers means you're making a conscious decision to give poor performers the majority of your time. So the best thing you can do today is stand up, lead well, do the work it takes to get them off your teams, and then? Watch what happens.

In addition to bringing your organization one step closer to becoming a High-Performing Organization, you'll raise your profile as a decisive leader.

As I used to tell my commanders in the Army, "When in charge, take charge!"

Demonstrating decisiveness is a great big part of building confidence. And when you allow poor performers to stay in your organization, it's a poor reflection on *you*.

Asking the poor performers to go seek happiness elsewhere, and doing it routinely, demonstrates a decisiveness that translates to the entire organization as, "Whoa. That person was asked to leave, and if I don't improve, then I'm probably next!"

It also highlights the fact that you're not showing favoritism. When I do 360s on senior executives, I get a *lot* of feedback that those individuals are showing favoritism left and right. It's easy to do, especially over time. If you're a leader and you've got an individual who's been with you for twelve, fifteen years, and that individual isn't doing well these days, it's easy to overlook it just for the sake of the friendship. You've likely developed a sort of symbiotic relationship, maybe a father-son or mother-daughter kind of thing that's so close, it almost feels familial. Well, remember how that worked out for General Lee and his young Cavalry star, Jeb Stuart? If you let a poor performer get away with stuff and won't let a person go because of a personal relationship, everybody sees that. If you're taking a person who's no longer doing their job and promoting that person only because of their personal relationship, when they shouldn't be getting promoted, the animosity that's going to build on your team is either going to come back to bite you, personally, or it's gonna tank the morale and teamwork you need in order to get the job done.

So don't let anything personal get in the way of what needs to be done. Have the uncomfortable conversations. Do the routine counseling. Provide opportunities for employee development. And when the decision needs to be made, be decisive: Let the poor performers *go.*

CHAPTER 10

MEDIOCRITY MADNESS

I realized something shortly after transitioning out of the military and into civilian life: I enjoy playing golf.

I enjoyed it so much, I made it a routine to go out and play two times a week with my buddies. And it didn't take long for me to realize something else: I was a mediocre golfer. *And I was okay with that.*

I convinced myself, "I like to play, but I don't like to practice." And as a result of that, even though I was playing twice a week, I kept making the same mistakes. I didn't improve, because I didn't practice or take any lessons. And I truly was okay with the repeated mistakes I made, because I convinced myself that golf was more about the social experience than it was about the score.

My golf game is good enough, I thought.

But as I started to formulate ideas for this book, I found myself reflecting on one of the biggest weaknesses I see at so many corporations, and it struck me: They're suffering from a systemic acceptance and tolerance of mediocrity in their ranks.

I started to question: How can I ever get corporate leadership to do something to address the plague of mediocrity in their organizations if I, myself, remain complicit with mediocrity in my golf game?

I couldn't. So I changed my perspective. I started taking golf lessons. I spent more time on the driving range, on the putting green, and practicing my short game. And while I'm still a mediocre golfer at this moment, I've improved. Significantly. And I plan to continue improving for the foreseeable future.

Wouldn't you know it? I have found that the better I play the game of golf, the more I *like* the game of golf, which, as we say at West Point, is something that should've been intuitively obvious to any casual observer. But that's where I am. I'm improving. I'm fed up with being mediocre, and I'm no longer accepting that mediocrity in my life.

It's about time Corporate America wake up and stop accepting mediocrity in its organizations, too.

John Maxwell put it well in his 2014 book, *Good Leaders Ask Great Questions*: "It's OK to be average in many areas of your life. You can be an average golfer and still have golf as an enjoyable hobby. You can be an average cook and still keep your family fed. You can be an average driver and get from point A to point B. But you can't settle for mediocre in your marriage, for example, and expect it to remain solid. And you can't be mediocre in your profession and expect to be rewarded for it."

I mentioned earlier that, whenever a new soldier came into my ranks, I immediately made a conscious effort to partner that new soldier up with a great soldier. The greatness of that experienced soldier would wear off on the new soldier, which left me with two great soldiers. I saw just the opposite in some units, where a new soldier would come in, they'd partner him with a bad soldier, and that unit would then have two bad soldiers.

The very same thing happens in Corporate America with poor performers, of course.

But there's something even more insidious happening in Corporate America that we need to put an end to: the haphazard placement of new workers—and even seasoned workers—next to mediocre workers at all levels.

Just like with poor performers, if you've got a mediocre performer who's simply doing just enough to get by, and in the adjacent cubicle, there's another person working very hard, it's not going to take long for the hard worker to look over the top of the cubicle and realize that they, too, could do mediocre work and still bring home the same paycheck.

The reason it's more insidious is because it's harder to spot. A poor performer stands out. A mediocre performer? Not so much—especially in an organization without routine counseling, and in cases where leaders simply have too many direct reports to ever get to know their own people. Not to mention: Mediocrity is much more contagious.

Here's what I mean: While your strongest performers are unlikely to turn into poor performers just because they see some people on the team performing poorly, it is *very easy* for even your best people to a) leave, or b) dial it down enough to match the mediocre performers' performance when they see it. Why? Because they *can*. And clearly, if the mediocre performers are drawing the same paycheck and not getting fired, the top performers will be smart enough to know that they won't face any consequences for dialing back their efforts.

So in many ways, this chapter is really Part 2 of the chapter on tolerating poor performance—because the message is the same: You cannot tolerate mediocre performance if you want a High-Performing Organization.

Mediocrity has to be wiped out. Now.

' THE WHYS

Again and again, over the course of the past twelve years, I've seen corporate leaders tolerate mediocre people on their team for one reason: Because having the mediocre performer in place, they reason, is better than having nobody at all. They convinced themselves that a 70-percent solution generated by the mediocre performer was better than having an empty chair. And in today's environment, where it's difficult to hire people to put in that chair, their argument is, "Let's keep the mediocre performer because that person is better than nothing."

I don't buy into that.

However, I do believe that nobody comes to work *intending* to be mediocre. Most of them just don't know what it means to be a high-performing employee. In most cases, people have to be taught, coached, and mentored into being a high performer, and Corporate America needs to get better at providing the important development that everyone needs.

Sometimes that teaching and coaching won't take, and, as a result, some people are just not nearly as effective as they could be. In those cases, letting someone move on to a different role or to a different corporation is necessary for the High-Performing Organization to thrive. But whatever we do, we have to be careful, as leaders, to keep ourselves in check and actively make sure that we are not systemically encouraging mediocrity in our ranks.

Case in point: When I was a cadet at West Point, my class went through a major honors scandal. A whole bunch of cadets were caught cheating, and a lot of my classmates were either kicked out of the Academy or turned back.

The scandal was so big that Congress stepped in and decided that we needed to look closely at the military academy to find out what was going wrong. They—and we—created a commission led by astronaut Frank Borman. It was called the Borman Commission, and one of the conclusions we came to was that West Point itself had been advocating mediocrity. That sounds counter to everything we know about West Point, right? It's the top military academy in the country, with extremely stringent admission requirements. It serves as the pinnacle of high performance and honor. So how could this happen?

It happened because the Academy had initiated a 3.0 grading scale: 3.0 was as high as any cadet could get, but 2.0 was "passing." So the theme that the commission encountered across interviews with hundreds of cadets at West Point was that they lived by a code of "Two-Oh and Go." In other words, 2.0 is "passing," and that's good enough. So do whatever you need to do to get 2.0, and then drop it. Just get by. That's good enough. And in a school with as difficult a curriculum as West Point, there were a lot of reasons for students to incentivize themselves into believing that lie.

One of the reasons was because the cadets at West Point were required to do so much. They simply had too much on their plates. In many ways, they weren't given the time and space to excel in any one area. They were expected to excel in all areas, and we know, I think, that, in life, that's an impossibility. When people try to do it all, about the best they can possibly do is to be "good enough" in all areas.

In this case, a number of students convinced themselves it was best to take shortcuts and do only what it takes (including cheating) in order to get by, so they could pass all their classes.

The very system itself encouraged mediocrity and, ultimately, unethical and dishonorable behavior.

I'm all about the culture of the organization. And if the culture of any organization is "do enough to get by," then that just spawns additional mediocre behavior, which can lead your people down some ultimately dark paths. If you put an individual in a company where all they're ever told and shown to do is to strive to be mediocre, then everybody will wind up being mediocre.

On the other hand, if the culture of the company is, "We can always do better. It's never good enough," the paths ahead get a whole lot brighter. And it doesn't really matter what the "do better" is about. Maybe it's about improving stock prices or improving the product. In the world of the pharmaceutical industry, the "do better" is often about improving patients' quality of life or lifespans. The do-better culture can help any organization thrive, from sports teams to churches to schools and nonprofits, too. My friend and actor Gary Sinise, who played Lieutenant Dan in the Academy Award-winning film *Forrest Gump*, started The Gary Sinise Foundation as a way to use his good fortune and talents to rally support for our nation's military, including active members, veterans, and their families. He was inspired to do so after devoting time to those who were sent to defend our nation in the wake of the 9/11 attacks, and he puts it like this: "We can never do enough for our service members and their families, but we can always do a little more." That's exactly the kind of positive attitude it takes to push organizations into greatness.

There has got to be a general culture across the company that chooses to be high performing—not mediocre—if you want to have anything other than a mediocre organization. And the problem of accepting mediocrity, as with all problems (in my opinion), comes down to leadership—and, yes, as I'm sure you're aware, there are such things as mediocre leaders.

Donald Rumsfeld wrote a book that, among other things, shines a light on one of the reasons mediocre leaders wind up creating mediocre performance and even complete failures in the organizations they lead. The book is entitled *Rumsfeld's Rules,* and in that book, he talks about the remarkable patterns he saw, everywhere he worked, from his time in the Navy, to his decade in Congress, and all the way to the White House, where he served as the youngest ever Secretary of Defense under Nixon, and the oldest-ever Secretary of Defense under George W. Bush.

What Rumsfeld noted was this: Type-A people tend to hire Type-A people, while Type-B people tend to hire Type-C people.

Now, I don't know about you, but when I share this observation with people, it's almost like a lightbulb goes off in their mind. They recognize it as something they themselves have witnessed but could never put words to. So let's peel the onion back on that.

A Type-A person is a high-performing individual himself. He's always trying to improve; she's always trying to be the best she can be. So the Type-A people intentionally surround themselves with people smarter than them, people with more passion than them, people more aggressive than them, because they recognize: if it's good for them, it's good for the organization and vice-versa. Type-A's are comfortable in their skin, so they don't feel threatened by people who, candidly, might be better than them.

On the other hand, Type-B people are uncomfortable in their own skin. They're always looking over their shoulder, worried about getting fired, worried about being shown up by somebody smarter or more skilled than them, worried about whatever might happen that they can't control. So they intentionally hire Type-C people: people that they can bully and boss around, people that will provide no pushback or original ideas, people who will simply do what they're told by their Type-B boss. That Type-B person, therefore, sets up a chain of command and a team full of subordinates who suffer from situational mediocrity in terms of what their leader looks like. And this, indeed, impacts the entire organization.

It's shocking, right? To think that one "Type-B" leader could basically be tanking everything? But we all know they're there. We all know they exist. We all see them right in front of our eyes, whether we work for them, or with them, or we come in from the outside to do a little research and consulting on why a particular team isn't doing so well.

There are cases where I've worked for certain companies or been asked to speak by certain companies, and I was so enamored with the good work they're trying to do—their mission, as it were—that I've volunteered to come in and consult or offer additional advice to a particular leader *for free.* I offered purely out of the desire to do a little good in the world, and because I knew they needed additional help that, in some cases, they didn't have enough of a budget to cover. And the most frustrating thing in the world to me is that some of those leaders, be they presidents, CEOs, or executive-vice-president types, have failed to call me back. They won't even return my calls! And I know, to a person, it's because they're a Type-B leader: They don't want to hear my ideas to improve their situation, because they would then feel that they'd been shown up by somebody smarter and more experienced than them. And God forbid anyone ever find out that they're not the smartest one in the room.

The last thing they want is to have somebody make them "look bad."

What they don't realize, which Type-A leaders *do* realize, is that having someone smart come in to offer advice to help your organization rise up to a higher level will never, ever make a leader look bad. In fact, there's hardly a faster way I can think of for an engaged leader to look *good* to their people than by finding a strong mentor and taking legitimate shortcuts to operational/organizational improvement.

You can also bet that the Type-B leader is going to be the last person to fire a mediocre performer, because they want those mediocre performers to stick around, to make them feel better about themselves.

Well, guess what? Any leader who allows mediocre people to stay on the team loses a lot of personal credibility. Without fail, the folks on the team will question, "Why is this leader allowing this person, whom we all know to be mediocre, to stay on the team?" Then, they will start questioning everything their leader does. It seems ironic, right? The actions the Type-B leader takes to protect himself and glorify himself turn out to be the actions that destroy his team.

I don't call it *ironic*. I call it *predictable*. And if you want to create and maintain a High-Performing Organization, you've got to stamp out this type of behavior and "leadership," wherever it exists.

A SCOTTISH TALE

One of the most fascinating Leadership Tours I've had the pleasure of leading took place in Scotland, where we walked the battlefields of the War for Scottish Independence in the late-1200s, exploring some of the fields, forests, and castles featured in the award-winning Mel Gibson movie, *Braveheart*. What a way to learn the truth about the real-life warrior behind that film's character, William Wallace, who fought so hard to try to free his country from British rule.

It was fascinating, in part, because so much of what was depicted in *Braveheart* is just plain wrong. It's an entertaining film, for sure. But it's historically inaccurate in at least ten different ways (which the Scottish people will gladly point out to you, if you ever have a chance to visit their country).

It was also fascinating because what my corporate clients learned is that William Wallace's greatest failure didn't occur because of anything he himself did wrong. It was because he was constantly held back and held down by the actions of passive-aggressive, mediocre performers.

The First War for Scottish Independence began in the year 1296, and Wallace was a young knight with some military experience when he stepped forward to lead the fight in 1297. He rallied the locals, gathered together advisors, and approached the battlefield with an open mind—willing to train and try new techniques and strategies as a way to defeat King Edward I's forces. And straight out of the gate, he won, in a tremendous victory, for which he became famous: The Battle at Stirling Bridge, which took place on September 11, 1297. (Inaccuracy number one in Gibson's film: There is no bridge at Stirling Bridge. It's the name of a place, not a structure. There also was never a law in Scotland that allowed nobility to sleep with other men's wives; and Wallace didn't father a child with the Queen of France—Wallace would have been three years old at the time of the child's birth, etc. But those film errors are beside the point.)

With a decisive early victory on his side, Wallace was appointed Guardian of Scotland, and set about gathering the support of the Scottish nobility. He would need their assistance in gathering the resources—men, money, weapons, etc.—to continue the fight for the one thing he believed every Scotsman wanted: to live free in an independent nation. And to his face, the nobility were all-in. But back in their fancy estates, on grounds that had been gifted to them by the King of England, these same noblemen were less than enthusiastic to throw their weight behind the fight. In truth, they weren't willing to risk the good lives they had for the potential of a life that would be better for their fellow countrymen. So they would tell Wallace that he was the boss and say they were prepared to do whatever he asked, but then they would fail to rally support as promised. They would fail to have their men show up on time for the next fight. They took a laissez-faire, passive-aggressive stance that left Wallace and his dedicated foot soldiers never knowing whether they would have the support they needed on the battlefield or not. As a result, he and his men were left under-supported at the most crucial moment of all: the Battle of Falkirk in July of 1298. That defeat would force him to step down from his Guardian position, and in 1305, he would be captured and handed over to King Edward—who promptly had him hung, drawn, and quartered for the crime of treason against the crown.

Wallace's head was dipped in tar and placed on a spike on the London Bridge for all to see, and yet, his legacy as a fighter for freedom would live on strong. The campaign for Scottish independence would continue for the next 58 years, and Wallace's legacy would become the stuff of legends. But the campaign would never be truly won. Scotland is still a part of Great Britain to this day.

I've said it before, and I'll say it again. The biggest threat I see in Corporate America today is the very same threat that cost William Wallace his life and Scotland its true independence: The threat of the passive-aggressive, mediocre performers in our midst. These are the ones who seem to have your company's best interest at heart, who promise to follow orders, but who then turn around and do something else—the ones who say "sure" to any new initiative you put forward but then refuse to do what you've asked. And if you aren't continually counseling and reviewing your people's performance, then, like Wallace, you're never gonna know when your people are off doing something else. And in the corporate world, as on the battlefield, what you don't know *can* hurt you.

> In the corporate world, as on the battlefield, what you don't know can hurt you

A LARGER IMPACT

I have to say, I'm worried about how the plague of mediocrity in the workplace winds up spilling over to how we're raising our families as well.

Going back to the West Point example (and this isn't to malign West Point; they've improved massively over the years by conducting After-Action Reviews on their past failures), when I went to school there, the goal was to intentionally to expose us to *everything.* So, for example, we found ourselves exposed to every sport. Over the course of the four years I did gymnastics, I did swimming, I did boxing, I did wrestling, I did squash, I did handball, I did tennis, I did golf, and on and on. And that made me knowledgeable of every sport but not good at any sport—a jack of all trades, but a master of none. And I think that's what's happening today with families. It seems like we've been in this era of handing out participation trophies for a little too long now. And participation is important, but over the long term, what we're teaching our kids is, "It's okay to be good enough. It's okay to be on a losing team." And my fear is that, as a result of that, our youngsters are basically being encouraged to be mediocre. They're certainly not being encouraged to *not* be mediocre, right?

Exposure to a bit of everything is important. It's good. With our own grandkids, we're trying hard to allow them to have the opportunity to experience lots of things. But when they pick the thing that they've got the most passion for, then we just want to pile on—to help them pursue that passion, with equipment and training and clinics and camps, so they can indeed be the best they can be at that particular thing. So this whole idea of mediocrity affects all aspects of a person's life, not just what happens at work.

So what are we gonna do about this?

I've already spoken about the need for effective counseling, and here's how it applies to mediocrity: We've got to be sitting people down routinely to say to them, "Okay, here's where I see your strengths. Here's where I see areas in which we should improve. And here are the objectives for the next thirty days," or whatever timeline you feel is appropriate, as long as it's no less than once a quarter. And then, thirty days later, bring them back in and say, "How'd we do?" and start the process over and over again. That gives us a chance to elevate poor performers *and* mediocre performers, to allow them the chance do better, because they're getting exposed to good, consistent feedback.

I am also an advocate, as I've talked about before, of 360 Assessments. If you really want to know how you're doing, don't just ask your boss or ask yourself when you look in the mirror. Ask your peers, and ask your direct reports, in an environment where they can give you candid feedback. Then you can see those things that you need to improve on. And we should always improve.

If we're not improving, then we're embracing mediocrity.

For example, let's think about the 360 Assessments I've done with senior executives who refute all the findings of their assessment. I'll come back to them with a detailed report, showing that more than half of their subordinates and colleagues feel they're failing to live up to certain leadership traits and goals, and they'll flat out tell me, "I refuse to believe it. I'm not like that. I don't do those things." Hate to tell you, friend, but when six out of ten people around you say you're failing, you're failing! It's not made up. It's the impact you're having, and it's something you need to address. Being good in one area and letting others slide means you're surely one heck of a mediocre performer.

> **If we're not improving, then we're embracing mediocrity**

Is that what you want to be?

As we teach people, including ourselves, to be more self-aware, we also have to insist upon reminding ourselves and others to embrace individual improvement—to take on an attitude of constantly improving and wanting to be a winner. In order to become a winner, you've got to act like a winner, you've got to believe you can succeed, and you've got to choose success over mediocrity. In all aspects of your life—not just how you're doing in your chosen profession, but how you're doing at home, and how you're doing on the ballfield or the golf course. Be humble. Acknowledge that you've got work to do, but simultaneously believe that you are a winner. Choose success over mediocrity. Believe that you can succeed.

And then, candidly, always seek criticism instead of praise.

People can tell you how great you are all the time, and that does absolutely nothing for you. It doesn't make you a better person, and it doesn't make you a better professional. It just reinforces (probably) bad behavior, because you're only hearing what you want to hear. So you should always seek criticism, not praise.

Keep going back to the idea of being humble, and acknowledge that, on this new path to improving, you're going to make mistakes. I mean, there's so many folks out there who remain mediocre just because they don't want to make any mistakes. They're afraid of failure. And I don't believe that's useful. Failure brings humility and helps us develop character. We can learn from our mistakes. So it's okay to fail—as long as you're doing your After-Action Review.

And then? You just have to advocate self-educating.

If you want to lift your people up from being mediocre, lead by example. Let your people know that you've got work to do, and show them how you're trying to do better.

One way I do that, candidly, is by reading. I keep coming back to this because I read a lot, and I've seen the results of increasing the number of books my subordinates have read in every leadership role I've pursued.

In my case, I tend to read about one book per week. And people say, "That's impossible. I could never do that!" And that's when I let them in on a little secret: It's not impossible if you read like I do. When I pick up a book of interest—and I don't read fiction, only nonfiction, because I'm trying to learn from history and become a better leader—I'll read the front cover and back cover, the front flap and the ending flap, and I'll read the introduction, word-for-word. But then, when I get into the meat of the book, I read the first line of every paragraph. And if that first line interests me, then I'll read the rest of the paragraph. If not, I'll jump to the next paragraph, and the next. People say, "Well, you're really not reading the book then, because you're not reading every word." And I say, "Who made that rule? I want to read as much as I can, and I want to get the gist of it all. I don't care what book it is—not everything in that book is going to be of interest to me. So I don't want to dwell on things that aren't interesting. I want to jump to things that *are* interesting and *learn* from that."

There are lots of ways to get things done, and developing your own aggressive reading program will start you down a road of rising up from mediocrity, for sure.

It also comes down, once again, to time management: Actively making decisions about how to spend the fifteen hours of work and free time you have, each and every day.

In my fifteen hours, for example, I very rarely ever watch television. I don't watch the news, either. I do believe that the national media is a national embarrassment. I do believe that what you get on news stations these days is not the facts; what you get is mostly opinions. They don't say, "Hey, this is my opinion." They say, "Here's this new bit of information," leading you to *believe* it's a fact when it's probably not. So there are a lot of people out there who are tainted by spending too much time watching the news and TV programs that may or may not have any effect. They can be fun to watch. I get that, and I do watch some of those, but a person who wants to be a high performer ought not dwell on television. And I believe social media has become a major problem, too. I can't fathom how people spend so much time just staring at social media. How's that making you a better person? I mean, you can see 'em all the time, sitting in a place scrolling through Facebook, TikTok, and Instagram postings. Unfortunately, you see it all the time—they're driving a car and looking at their social media at the same time. And I don't see the utility of any of that, at all.

Clean up your calendar. Spend some of your time every day concentrating on learning, on self-educating, and you'll be well on your way to becoming a better performer who's less mediocre. That then allows you to become a lifestyle evangelist, to show your people what you're doing to become a better performer, so they can follow suit. And if they really don't want to read, there are many apps out there now that can help them (and you) learn a language or be a better athlete or eat better. Those apps are useful. There are many webinars out there, too, that let you spend twenty minutes on a particular topic, and learn, and be better.

There's a secondary advantage to doing this sort of self-educating too: You quickly become a more-interesting individual.

We've all been to social events where, after a person talks about the weather, they run out of things to say. And a lot of times in a social setting, they'll divert to talking about work, because all they've got in their life is work. And that just can't be. I mean, I do read the local newspaper in the morning, to stay attuned to what's going on in the local community. And I read the *Wall Street Journal* in the evening, to understand world affairs. I'm not saying the *Wall Street Journal* is perfect, but I do believe it gives me more facts and less opinions, depending on what part of the newspaper I'm reading. Doing anything similar allows you to go to a social event and talk about current affairs, a recent book that you read, or the recent app that you discovered. All of that has helped me be a better person, and when you become a better person, you quickly appear to be less mediocre to others.

I mean, truly: Does anyone who aspires to be a leader really aspire to be mediocre? The characteristics are obvious. It goes back to the Type B people and Type C people. Mediocre leaders are quick to blame others. Mediocre leaders are selfish. All they can think about is, "How does this affect me? How does this make me look better than I truly am?" Mediocre leaders, because they're not comfortable with who they are, tend to be uncivil and even cruel. They tend to be demeaning. They tend to put people down. They tend not to be nice people. Who aspires to that? I hope not you.

I do think that some mediocre leaders are unaware of their incompetency. They're the guy or gal who looks in the mirror and says, "How great am *I*?" and then talks to their boss and only hears the boss talking about how great they are, too. Just remember: You can always fool your boss, but you can't fool your peers and your direct reports.

If you want to be sure you're not that mediocre leader who's ignorant of the fact that they're a mediocre leader, do some 360s, and actually pay attention to the results. And then? If you want to lift yourself from mediocrity, do what I was taught as a young Lieutenant. Our Division Commander published a paper and gave a presentation on how to be successful, and he subtitled it, "Stairway to the Stars." It was specifically designed to pique the interest of us Lieutenants who may aspire to be General Officers someday, but I think its lessons apply to Corporate America as well—to the worker bee, the VP, or anybody else, who might one day aspire to be CEO. And the primary lesson was this: Do every job superbly. Then? Be visible and widely known. In other words: Whatever job you got, be the best. If you're a dishwasher, be the best dishwasher. And then, make sure people *know* that you're the best dishwasher.

Of course, there's a real skill set to being visible and widely known while not being an in-your-face braggart or obnoxious kind of person. But I guarantee that skill set will remain well-checked if you're working in an organization that embraces routine counseling and 360s—because you're gonna get counseled on it, and quick.

When everything's working right, it all works together for the greater good. And that's what we're after here: To develop ourselves, and to develop our teams, so the organization itself can develop into the High-Performing Organization both we and our shareholders—and, frankly, our country—deserve.

But there are still two more areas we need to address in the realm of employee development if we're gonna get there, and they deal with how people at all levels are treated by the organization and how we can get our people to better serve the organization in a fast-changing, post-COVID, hybrid-workplace world.

CHAPTER 11

PLATE MANAGEMENT

When I was a Brigade-Level Commander, we had a Corps Commander who got all of the Colonels together. He was the Three-Star of the same Corps that I would come back to command later in life. And he said to us, "It's said that the best juggler in the world can only juggle seven things. Well, I expect you all to be like Chinese plate spinners and be able to spin 200 plates at a time without any of those plates breaking."

There is nobody who can keep 200 plates in the air at any one time forever. Nobody. It's a ridiculous demand and an order that cannot be followed.

You can't just keep piling plates onto the end of some pole 'til they reach up into the sky and expect that no one's gonna drop one.

To use a different plate analogy: You can't keep endlessly piling food onto somebody's plate, to the point where it's ten-feet high and spilling over the sides, and expect them to walk across the mess hall without spilling any of that food.

Either way you look at it, plate management needs to be a discussion in Corporate America.

As leaders, and as organizations, we can't keep adding things to everyone's plates all the time without consequences. Big, crashing, messy consequences. And the primary goal of most corporate organizations I see today ought to be clear: We need to be taking things *off* our teams' plates, pronto. Especially in environments where our resources (of people, time, and/or money) are constrained. We can't keep telling people to work harder and do more with less, which just leaves people in dire straits, burned out, dialing down, and passive-aggressively taking out their frustrations by not getting the job done. We need to take things off the plate that simply no longer need to get done.

It's, frankly, amazing to me the number of things that workers in Corporate America have on their plates that do not need to be there. And the only reason it's on the plate is because it was *always* on the plate. Somebody put a task on the plate a long time ago, for whatever reason, and nobody's ever taken it *off* the plate—to the point where the plate itself is beyond its breaking point, let alone the person tasked with carrying that plate, or juggling a bunch of plates.

In *Adapt or Die*, I talked about the extensive work I did to try to make the Army's Installation Management Division more efficient. I started a program asking all 120,000 employees to send me emails and tell me how we could "Stamp Out Stupid." I basically asked everyone to explain the things we were doing that made no sense, which eventually led me to eliminate the creation of a whole lot of government reports that were completely unnecessary and wasting everyone's time.

I went around and told this story of how I came across a young civilian employee working in an office one day; I asked him what he was doing, and he told me: "I'm filing this report." So I asked him, "What happens to that report once you're done with it?" And he said, "I put it in this filing cabinet."

"Well, who reads those reports?" I asked.

"No one that I'm aware of, sir. Not that I know of," he responded. "It's just my job to generate these reports and file them, so that's what I'm doing."

That sort of thing was happening all over IMCOM, and I know that *you* know it's happening all over Corporate America as well. It is amazing to me how much stuff is going on day to day that needs to stop, and yet nobody stops it. Why? Well, in part because Corporate America is failing to develop its people. Nobody's doing the routine counseling and honest performance appraisals, and not nearly enough leaders are walking around enough or engaged enough to realize what's really going on with their people.

Routine counseling cuts directly to the issue of plate management: If you're constantly aware of what your people are doing well—*and* what they need to improve on—then you can't help but notice what sorts of things they're tasked with, and how many of those tasks either aren't getting done, or don't need to get done. You might not even realize how much has been piled on your direct report if you're not talking to them during the year.

At one point, we had a massive exodus of Captains from the Army. I was put on this blue-ribbon panel to study the cause of the exodus, and what we found when we interviewed our Captains about why they were leaving was every one of them, to a person, said, "We can't do it. We can't get it all done. If we were to do everything you tell us to do up at headquarters, we would have zero time to do the things that we *know* need to be done."

Over and over again, these Captains were being told, "The General said we need to do this." That meant to them that *everything* they were told to do was important and needed to get done. There was just one problem: I was the General, and I wasn't aware of most of the things they'd been told to do in my name!

171

I see the same things happening all over Corporate America, only instead of "The General," it's "The CEO said this has to be done." The employees go around thinking they're following orders from the CEO, when the CEO isn't even aware.

Guess if that isn't part of the reason we saw a mass exodus of employees in the post-COVID world? "The Great Resignation," as some people called it. All through the pandemic, executives kept adding stuff to everyone's plate, so the people who were supposed to be doing a job, based on what they acknowledged was their job, became overwhelmed by so much miscellaneous plate-piling that they had no time left to do the job they were supposed to do. That's too stressful for anyone to endure. So they quit and sought happiness elsewhere. I've seen it again and again, and I've had this conversation at least twenty times with CEOs and other top leadership across multiple organizations in just the last couple of years, as resources and hiring have been squeezed in the post-pandemic world.

So here's what we did in the military to solve the mass exodus of Captains: We took a good, hard look at all the things we were telling the Captains they had to do, and then we eliminated half of those tasks. Half! Not 5 percent or 15 percent. We chopped off half of their duties—and the organization didn't suffer one bit. In fact, it started working again, and working well, because what we realized was that half of their tasks were stuff that had been added to their plates in times past that were no longer necessary.

What I found when I was trying to reduce our budget from $20 billion to $15 billion at IMCOM is that we, as an Army, were great at starting programs. But we were lousy at *stopping* programs.

It's the same thing with Corporate America.

If your staff is overtaxed and burned out, your best people are leaving in droves, and the rest don't seem to be pulling their weight, it might be time to stop and take a serious look at what's on their plates—and eliminate everything that doesn't need to be there.

PET ROCKS

I also find that a lot of individuals in Corporate America are out there pursuing their own pet-rock programs. They're working on projects and completing tasks that have got nothing to do with the company's overall purpose and VVOP. They're just out there in some quiet corner, doing their own thing, and nobody's stopping them or getting them refocused. Why? Usually because whoever's in charge of them has too many subordinates to look after, so they're really not supervising any of them. (In other words, even the *leaders* have too much on their plates!) When one supervisor has twenty or fifty direct reports, it's really easy for number eighteen to just go rogue and do their own thing, because they're not getting any direct supervision or counseling.

I cannot tell you how many people I've encountered during my 360 Assessments who were out there doing something totally opposite of what needed to be done, simply because nobody was supervising them. And they were drawing a paycheck, just like everybody else, all because the company's plate management was so poor.

If you want to improve your organization's performance, you've got to get your priorities straight, not just in terms of values but also in terms of how and when you distribute the workload.

If you're having trouble prioritizing what needs to get done and when, do what I suggested back in Chapter 3, and take a few minutes to study the Eisenhower Box, which, as its name suggests, is based on something our 34th President, Dwight D. Eisenhower, invented and relied upon in his efforts to run our nation (and, I might add, as the Five-Star Army General who planned the liberation of France at Normandy Beach during World War II).

Since some of you might not have taken the time to look it up, I'm going to take a moment here to explain how the Eisenhower Box works. If you already know, then you can skip ahead to the next section.

The Eisenhower method involves breaking tasks down into four categories, or "boxes": Urgent and Important; Urgent and Less Important; *Not* Urgent but Important; and *Not* Urgent and *Not* Important.

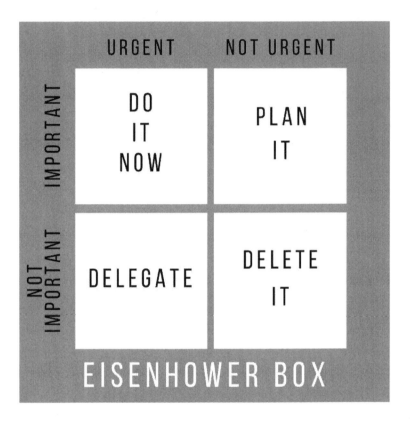

When you categorize what needs to be done into these four boxes, it becomes clear that what's *Not* Urgent and *Not* Important should be treated as such—they need to be put on the back burner or maybe even eliminated from consideration entirely. On the other hand, tasks that are Urgent and Important need to be dealt with right away and with the utmost care and attention. The Urgent and Less Important require quick action but shouldn't take precedent over the More Important tasks. And the Important but Less Urgent tasks should be delegated appropriately to get finished after the Urgent tasks are completed.

Simply using the Box to help you stop from plate-piling will help show your people that you care about not wasting their time, while also showing that you're not losing sight of what's important and urgent for your organization.

IT'S MORE THAN JUST THE WORKLOAD

Also remember: What's on a worker's plate is more than just the workload. Forward-thinking leaders at High-Performing Organizations recognize this and adjust their schedules and even their benefits packages accordingly.

For example, a team from one of the major pharmaceutical companies I work with came on a Leadership Tour with me a couple of years ago, and one of the young men who came along told me he was getting ready to go on a three-month paternity leave after his wife gave birth. His wife works as a lawyer for a big law firm, and she was afforded six months' maternity leave, but the young man, as a father, at his company, was *also* afforded three months. I think that's pretty cool. That's not paid "vacation." He was being paid to go help take care of his new baby—an American child. The leadership at his company believed it was worth their time and money to invest in employees taking care of their children, whether it's the mom or the dad. I find that intriguing and refreshing. We didn't do that in the military. We gave two weeks at most to the dads. But how great is it for a company to say, "Hey, take the next three months, welcome your new baby into the world, and work through your family's transition"? I think that's pretty powerful. And the ultimate beneficiaries of that are the children themselves: our next generation of Americans. But it also fosters a whole lot of trust and loyalty in that employee, and shows all the employees that you care. And that's good for the *company*.

When you've created a vision—a mission—with Values and Purpose driven by Taking Care of People, these are the kinds of things great leaders not only come up with but support.

Which is a very good reason for each of us, as leaders, to pay attention to managing our own plate, too.

As leaders, we need to make enough time in the day to actually *think* about what we're doing. Too many of us are moving from one event to the next to the next, without stopping to think. And that's irresponsible.

I had thirty-two years in the Army before I was assigned to the Pentagon, and the moment I walked in, I saw that something was wrong: Life in the Pentagon was always moving at a crazy pace. There are General Officers, Three- and Four-Star generals, moving from one meeting to the next all day long; and while they're meeting, there's some Colonel sitting next to them, feeding them the notebook, saying, "When this question comes up, here's the answer."

Because of the way we had failed to organize our days, even our Generals didn't have enough time to think. And we needed their thoughts. We needed their leadership. It's why we were all there.

Astoundingly, I've found the same thing is going on all over Corporate America: People are moving from meeting to meeting, day after day, with no time to assess or properly review the big questions and look at the big picture in between dealing with all of the minutiae.

Which means we've got to work harder to get the minutiae under control.

EMAIL IS NOT COMMUNICATION

For example: Ask anyone in Corporate America how they feel about email, and their answer will probably be, "Overwhelmed." Well, there's good reason people are overwhelmed by it. There's too much of it, it's poorly worded, it's not being read, it's being misinterpreted, a lot of it is completely unnecessary (but takes time to read, regardless), and it's coming at all hours of the day and night, putting stress on people when they should be enjoying their leisure time or time with their families. And that's just the half of it.

People are not robots, and they have no way of efficiently sorting, reading, responding to, and understanding the volume of email that changes hands on a daily basis in most organizations. Therefore, this modern communication tool that's meant to speed things up winds up *slowing things down*, causing headaches and burdens where there formerly were none.

It's up to leaders to put a stop to it, and rein things in.

That is why, in my consulting work, I encourage leaders to put together an email-policy letter to help bring this one area of concern under control—and every High-Performance Organization I've worked with has taken the time to take this step. Because it works.

And the following is the email policy I suggest. Take it, and use it freely.

You're welcome.

EMAIL POLICY LETTER

Remember that email is not communication—it is simply typing and then pressing "Send." You are never sure that the intended audience received the email, understood the email, or properly interpreted the intent and passion of the email. Always defer to face-to-face communication if possible. If you are going to use email, remember these eight rules:

1. Ensure all email communication is clear and concise. Put the critical points of the email in the first three sentences.

2. Never type an email when you are angry or frustrated.

3. Always type your email before you put in the names of the folks you want to send it to.

4. Always proofread emails before sending them.

5. Never use "Reply All" as a response. Be focused.

6. Assume your email is going to end up on the front page of *The Washington Post*, because it probably will. Emails never go away.

7. Use a signature block on all your emails. Include contact information.

8. Always be aware that your emails are subject to IT issues (phishing, ransomware, anti-spam programs that could keep them from being delivered to your intended recipient, etc.).

Taking time, as leaders, to think about the issues that are plaguing our people and causing them to try to keep too many plates in the air at once is important.

Taking action to eliminate or improve those issues is critical.

As leaders, too many of us are moving so fast and thinking so little that we're losing track of what we're doing and not doing. As a result, we're often not following through on our promises to our people—promises big and small. And because of that, we're losing trust and faith in each other as human beings.

In short, we're moving so fast and thinking so little about the very real effects of our actions, decisions, and communications, it's costing us our integrity.

And without our integrity, we don't have much of anything.

I'll tackle this last topic further in the very first chapter in Part III. But before we get there, let's talk about one last, rather controversial topic that I feel is getting in the way of allowing our employees—and therefore our organizations—to turn into high performers.

CHAPTER 12

THE IMPERATIVE TO RETURN TO WORK

In all my books, I've made it a point to mention that *leadership is a contact sport*, and I've made that point again and again in the pages of this book, too. But I cannot stress enough just how important it is to reiterate it here, because it's a fact: Being a leader is face-to-face work. It's handshakes, it's hugs, it's physical contact. It's cups of coffee. It's meetings. It's meals. It's sharing experiences. But most of all, for leaders who care, it is human to human.

Now, I realize that a lot of things have changed, a lot of things are still in flux, and that a lot of my readers are gonna disagree with me on this point, but I gotta tell you: My feelings on this matter have not changed. Despite what happened during COVID; despite the invention and implementation of Zoom and Microsoft Teams; and despite the impact of an increasingly mobile, spread-out, even international work-force, everything I stated in my prior books and everything I stated in the paragraph above remains true.

In fact, seeing leadership as a contact sport is even more important now, precisely *because* of all of these massive, sweeping changes that washed over us like a tsunami in the past few years.

Even though people act like it's all over, I believe we're still experiencing the impact of the COVID pandemic—when we sent everybody home. There were a whole lotta months there, given the contagion of the COVID pandemic, when people had no choice but to figure out how to work from home. And now that the immediacy of that danger has passed, a whole lot of those people are *still* at home. They're hesitant to return to work, because they became pretty comfortable.

For one thing, working from home negated the need for a long commute. Many of the people that I work with in Corporate America had commutes that were an hour or two back and forth to work. Yet when they were allowed to work from home, they discovered the joy of not having to deal with that commute. And they loved it.

Of course, they also discovered (like everyone else) that working from home meant they could spend more time with their family, and spend more time on their own personal fitness, etc. And I get all of that. I love being home and working from home, and spending time with my family as much as I can. I've read the studies, and I truly believe that working from home was okay in terms of individual productivity.

But Corporate America is not about individual productivity.

Corporate America is all about *collective* productivity. Which means that, in order for any corporate organization to work at a high level, it's imperative to get its people together, routinely.

Different organizations have taken different approaches on this since COVID quieted down, but the first ones I want to focus on are those who said, "You know what? We're gonna allow people to work from home from now on, full-time. We can save ourselves a bunch of rent and expenses for office space, and we can easily rely on Zoom calls and Microsoft Teams to stay connected."

Well, that was a nice experiment. But the result I've seen is that the collective productivity of the companies that have tried it has plummeted. Why? Because in order to truly work together, people have got to get face to face. In order for teams to truly be productive, there have got to be opportunities for folks to get together, break bread together, have a cup of coffee together, and just to be able to enjoy each other's company in between sharing ideas, insights, and information in a way that happens, naturally, in post-meeting meetings. The important talks that happen around the water cooler. Down the hallway. At lunch. Over drinks, after hours. Whatever it might be. That collective discussion cannot happen when people are sitting around in their pajamas after the cameras are turned off in a Zoom meeting. And that collective discussion is a big part of what gives High-Performing Organizations their power.

I'll get deeper into this as we go along, but first, I think it's important just to kind of lay out the statistics. A lot of surveys have been done with the American population and the workforce these past few years to get opinions about the idea of returning to work. And from what I've gathered in my observations of a number of these surveys is that only 18 percent of the people who participated want to come to work full-time (meaning to go back to five days a week, 40 hours a week, in the office). Only 18 percent! So 82 percent of the population is saying, "No, I don't want to do that full-time. I've become enamored with the opportunities and options that working from home gives me, and I don't want to lose them."

Of those 82 percent who don't want to return to work, only 27 percent say they want to stay home every day and *never* go in to work. So that should tell you something: There's actually a large percentage of the workforce who say, "Yeah, I need some contact. I need some collaboration.

I need some opportunities to return to work." Statistically, 50 percent of those people surveyed agree that collaboration and building relationships are important.

They realize they can do that only if they come into work every now and then.

Plus—and this one is especially telling, across all of the surveys I've seen—fully 70 percent of Americans say they're missing the social relationships of being at work. Now, robots could work from home just fine. They don't care about social engagement. But they also won't commute to the office when needed, can't participate in collective thinking over coffee, and will totally fail to do their job if the electricity goes out. Which is why we don't hire robots.

At the same time everyone's wringing their hands about what to do with this new work-from-home workforce, a Gallup poll released in April of 2024 showed that employee engagement had dropped to its lowest point in more than a decade. Coincidence? I don't think so. Even if people can't articulate it, the changes that happened have all been too much. They've disrupted things in a way that we haven't been able to wrap our minds around quite yet. So this is a topic that has to be looked at and has to be addressed.

I think we can agree on a few things. For instance, some organizations that I deal with had no choice but to bring everybody back to work full-time. If you're a grocery store, your people need to be at work; if you're a healthcare organization, the nurses and doctors need to be at work; if you're a university, most of the time, the staff professionals need to go to work. The question is: how much, how often, and how? And that's a dilemma that the corporate leader has to deal with now.

In the past, for example, the sales forces of a lot of my clients have worked from home anyway, because that's what sales forces do. They're scattered across the nation, and they visit their respective districts and regions to sell stuff. They come into the corporate headquarters only as required. But the corporate folks? They come in. That's where they work. They work at the corporate headquarters. So let's just kind of talk about the options here and then see how best to pull this off.

The bottom line, up front, is that it's important to have measured productivity.

We all seem to have fallen into a habit of using general comments about productivity. "I'm more productive working from home," or "I'm more productive when I'm working at work," but what are the measurable outputs that leaders ought to establish, so that people have actual productivity goals?

Candidly, I think most leaders ought not to be micromanagers. They ought to say things like, "How you get this done is up to you. But this needs to get done." I mean, I do have corporate executives now who, when their folks are working from home, put some kind of rigid monitoring devices in place so they can make sure they're working eight hours a day. They watch when they open up their computer, they watch when they turn off their computer, they watch the number of keystrokes over the course of an eight-hour period of time. That's just a waste of time and energy for the leader, if you ask me. Instead, I advise them to just give their people measurable outputs. "What are you required to accomplish over this particular period?" And see what happens. If the person working from home works better at three o'clock in the morning, or eight at night, let 'em do that. I mean, that's the whole key—to allow 'em to play to their strengths.

I tell the story these days that pre-COVID, me, the old guy, could go to a movie once a week, primarily on a Tuesday, and have the entire theater to myself. The entire theater. These days, I go to the movie on a Tuesday afternoon, and the theater is full of people who are supposedly working from home. The other day, one of my corporate teams was having a Zoom call when everybody was supposed to be at work, and in the background of one of the corporate executives was a ski slope.

And it wasn't a generated background. It was an actual background. He was at a ski slope, which caused some post-meeting concern. "Why is this guy at a ski slope while he's working?" And again, I think those are irrelevant questions. If that guy found himself more productive working from the ski resort than working from home, who cares where he's working from? As long as he's not charging the ski vacation on a corporate charge card. So the point is, leaders ought not overly concern themselves as to *when* the person is working. More importantly, they should focus on outputs—clearly defined, measurable outputs: What did they get accomplished, in terms of what they *should have gotten* accomplished?

That's crucial if we want people to really get the benefits of working from home, which include things like being better parents to their kids, getting in better shape, having more time on their hands because of the lack of commute, and generally feeling healthier and happier.

When work-from-home isn't managed properly, and especially when it's micromanaged, it brings up all kinds of other issues. For example, I've had a few clients over the last several years who failed to set boundaries. And when you fail to set boundaries, then you're not working from home; you're sleeping at work. You're *always* at work: you turn on your computer, you turn on your cell phone, you make yourself available 24 hours a day, and people will take advantage of that. So you've got to set boundaries if you're working from home. You've got to say, "Okay, I'm available for calls between this time and this time. And during this time, I'm not available," because you're at the gym, or picking your kids up from school, or at a family dinner, whatever it might be. There must be boundaries that are set by people who are working from home, so they can, indeed, be more productive.

Part of what people complain about in the workplace is that there are too many distractions. In my surveys and in much broader surveys alike, people say that, when they go to work, they're distracted. "Bob wants to talk about football, Sally wants to talk about her weekend, and all those folks are taking my focus off my work! When I'm working from home, it's just me and the computer and the work. I like that better."

Now, an issue with this, obviously, is small children. If the small children stay home while the individual is working, that's just another form of distraction. And in reality, there are all sorts of distractions that are taking place at home that cause people to lose their focus on their work. So all of those things have to be taken into consideration.

Even with all of that, I am convinced that, in general terms, individuals are more productive working from home. They're healthier, they're happier, they're more engaged, and they're less distracted. That's wonderful. Unfortunately, the sacrifice corporations are making comes in terms of collective productivity. And you simply cannot get that back by holding virtual meetings.

People are enamored with Teams and Zooms. I understand the technology. I use the technology on a daily basis. It's better than email for sure. It's better than a phone call if the cameras are on, so you can actually see the other person, see their demeanor, see how they're looking, see how their body language is. So I understand all that. But I do know there's an important aspect of collective productivity that happens when everybody gets together.

I remember vividly, during my time in Iraq, I was a Two-Star General on the Four-Star staff. We'd have routine meetings, daily meetings, in which the Four-Star would articulate his passion and his vision. And then, after the meetings, all of us Two- and Three-Stars would get together and say, "Okay, what are we going to do now? How are we going to make that happen?"

I'll go so far as to say we might never have accomplished the positive things we accomplished in Iraq had those post-meeting meetings never happened. And that's what we're losing with people working from home. There's no collective post-meeting brainstorming taking place. There's no bonding taking place, either. And that's a loss, especially when you get new team members. I mean, I've done all these surveys over the last several years where I talked to team members who came in post-COVID, and they've never even met their colleagues. They've seen them on a computer screen, but they've never met them face to face, and that is just not enhancing anyone's collective productivity.

SO WHAT'S THE ANSWER?

I do believe that the answer to all of this is some kind of a hybrid model—one in which people don't come to work full-time, all the time, like they did pre-COVID. But they do come to work at certain occasions for certain events, to be able to improve their collective productivity. I think that's important. And as we move forward, what's really going to be called for is a new, adaptive kind of solution.

Here's where the essence of adaptive leadership comes into play: In order to entice workers to *want* to come into the office and contribute face to face again, leaders will have to be adaptive in terms of constructing that work time.

I've had some clients say, "I've got this brilliant idea: Everybody work from home three days a week, and come to work two days a week," for example, which is a hybrid model; or, just the opposite, they say, "Come to work three days a week, stay home two days a week," which is what a lot of my clients are doing, and, at first, everyone thought those ideas were great.

Here's where the reality sets in: On those days when people are required to come to work, if you just have them do at work what they could have been doing at home while avoiding the commute and all the other negatives, you wind up with a demoralized workforce. They're going to spend all day in the office thinking, *Why am I here? I'd much rather be home, petting my dog, focusing on the work without these all these distractions.* So an innovative leader, an adaptive leader, has to say, "What do I do to make it so attractive that they *want* to come to work; so they wake up in the morning, bright eyed and bushy tailed, get dressed, go to work, enjoy their time at work and come home, uplifted, spirited"—all that kind of good stuff.

I've been watching and trying to help my clients try to figure this all out, and there are quite a few options I've encountered already that seem to do the trick.

One example: catered lunches. The folks working from home are probably not eating much, or maybe eating a bologna sandwich while they're working. So if you have catered lunches available at the office, at minimal cost, where those folks coming to work can all gather together and break bread together—man, that's powerful. That's worth every cent. Food is a great gathering incentive.

If you say, "Okay, we're gonna come to work on Tuesdays and Thursdays. But on Thursdays, we're all going to get together with the corporate executives, and we're going to talk about what's going on to improve communication," that's powerful, too. Especially in a High-Performing Organization, your people are gonna want to come to work because they want to listen to and participate in what's going on.

Little incentives like that really work.

When I was a Corps Commander, I required all of the officers in the Corps—and that's *a lot* of officers—to join me at the officer's club every Friday at 4:30 (assuming they weren't deployed). I had a gazebo set up, a sound system set up. So from 4:30 to 4:45, I talked to all the officers in the Corps: "Here's what's going on. Here's what we're dealing with. Here are the issues." Total transparency, so everybody knew what the Corps Commander was dealing with, so they could be value added. And then at 4:45, the band started playing, the whiskey bottles got open, the cigars came out, and we just had a hoot and a holler for probably an hour and 15 minutes. Spouses were invited, and they would show up so they could enjoy the festivities. It just became something that the officers of the Corps looked forward to. Because it's okay, like I say in book number one, to have fun.

I still get notes fifteen years later from people, highlighting how much they enjoyed those socials on a Friday afternoon.

That's why, for twleve years now, I've been advocating for Corporate America to include spouses on some events. For example, a number of the major clients I have hold annual national sales meetings, and every national sales meeting takes place in some exotic location. It's always at Margaritaville in Florida, or a resort in Aruba, or wherever, and I often get invited to those. But what I see once I get there is a great big, missed opportunity.

What I tell the leaders is that, at no cost, they can include their spouses in these fun and productive trips. You just make the employee pay for their spouse's plane ticket or other travel arrangements. You've already paid for a room for the employee, so there's no additional costs there; and there's always a social function or two that the husbands, wives, or partners can attend. They're not going to attend the business part of the national sales meeting. They're not going to disrupt activity. During those times, they can be free to go out sightseeing or relax by the pool. But when you bring people's spouses along, three things are gonna happen. One, the spouse is going to feel *included*. It's going to be blatantly obvious to the employee and the spouse that you actually care about them—that their familial relationship is important. Number two is that their marriage is going to be strengthened, because absence does *not* make the heart grow fonder, and the old saying is true: "Happy Wife, Happy Life." Take out the sexism part of that, and it doesn't rhyme, but it still applies: "Happy Partner, Happy Life." And that makes for a happier employee. And number three is that you eliminate what we all know happens on some of these trips. We've all seen it, when there's a social event, complete with open bar, and the spouses aren't there, and as the night winds down, some people go back to their respective rooms, and some people go back to *other* people's rooms. Early risers like me tend to catch 'em in the hallway doing the *Walk of Shame* the next morning. So why leave room for that sort of temptation to happen on your watch, knowing it will cause all kinds of heartache and difficulty at home, which will inevitably spill over into the workplace once everybody returns?

It goes back to Abraham Lincoln being smart enough to send General Ulysses S. Grant's wife along with him as he traveled, as a means to help temper Grant's drinking. If it was a smart thing for Abraham Lincoln to do, you can bet it's a smart example for a corporate leader to follow. Having spouses around tends to temper things a little bit. Plus, it fosters camaraderie and friendships that may well carry on back home, which will only make your team that much stronger.

So that's the key to all this: Go ahead and make the decision in terms of what you want to do about returning to work, but consider all aspects of it before you make that decision. What can you do that will turn this new obstacle of "coming into the office" into an opportunity to make your team even better than it already was?

What you don't want to do is make decisions in this area without thinking them through, thoroughly. I've already mentioned some organizations that canceled full-time office work altogether and noted that they were having some very real struggles. But on the other end of the spectrum, I have CEOs who didn't want to adapt at all. They said, "Nope. Everybody come back to work. *Now.*" And, candidly, that didn't work very well, either, 'cause those folks who were enamored with working from home just went and found a remote job somewhere else. They voted with their feet and became part of what the business press commonly refer to as "the Great Exodus." And that's probably going to continue to happen to anybody who takes a draconian approach that's 100 percent "Come back to work."

So the combination/hybrid-type model seems like the obvious solution. You decide whether it's two and three, or three and two, or you decide whether people always come in on Fridays, or whatever it might be, but there's got to be some adaptation involved. It can't just be the way it used to be. It can't be. You've got to make it so attractive to your people now that they *want* to come to work. Making the event of going to work something that they *want* to do is absolutely essential.

When you care about your people, you listen to their needs. You step back from the map and look at trends. You adapt as necessary. You show them that you're decisive. Again, all of these various parts work together in a High-Performing Organization, which makes each part of the puzzle a little easier as you go along.

As long as you pay attention, follow the steps of what I've laid out so far, and do all you can to lead with integrity, you'll soon find that you're no longer worrying about all of these day-to-day problems and, instead, easily adapting to and taking advantage of these obstacles and sweeping changes that inevitably come out of nowhere, no matter how much you've planned and tried to anticipate what the next few years might look like.

The idea of switching over to a hybrid workforce? After all these years of knowing exactly what your workplace looked like, and felt like? If you and your team find this sort of a brand-new, unexpected challenge to be invigorating and exciting, rather than daunting or devastating, then there's a very good chance that you've made it.

You've already started to unleash the incredible power of what a High-Performing Organization can do.

PART III

Unleash the Power of Your HPO

CHAPTER 13

TRUST IS A MUST

Of all the Army values, Integrity is the most important. Why?

Because if the people in leadership positions don't have Integrity, we *lose*. And in ground combat, if we lose our integrity, our Army loses *lives*.

Our Army teams have no choice but to work together; we have to trust each other at the deepest level in order to accomplish our missions. And in order to do that, we need to trust that the commanders in charge are leaders of great integrity—from the lowly Lieutenants all the way up to the Commander in Chief.

Without Integrity, our leaders can't be trusted. And it goes both ways: In the Army, we're taught from day one that the only way to build cohesive teams is through *mutual trust*.

There is no part of that principle that can't be applied to Corporate America as well.

How do we build mutual trust? It's not by putting a slogan on a poster. It's not by making grand gestures once a year, or once a quarter. It's through everyday actions and interactions. A leader builds trust with his or her people *automatically* just by being engaged with them, by communicating clearly, by "Leading by Walking Around," and simply "Walking the Walk," in Deeds, Not Words—so much of what I spoke about in my books *Adapt or Die* and *Work Hard, Pray Hard*, and so much of what I talked about in Part II of this book.

But the biggest way to build trust should be obvious: By being honest and dependable.

There's really no other way.

The Army, after all of its years of study and practice, at home and abroad, knows for a *fact* that integrity—the simple act of being honest and dependable, anchored by a strong moral code—creates and enhances trust in the organization.

And I am telling you, here and now, that trust and integrity are also the fundamental components required, the values that we need to demand from ourselves and from others, first and foremost, if we want to build High-Performing Organizations in Corporate America.

Don't just take my word for it. This fundamental principle also comes from the mouths of the world's foremost business experts.

Stephen Covey released an entire book on this subject back in 2008, called *The Speed of Trust*. In it, he shows how trust—and the speed at which it is established with clients, employees, and stakeholders—is the single most critical component of a successful leader and organization. He talks extensively about how, when trust increases, the speed of your operation increases, and your costs go down. But if trust goes down, the speed of your operation goes down, and costs go up.

The Speed of Trust is one of my favorite business books, and if you haven't read it, you should, because what Covey talks about is the fact that organizations that are built on a foundation of trust are generally

80 percent more effective than those that aren't. *Eighty percent!* That's not a minor amount. And I've seen it play out: The companies I work with that foster trust at all levels are the very same companies that thrive; and the clients without that foundation, the ones full of people who just don't trust each other, find themselves floundering and faltering all the time.

Wherever there *isn't* trust, we run into problem areas full of passive-aggressive behaviors. And when everything's gummed up and slowed down at every turn, you can forget about making your quarterly results.

Let me repeat Covey's findings: Organizations that are built on a foundation of trust are *80 percent* more effective than those that aren't. And after working in Corporate America for the last 12-plus years, I am convinced that trust is the ultimate discriminator between a highly effective organization and a marginally effective organization, every time.

Does building trust guarantee better quarterly results? Of course not. No one thing is the determiner of that, and nobody can win all the time. But with trust in place, it becomes a whole lot easier. And trust is built, first and foremost, by engaged leadership.

LEADING FROM THE FRONT

I spent a lot of time looking at the importance of building and restoring trust in the expanded 10th Anniversary Edition of *Adapt or Die*, and the long and short of it is this: It's nearly impossible to win a battle, let alone a war, without engaged leaders, leading with integrity, and leading from the front.

In High-Performing Organizations, leaders cannot lead solely from behind a desk, far from the action. You have to be in it to win it, and your people have to see it, feel it, and know it. All the time.

When times are tough, are you hugging your people? Are you putting your arms around the people in your charge—whether they're your children or the people who work on your factory floor—and saying, "We can get through this together"? Or are you sitting back in your cubicle, typing vicious emails, blaming others for mistakes, and staying out of the fray? Where are you leading from right now? Are you sending instant messages from a cushy office or bedroom somewhere while people do your bidding, possibly suffering real consequences from your non-engaged decisions?

There is no faster way to erode trust and destroy your integrity than by failing to lead from the front, or failing to stand beside your people.

I've spent a lot of time talking about this one issue of building and restoring trust in open forums from West Point to corporate boardrooms, and when I talk about the fact that "people don't care about how much you know until they know how much you care," I remind my audiences that, in order for people to *know* that you care, they need to *trust you*.

It's a really big deal.

Do the people who work for you and look to you as a leader believe that you're really going to take care of them? Not just in good times, but when the chips are down? When things aren't going right? When the battle comes to *you*?

As an engaged and empathetic leader, both at work and at home, I concluded a long time ago that there's no such thing as a casual conversation. If you say, "I care about you" to anyone in your circle, in your family, or on your team, and the person says, "I'm glad you say that, because I need help," you have to respond. Your actions had better not say to them, "I was only kidding. I'm really not going to help you," because that is the ultimate act of breaking trust.

When you say you care, you've got to demonstrate empathy—with actions.

And don't you *dare* say to me that you don't have time or space to care.

In Iraq, during the Surge, I had sixty-two patrol bases spread across the region. My headquarters was in Baghdad, in a secure area. I could have easily sat in my office and just directed activity between trips to the gym. I could have done that. But I didn't.

Every morning, after my morning routine—which, in my case, typically involved some Bible study, breakfast, and meeting with my leaders—I got into a helicopter, and I flew out to places like Patrol Base Whisky 1, to be out there with our soldiers and go on patrol with them.

Now, please don't think I'm telling personal stories in order to glorify myself, because every leader that I dealt with in Iraq did the same sorts of things that I did. We *all* led from the front, which is why we accomplished the Mission.

At our forward operating bases, soldiers simply could not accomplish their mission by staying on base, either; they *had* to go out on patrol and engage with the population, with the Iraqi people. So as engaged leaders, Army leaders who wanted to instill a sense of trust in our teams, guys like me would actually go on patrol with them, so we could get a sense of what was going on. That meant suiting up in body armor and driving on roads where Improvised Explosive Devices (IEDs) might be buried in the dirt under our wheels; walking into villages where a sniper might be hiding on a rooftop, or somebody's house might be wired with an IED just waiting for us; helicoptering into locations where we were regularly fired upon with machine guns or anti-aircraft weapons. We had great people who were clearing and securing the routes we took, and we tried to make sure the locations we entered were safe, but there was always, *always* a risk.

I took that risk knowing it was the right thing to do—and trusting my safety, first and foremost, to my trust in God. (You can read more about that in my second book, *Work Hard, Pray Hard*.)

So, really: How hard is it to go down to your factory floor or your research lab? To go out on the road with your salespeople, or to go meet customers, firsthand, if that'll serve you well? It's not. Get up off your rear end, and do it! And never forget: Being widely seen matters. Just being *present* matters. That alone builds trust, in and of itself.

It's also harder to fail your people once you've looked them in the eye and shaken their hand.

Remember: You can't shake hands on Zoom. You just can't. And the handshake has been an international symbol of greeting and trust for nearly the entirety of human existence. It's stupid to think we can just drop the importance of that gesture all of a sudden and replace it with screens and emojis.

THE COST OF LOSING TRUST

Fair warning: If you're currently working in an organization that *doesn't* foster trust, there could very well be passive-aggressive people either under you, over you, or right beside you, who will deliver inaccurate or purposefully misleading information your way just to mess things up, or maybe even to mess with you personally.

As the Engaged Leader you want to be, you have to be aware of this and start working to change things right away.

If there are people within your organization who don't agree with what you're doing, who smile and nod and say, "Yeah, OK," or, "Good idea, boss," and then they go do something totally different, you're in trouble. When passive-aggressive workers are present, communication breaks down, performance breaks down, and the organization becomes dysfunctional, fast. (Remember what happened with some of Gen. Robert E. Lee's passive-aggressive and less-than-honest subordinates at Gettysburg?)

The primary cause of passive-aggressive people in the workplace is that the employees do not trust the people who have been hired to lead.

They don't believe that the company or the leaders care about them. Don't let that leader be you.

And don't forget: Companies that promise to Take Care of their People—and then live by it—do better than companies that don't.

I had one company in the last twelve years that was struggling, big-time, with their employee-turnover rate, and when I started looking into it for them, I found out that people *leaving* the company wasn't their biggest problem at all. Everywhere I looked, I found passive-aggressive people who *weren't* leaving, because they were too scared to cut and run. They needed the paycheck, but they hated their bosses and hated the culture. So instead of making their exit, they stuck around and actively worked against the interests of the company, just to spite their bosses.

As I observed those bosses in action, it became clear to me why the workforce was so disgruntled. Not only did this firm have a bad habit of not taking care of its people the way they promised—they cut employee healthcare coverage as a "cost-savings measure," and that was just one of many brazen displays of disregard for the wellness of the people in their charge—but leadership itself was prone to infighting. The leaders at the top couldn't stand each other, and they let it show. Some of them even took it out on their workers, waltzing into the hallways and berating them, demeaning them in front of their colleagues, just for fun. I think some of them did it as a way to "kick the cat" and get their stress out.

They were breaking the Golden Rule: "Do to others as you would have them do to you." A rule so important, it's found in the Bible twice: In Matthew 7:12 and in Luke 6:31.

It's hard to know where to start with an organization that's in that much trouble. Individual leadership training, collective training—the fact that they brought me in to even try was a good sign. But they really had no choice. Leadership had to recognize that their workplace culture—and, especially, the lack of trust—was keeping them from growing. And we all know how important quarterly growth is in today's world.

Once they'd exhausted all other means, they finally turned to following my lead as a potential way to increase earnings per share. They followed the steps I've outlined in this book, and guess what? It worked.

I'm proud of the progress they've made—but they've still got a long way to go.

What I'm trying to say is that we have to strive to establish a foundation of trust within our organizations in order for *any* of this stuff to work.

Now, remember, trust comes in two different categories:

1. We trust people based on their character.

2. We trust people based on their competency.

Now, frankly, I don't see a lot of issues in Corporate America where individuals aren't trusting each other based on their character (outside of a few really troubled organizations). But I see all sorts of issues with folks not trusting each other based on competency. People observe their fellow workers acting in an incompetent fashion, and as a result, they don't trust them. They don't want to give them work to do, primarily because they don't trust their ability to get the work done successfully. That's a major, major issue. We can't have people on the team who aren't competent. And if we've put in the time to establish detailed job descriptions, and we're following through on our routine counseling and performance appraisals, and there are still incompetent people on our teams? In the name of trust, it has to end. Leaders *must* step up and either get those people in line, or let 'em go.

If we have somebody on the team who is just incompetent, and we allow them to stay on the team, that's going to erode our trust across the entire organization.

And once it's gone, trust ain't easy to get back.

Trust is a remarkable thing in that way. It takes a long time to build it, but it can be broken overnight. In fact, it can be broken in an instant. Flicked off like a light switch. The examples of how it happens in Corporate America are too many to list, but it usually comes down to basic truth-telling. For instance, if a boss tells you you're not getting a bonus this year because revenue wasn't high enough, and you later find out the boss himself got a bonus that very same year, your trust in that boss is now *gone*. And a lot of folks I talk to in the workplace place tell me "Once that trust is broken, it can never be rebuilt." I try to explain to them that it's not true.

I spent a lot of time in the expanded 10th Anniversary Edition of *Adapt or Die* talking about restoring trust, and the long and short of it is, you *can* restore trust—but it takes a long time. Even in personal relationships, let's say somebody decides to be unfaithful to their spouse, that doesn't mean that the marriage *has* to end—no ifs, ands, or buts. But the act of cheating cannot be erased. There's a major trust issue in the marriage now, because every time that spouse leaves on a trip, the one left at home is going to wonder if they'll be unfaithful again, right? Even if the cheating spouse promises it'll never happen again, their spouse is going to take it with a grain of salt, because the first promise—the marriage contract itself—wasn't worth the paper it was printed on. But with marriage counseling, extensive proof of fidelity, and lots of time, it is possible for trust to be regained.

Still, if an employee isn't willing to give you the time or benefit of a second chance the way a spouse might (if you're lucky!), then you're outta luck. In many cases, once trust is broken, your people aren't gonna sit around and wait for that trust to be rebuilt. They're going to leave. Or worse. (See the example of the passive-aggressive workers I shared above.)

And don't be fooled into thinking you have a good record of trust if you don't. If there's a lot of turbulence and turnover at your company, you can bet, 99 percent of the time, there's a trust issue happening somewhere. Maybe it's not at the top. Maybe it's one poor performer or one bad leader somewhere down the chain of command, like it was with my client that had a first-year turnover rate of 35 percent with new hires. Which is another reason to stay on top of the counseling and appraisal process, and to do 360-degree Assessments from time to time, too. I advise clients all the time that it's important to develop metrics, just to make sure you're watching for things that might get overlooked—like exit rates.

What I'm saying is that one way to build trust is to stay on top of what's actually happening. Which all goes back to continually asking ourselves:

"Are we doing the right things?"

"Are we doing things right?"

. . . and most importantly:

"What are we missing?"

If an unusual number of people are leaving your company all of a sudden, that's a metric that you ought to be aware of. And getting on top of it, rooting out the problem, and setting things back on course is absolutely a way to build trust throughout your company.

BUILDING TRUST THROUGH COMMITMENT

Another indicator of trust, and one way in which trust can be built, or rebuilt, is simply through commitment.

In the military, I had ultimate trust in all of my leaders, peers, associates, and subordinates, because we were all committed to the mission. An important mission: to protect our nation's freedoms and our way of life; and to support and defend our Constitution (not to mention the fact that lives were involved). So I don't ever remember in 35 years having someone violate my trust, in part because what we were doing was so important.

Historically speaking, there are all kinds of examples of military leaders showing commitment beyond the pale to accomplishing our military goals. One that immediately comes to mind is one I share in detail on Leadership Tours to the Civil War Battlefield at Chickamauga, Georgia.

The Battle at Chickamauga took place in September 1863, a few months after the Confederacy suffered its biggest blow ever, at Gettysburg. What some people don't realize is that Gettysburg, despite its crushing blow, didn't put an end to the War. It stretched on for nearly two years after that, and in fact, the backlash it created fired up what remained of the Confederacy and propelled them into winning some pretty big battles in the ensuing months.

In this case, in Chickamauga, the Confederate forces under Braxton Bragg took advantage of a gap in the Union lines. They rolled up to Union forces and forced them back to Chattanooga, which could have resulted in a bloodbath for the Union. But rather than retreat right away, even though he was greatly outnumbered and in mortal danger, Union General George Thomas gathered what was left of his available forces, established a defensive line, and allowed the Union forces in Chickamauga to safely evacuate back to Chattanooga. It was such a heroic act that he was given the nickname, "The Rock of Chickamauga." In the face of grave danger, he was *so* committed, he was so focused on gathering gear and available forces, and to stopping the Confederacy from advancing, that what he did became a legendary example of commitment in action.

It was that kind of commitment that instilled trust up and down the entire chain of command in the Union Army—which, of course, is the Army that eventually won the War.

And as we discuss at length on my Leadership Tours to Chickamauga, the lack of trust on the Confederate side cost lives. Big time. Braxton Bragg himself, who was a Four-Star General in charge of the Confederate Army of Tennessee, had a reputation for retreating. Again and again. He was considered by many to be the worst-performing General in the South, and that wasn't just because of his big faults in battle. It was his everyday actions that made people mistrust him.

Just before the battle at Chickamauga took place, Bragg made it known that he needed reinforcements. At that point, he called upon

General James Longstreet—who you may remember from the Battle at Gettysburg. Longstreet was critical of General Lee after that massive loss in Pennsylvania, and so Lee re-assigned Longstreet to go work for Bragg, which Longstreet knew was a slight. Anyway, when Bragg called on Longstreet and his men, they were 775 miles away. So Longstreet hopped on a train and went ahead to go have some face time with Gen. Bragg, as his entire 1st Corps loaded up and got ready to move by rail to Georgia as well.

When he arrived, Bragg failed to send anyone to meet him at the train station. As Longstreet wandered around trying to figure out where Bragg's headquarters was, he was nearly captured by Union Soldiers. After that, there was no love lost between those men. What little trust might have existed between the two, based on position and loyalties to the Confederacy alone, went out the window. In fact, Longstreet was famously quoted as saying, "Nothing but the hand of God can save us as long as we have our current Commander."

And yet, being the dedicated General Officer that he was, Longstreet didn't let the bad faith get in the way of protecting his men and serving the Confederate cause as best he could. Instead, while Bragg sat in his office and made demands from behind a desk, Longstreet was the one who ignored Bragg's orders and—in this case—did the right thing. It was Longstreet's men who ultimately pushed the Union forces back into Chattanooga, even though Bragg took credit for what happened that day.

Longstreet saved the day *despite* his lack of trust of Bragg. Why? Perhaps because he had been well-developed as a young soldier at the hands of General Lee. And when your people are developed and nurtured, they respond positively when the chips are down.

That, of course, rarely happens in the corporate world. In the corporate world, a guy like Longstreet might have let Bragg fall flat on his face, and then taken his position, or gone to work at some other company. Or maybe not. Maybe Longstreet would have remained the loyal soldier no matter what the circumstances. But there was only one Confederacy at the time, and in some industries, you'll find that the best workers will often work hard *despite* a lack of trust with those at the top. It's a matter of their own integrity, which is why we want guys like Longstreet in our midst.

Ultimately, though, while a company that suffers from a lack of trust may survive a few battles, they have little chance of surviving the war.

Companies that are filled with trustworthy individuals are the ones who will win in the end.

When it comes to building trust in the modern corporate world, I liken Gen. George Thomas's actions to some of the actions that were taken by first responders and front-line workers at the outbreak of the pandemic. The doctors and nurses, the grocery workers, the delivery people and others who refused to give up and go home, despite the impending fear and danger that was spreading all over the globe. They helped instill trust, while many of our political leaders were caught floundering around and not knowing what to do. Kind of like General William Rosecrans, who was actually the man in charge of Union Forces at Chickamauga. He served *above* General Thomas. But when the Confederate forces had them cornered, Rosecrans fled the battlefield. It was Thomas, the well-developed subordinate, who stayed and saved so many Union soldiers from losing their lives.

Corporate America rarely deals with the same intense matters of life and death, or the safety of our country, or our Constitution that's at stake in times of trouble and war. And yet, as we saw during the pandemic, the power of shared commitment can *absolutely* help to build that same sort of unwavering trust that causes High-Performing Organizations to survive and thrive.

In general, if you're hiring good people—as in people who care about other people—they're going to be folks who are committed to the greater good from the start. They're people who don't just worry about what's best for them—they also worry about what's good for all of us.

And to really get things going in the right direction, everyone in your organization needs to trust that everyone else is just as committed as they are. Which means that all those things that I talked about in Part I have to be well-established. The same way the Army is a values-based organization, your company needs to establish its values. The same way the Army has a mission, your company needs to have a mission. And then, through routine counseling, etc., we need to make sure that everybody on the team is committed to the same mission and values.

I know that sounds like a big task, especially in a large organization. But the Army's got somewhere around a million people in it at any given time, and if the Army can sustain that sort of commitment, I have no doubt that your organization, of *any* size, can do it just as well.

Sharing your vision, values, and operating principles with every new hire is a great start. And if they're straight out of school, like so many of our Army recruits, they'll most likely be willing to take it all in, like a sponge. But for the long-term employees who are hearing about these things for the first time, or those hired from other organizations who might be coming in the door a bit jaded from past experience, they might start out thinking, "Yeah, we've heard this stuff before about vision and values, but it doesn't really happen. Leaders simply post the vision and values on the office walls, and then they do something else."

Those folks will take some convincing.

Trust is built by letting everyone see that the senior executives are committed to living the Vision, Values, and Operating Principles every day. There can never be an indication, at any time, that one of the executives is seen intentionally violating the vision and values, or isn't living by the operating principles. And then? The whole team has to be held to the same standard.

This is where leaders can have a big impact—by not allowing someone who isn't committed to the VVOP to stay and by telling them to go find happiness elsewhere.

Because when *everybody* is committed, trust is gained.

Now, I'm not saying that every corporation needs to live by the West Point Honor Code ("A cadet will not lie, cheat or steal, or tolerate those that do"), but I don't think it's a bad code for every decent human being to live up to. And I have done everything in my power to live up to it. In the last twelve years in Corporate America, whenever I came across a person who lied or cheated or stole, I would not tolerate it. I would confront them and ask them to change their ways, and if they *didn't* change their ways, then I left the organization. I don't want to be around people like that, and if I chose to stick around or do anything less than leave, my personal integrity would be out the window. As it says in 1 Corinthians 15:33: *Do not be misled: "Bad company ruins good morals."*

Of course, we're not all in a position to just walk away. We've got families to feed and mortgages to pay. Which is why, as leaders, we need to be doing 360s, managing by walking around, and listening to our people—so we can foster environments where employees aren't afraid to stand up and call out bad behavior. When any of us deals with people, we can pretty much codify their character, right? We can tell: Do they have character? Do they lie? Do they cheat? Do they steal? Do they have affairs? Do they steal from this organization? Do they misuse the corporate credit cards? So it's pretty easy to categorize folks based on their character, and then folks have just gotta decide if they want to trust the individual. And the company itself should be committed to one thing: Anyone who can't be trusted should be gone.

By the way, the response I get to this from leaders and workers at all levels is usually, "Wow! What a relief that would be! That one commitment would solve so many problems!" So ask yourself: "Why aren't more companies willing to commit to that?" Or, more specifically, "Why isn't *my* company willing to commit to root out bad characters?"

The answers you find just might lead you to make some changes.

As I've said, trust is built through the shared understanding that everybody in the organization is committed to embracing the Vision, Values, and Operating Principles. And if that's not happening, then it just goes back to the issue of tolerating poor performance and mediocre behavior. If you don't believe somebody is competent to do the assigned tasks, then why are they still on your team? All they're doing is bringing down everybody around them, and, as a result of that, there's a lack of trust.

When everyone shares the commitment to the vision and mission of the company, then it's much, much easier for everyone to share a commitment to the *success* of the company. And that's what makes a truly High-Performing Organization stand a cut above the rest. In HPOs, everybody's committed to saying, "How far can we take this?" Everybody's interested in making sure that goals are achieved, and then re-looked at and re-highlighted, so that we're always doing better. They move beyond the feeling that something is "good enough" and keep asking themselves and each other, "What else can we do? If we've accomplished this goal, then what would happen if we provide you with additional resources—people, time, and money—and raise the bar even higher?"

Doing more and aiming higher in HPOs is never about abusing people. It's never about doing more with less or forgetting that "vision without resources is hallucination."

It's about commitment. Shared purpose. Shared desires to keep getting better.

And, oh, by the way, you can be committed to more than one thing. You can be committed to mission accomplishment with your company, but at the same time be committed to your family, your church, your community, whatever it might be. This is not a one-trick pony. High achievers should be committed in all aspects of life. "I want to be the best employee, the best partner, the best manager, the best leader that I can be. At the same time, I want to be the best father, the best mother, the best spouse I can be," and on and on and on.

I've observed three major categories of commitment in my work and private life, and when we think about the types of committed individuals we want working in our organizations, I think all three of these areas are worth noting.

Number one is work ethic, which is simply a matter of taking care of every task you have to the best of your ability. That applies to whatever job you have, as I've mentioned before: Whether you're a dishwasher or a CEO, you should do that job to the best of your ability. But it also applies at home. I think back now to the work ethic instilled by my parents, and it wasn't just about going out and earning a paycheck or getting good grades. My mom was the hardest-working person I know, and when times were lean, and she wanted to be the best mom she could, she would go ahead and put dinner on the table for me and my brother, and rather than sit down with us, she'd say, "Oh, I'm really not hungry." I realize now, of course, that her refusal to eat had nothing to do with a lack of hunger. She was sacrificing her own comfort for the sake of feeding her children. She was being the best mother she could possibly be and exceeding the basic job requirements at every turn. That's just the way she was. That's the way she was wired. And while I don't advocate neglecting your own needs as a routine course of action, anyone who is that committed to whatever job they have is certainly someone we can look up to, and be grateful for, in every way. That's someone who is as committed as a person can be.

The second thing that we've got to make sure we think about when it comes to commitment is never to mistake activity for achievement. Back when I worked at the Pentagon, I made up a story to illustrate this point: "I was walking on an installation one day, and there was a gentleman digging a hole. And he was working hard. I mean, he was digging a *hole*. It was hot outside, he was sweating. And I said, 'What are you doing, young man?' And he said, 'I'm digging this hole,' so I said, 'Good job, keep it up.' The next day, I came across the same guy in the same area, and once again, he's working hard. He's sweating. He's doing the best he can. And I asked him, 'What are you doing today, young man?' and he replied, 'I'm filling in this hole.' So the hole that he dug on one day was getting filled back in on the next day. For no reason. Which meant that there was a lot of activity, but there was absolutely zero achievement."

Frankly, I see that in Corporate America far too often. I see a lot of people just doing stuff that has no real focus on the end state. And that affects this idea of being committed. To be truly committed, in a way that inspires trust, means we're committed to actually getting things done—things that serve the collective mission, that help us all move one step closer to the next goal and the next, and not pull us off in some other direction, or slow us down for no reason. That's not commitment. It's distraction.

The last thing that can be a real killer of the sort of trust that's built by commitment comes in the area of overcoming inertia. In any endeavor, there are going to be impediments. If you've got an organization that's built on a foundation of trust, if you've got hard-working people, if you've got a shared purpose, if you've got values, vision, and set operating principles, there are *still* going to be impediments. There are gonna be things that get in your way. So organizations have to be committed to overcoming inertia. Being committed to the mission means never allowing things to get slowed up based on bureaucracy or on whatever the circumstance may be. Commitment is about perseverance. There have been so many times in the last twelve years where I've seen Corporate America slowed down by obstacles and unforeseen circumstances, when they could have just pushed through and charged on. They could have worked together to overcome the inertia, identify impediments, and then encourage people to overcome them. They could have committed to accomplishing what was assigned, even though things were going in a different way.

And so much of the trust that comes from commitment goes back to the idea of not tolerating mediocre performers. Because in times of trouble, if we allow mediocre performers to remain on the team, then, generally, morale for the entire company is going to be affected. When the chips are down, people are going to become more like those mediocre performers and won't be willing to put in the extra work that might be required to overcome the inertia—because why should they work hard, be committed, and overcome inertia if the person in the adjacent cubicle is not willing to do the same and is making the same amount of money?

Commitment matters, because it builds trust.

And trust matters, perhaps more than anything else, for all the reasons I've shared.

So whatever it takes to build it, it's worth it. It is always money well spent. It is always time well spent. Once you've built a foundation of trust under your High-Performing Organization, then you're free to get to the good stuff. Let's call them *The Big Three of Productivity*: The ability to delegate, the ability to foster teamwork and collaboration, and the ability to adapt and innovate.

CHAPTER 14

YOU'RE NOW FREE
TO DELEGATE

Even when I was a young Company Commander in the late 1970s and was teaching a course to aspiring Company Commanders, I made it a point to highlight the fact that the key to success is to surround yourself by competent subordinates and delegate.

You, the senior leader, don't need to be consumed by doing every task yourself. You need to be aware of your own plate management and get anything less than *urgent and necessary* off your plate. You need to allow somebody else to do it—acknowledging that maybe, just maybe, it's not gonna be done as well as you'd have done it personally, but it *does not matter.* That's a lot of letting go for a Type-A person to do, I realize, but it's crucial.

We can never let the perfect be the enemy of the good enough, or we'll never get the important jobs finished.

As a senior executive, you've got to free yourself up to be doing those things that only a senior leader can do. Things like thinking, researching, attending conferences, building teams, developing leaders—those kinds of things. And the only way you can do that is if you have an environment where you're feeling free to delegate. So I say, in the corporate world, just as it was in the Army: Surround yourself with competent people, and delegate.

The critical word there, of course, is *competent*. If you've decided that you're not going to expend resources (people, time, and money) to develop your leaders, let alone your other team members, then you're not going to build the competency that you need in your organization that allows you to confidently delegate. And that is why it is crucial to do all the things we've been talking about in this book so far: So you can develop competence and excellence throughout your organization.

One of the biggest payoffs for doing routine counseling and performance appraisals, and for all of the development you encourage your people to pursue—be it institutional (classes, conferences), organizational (on-the-job training), or self-development (reading, studying, etc.)—is ensuring you can delegate freely when it's necessary.

Delegating helps you not waste time on tasks that aren't worthy of your personal attention, so you can spend more time focusing on accomplishing the things that make you and your organization high-performing. For example: Maybe you could dedicate some time and planning to restructuring the way your company holds meetings.

I don't think I've ever spoken to any individual in Corporate America who doesn't feel that their organization holds too many meetings that last too long. If we free our leaders to do the work it takes to trust their own people, and vice versa, perhaps they would make time to think, plan, and step back from the map, to make some improvements to the process. For instance, they could insist that all meetings have a structured agenda. Or they could decide to follow the decision I made in the Army to allow only one person from each team to attend my meetings.

The way I saw it was, if you've got a team of ten, and you send two or three of your people to attend the same meeting, you've just wasted time—my time and your team's time. Instead, just take one person you know is competent, tell that one person they're going to represent your team, tell that one person they've got to take copious notes, and have that one person come back and back-brief the rest of the team on how the meeting went. What's great is that one person can usually condense an hour-long meeting to five minutes, because there was only five minutes of the meeting that was absolutely essential and critical to the existing team.

In case you didn't notice, choosing to send one competent person to attend a meeting is a form of delegating, too. It makes the whole process more efficient, for both the senior leader and for your team. And in any HPO, efficiency matters.

I recognize that there are some meetings that you have to attend yourself. There are certain times when delegating just won't cut it. And that's why it's important to use the Eisenhower Box (and your own common sense) to sort out when it's appropriate to delegate and when it isn't. When I ran all the Army installations, I had an office in the Pentagon *and* a headquarters in San Antonio. While I preferred to spend my time in Texas, I figured out immediately that there were certain meetings at the Pentagon that I had to attend. What I found at the senior level in the Pentagon was that, if you're not at the meeting, then you're on the menu. Most of those Pentagon meetings were about resource allocation, and if the senior leader for any division wasn't present, a lot of their resources would just get taken by other divisions. Every single one of those meetings was about, "How can we do what we have to do with limited resources?" And if I wasn't there in force to represent my organization, I knew I was going to lose resources.

So there were certain meetings that I attended personally. But in Corporate America, the majority of meetings—I would say 95 percent of them—can be attended by a representative that you hand select and tell what they ought to be looking for in the meeting. And here's where the trust comes in: You need to trust that delegate to contribute to the meeting on your behalf—to speak up, confidently, to share input on your behalf. You can't keep second-guessing them.

One of the most powerful examples I ever experienced of this sort of trust came from one my mentors, when I was fresh out of MIT as the robotics project officer at Fort Knox, Kentucky. I knew a lot about robotics—more than many other people in the Army at that time, including my mentor, simply because I had been given two full years of opportunity to study the technology at MIT. So that particular mentor trusted me and was humble enough to admit that, when it came to robotics, I knew a lot more than he did. So here's what he did: Whenever there was a meeting where robotics issues were going to be discussed, he would send me in his place.

He didn't coach me or tell me what to say, because he knew I knew better.

Instead, he told me: "Okay, go to those meetings, and tell them what *I* said. And then come back and tell *me* what I said." He allowed me to go to meetings and speak up in his place, as if the words I said had come *from him*—a General Officer.

Just think about that. I was a young Captain, and this guy was a General, and he showed so much confidence in my competence and capability that he said, "Go ahead and speak for me." Because he knew if I went to those meetings and said, "Hi, I'm just a young Captain, but this is what I think," my suggestions were unlikely to be valued by other senior leaders. But if I went into those meetings and said, "the General says this," you can bet those folks were gonna listen. In fact, everybody paid attention. They pulled out pens and started taking notes, writing down what I said because "the General said it."

What I never did was violate that trust. I chose my words carefully. I prepared well for every meeting. And as soon as I said something that "he said," I made it a point to come back and tell the General, either in writing or verbally, whatever it was. To make sure he was aware, so he didn't get caught unawares later by something that I *said* he said.

We got a lot done in terms of robotics development and deployment during my time at Fort Knox, and the way my mentor handled it made all the difference. So really, this whole idea of *delegation* makes all the difference. You cannot be an effective senior leader if you're trying to do it all yourself.

I have so many pointed examples of organizations that failed because the senior leaders failed to delegate. Either they didn't trust people, or didn't think anybody could do it as well as they could, or whatever it might be. But the long and short of it was this: The lack of delegation had a direct, negative effect on their bottom-line results.

> **You cannot be an effective senior leader if you're trying to do it all yourself**

ROBOTS CAN'T BE LEADERS

Continuing with the theme of my robotics experience for a moment: When I was head of UTARI, just after transitioning out of my military career, we did a lot of work aimed at getting robots to collaborate effectively—and we made some strides. And today, when I see the incredible drone displays they're putting up at Disney World and major sporting events, it's obvious that we've come a long way. Those drones are, essentially, robots that collaborate with one another in terms of situational awareness and movement, while adjusting to wind and weather and other factors in real time. It's the extension of what we were hoping to develop early on in the Army, too, in terms of situational awareness on the battlefield. We had to make sure that any automated or robotic systems would work together to keep constant awareness of our soldiers' positions, to help avoid friendly fire incidents, and more.

But getting robots to work together is about nothing more than developing the right algorithms to keep track of and adjust to a flow of changing data. They're not really "collaborating" for a cause, or the betterment of the company, or the shared mission of the Corps. They're just following commands, which means they cannot possibly adjust to variances that fall outside of their algorithmic abilities. They can't notice that one of your workers is feeling spent and maybe needs some time off. They aren't programmed to respond to the fact that your worker is about to give birth. We cannot program robots for every possible human scenario, and even if they're programmed to further program themselves (with the technology we refer to as Artificial Intelligence), it is impossible to program a non-living being with human empathy.

And that is why robots can, maybe someday, be *managers*—but they will never be *leaders*.

In a grocery store, robots could make sure that people are clocking in and out on time. They can make sure the produce that is delivered is put in the proper coolers and that other items are put on the proper shelves. They can do plenty of finite tasks. But can robots be mentors? Can they evaluate performance based on more than metrics and numbers? Can they develop their people toward higher goals, backed by vision and values? Can they see an employee's unique potential and worth, even if they aren't placed in the right position at this moment?

The answer to all of those question is "No," because robots don't exhibit empathy.

We cannot expect robots to lead. And we cannot expect our people to perform like robots if we ever want them to excel as leaders, either.

We have to be able to delegate to them, and leave them to their own human devices to do the jobs we give them. To learn on the job. To make mistakes, hopefully early on, so they can learn to be better next time. And we have to give them the bandwidth to flourish, with their own ideas, that we trust them to take on and promote as we all aim to keep getting better.

LEARNING FROM HISTORY

If you want to learn about delegation in action during some of the most crucial fights in our nation's history, I encourage you to come along on one of my Leadership Tours. Whether it's on a battlefield, or on the streets of Selma, Alabama, where America's Civil Rights leaders initiated plans to change the laws and attitudes all across this land, there are all sorts of stories that emerge from those trips about the importance of delegation.

Stonewall Jackson might be somebody you've heard of, whether you've studied the Civil War or not, and the relationship between Jackson and General Lee is a perfect example of the power of delegation. Throughout the early days of the War, Jackson served as one of the strongest leaders in the entire Confederate Army—culminating with his leadership at the battle of Chancellorsville. The reason Jackson and his Corps did magnificently at Chancellorsville is because he already had in mind what General Lee was trying to accomplish. So he went out and did it. He didn't spend a lot of time asking for specific guidance. He didn't spend a lot of time waiting on couriers to come from Lee to give him directions on what to do next. He just went out and did it because he was the utmost competent subordinate Lee had, whom Lee trusted to do what needed to get done.

Delegating to Stonewall Jackson was such an important part of General Lee's winning strategy that, when Jackson was killed after

Chancellorsville (by his own soldiers, unfortunately, in a fratricide), Lee said publicly, "I've lost my right arm."

His words were fateful, because when he got to Gettysburg without Stonewall Jackson, the Corps Commanders he had to delegate to were not as competent and trustworthy. And that hurt him *and* the Confederacy. Big time.

Which gets me back to why it's so important to continually develop your leaders and your entire workforce—so that more and more of them will be competent and trained well enough to step up to the task when needed.

One place where delegation played a crucial, important, nation-changing role in American history was during the Civil Rights Movement. We talk about this during our Leadership Tours to Selma, and I want to talk about it here, too—because it offers us a chance to look through a very different sort of historical lens.

At the end of the Civil War, we passed a series of Constitutional amendments that gave Black people (including the freed slaves, of course) citizenship, and also gave them the right to vote. It was powerful on paper. But 100 years later, Blacks still couldn't vote in the South. None of the things that were promised in the Constitution and through subsequent cases like *Brown v. Board of Education* were actually carried out, because the white folks in charge kept rigging the system, doing everything they could to make sure the Blacks stayed poor, segregated, and unrepresented in government.

Slowly but surely, over the course of the century, the underserved and unrepresented Black population had started to organize. They formed the NAACP in New York City in 1909, partially in response to race riots that occurred in Illinois. Things started to change, and as we got to the 1950s, tensions over these issues had mostly settled down in the North. The laws were (mostly) being followed. And most Northerners were oblivious to the systemic racism that was continuing to occur in the South, which included blatant acts of segregation, from lunch counters and water fountains to the busses—where Black people were always forced to give up their seats to White people and move to the back of the bus.

In December of 1955, a woman named Rosa Parks stepped onto a bus in Montgomery, Alabama, and refused to move to the back—and her actions made national news. This wasn't a coincidence. She wasn't there by happenstance. Ms. Parks was deeply involved with the NAACP, and her actions (along with the media presence) were meant to be the start of a movement.

It was just after that moment when a young, charismatic pastor in Montgomery was chosen to lead the charge, and to persuade the Blacks of Montgomery to boycott the bus system. That pastor's name was Martin Luther King, Jr., and he was only 26 years old. But from his pulpit at the Dexter Avenue Baptist Church, he convinced the population to boycott the busses for an entire year. That's a year of hardship, as thousands of men and women had to walk or carpool to get to work. But the boycott had an economic and societal impact that was heard around the world: It worked. The busses changed their policy to allow blacks to sit wherever they wanted. And in 1956, after seeing the result of his organizational efforts, King set his sights on bigger issues: ending segregation and making sure that Blacks had the ability to vote in the South—as they had already been promised, nearly a hundred years earlier.

It was more than any one man could do, and the Reverend King knew it. So MLK turned to the power of delegation to get the job done. He gathered people around him that he knew he could trust. Some, he had grown up with. Some, he knew from the church. Others stepped forward, so dedicated to the cause that he could not ignore their passion—including "The Boy from Troy," John Lewis, who came to the cause from Troy, Alabama, and would go on to become a long-term U.S. Congressman after standing on the front lines of the fight.

And it *was* a fight. It was a nonviolent "creative war," as King called it during one particularly moving speech in 1964, when he accepted the Nobel Peace Prize (at the age of 35) on behalf of the Civil Rights Movement.

The root of the voting problem seemed simple enough: the registrars in the South controlled who could actually register to vote, and they just wouldn't let Black people register. Change the rules the registrars followed, and Blacks could get registered and go to the polls. But it wasn't simple at all. In order to get around the Constitution, the registrars and their political leaders had come up with ways to restrict registration, in ways that didn't seem to be based on race at all. They added seemingly harmless requirements to the registration process, such as a "literacy test." But in reality, the literacy test that was given to whites was completely different from the one that was given to Blacks. This is shown in a great scene starring Oprah Winfrey in the film *Selma*, which is definitely worth a watch. In it, we see that a Black woman's literacy test involved impossible-to-answer questions, such as "How many jellybeans are in this jar?" or "How many bubbles are in this bar of soap?" Anyone who couldn't answer those impossible questions was deemed "illiterate" and not allowed to vote. So what really needed to happen was a national awakening. King knew that he had to show people in the North, in Washington, and around the world, what was really going on, so they could pressure the President to pass a Voting Rights Act that would make the manipulation of the registration process against the law.

While MLK was quickly recognized as a powerful orator, he could not be everywhere at once—and that is why he delegated. Not only to his immediate, competent subordinates directly, but by sending them out across the country, to build consensus, collaboration, and a true movement with the help of the NAACP, the SNCC (the Student Non-Violent Coordinating Committee), the SCLC (the Southern Christian Leadership Conference), and the Dallas County Voting League. His delegated leaders helped to pull all of these organizations into a powerful coalition.

When he needed to be somewhere himself, he was there: Talking to Presidents John F. Kennedy and Lyndon Johnson one on one at the White House, accepting the Nobel Peace Prize, making speeches that were covered by the national media on the nightly news, on radio broadcasts as well as the quickly growing, powerful medium of television. But everything else was delegated and built over the course of a nearly ten-year campaign, right up to and including a massive, televised march at the Edmund Pettus Bridge, in Selma, Alabama, in March of 1965.

I vividly remember sitting in my hometown in Hamilton, Ohio, watching the events of that march unfold on a little black-and-white TV—and it was horrendous.

I do not fully understand why Martin Luther King, Jr. wasn't present to lead that march himself. No one does. Perhaps we'll gain more understanding when the FBI and other government agencies release their classified files to the public in 2027. But John Lewis was the man who led that march—and who was beaten, along with hundreds of other marches, by Sheriff Jim Clark and his men.

It was a moment that moved me, as it moved viewers all across the nation. Sometimes a moment captured by cameras says more than a thousand speeches ever could. MLK knew this. He also knew how predictably volatile and violent Sheriff Clark's response to Black protests had been in recent months. There are those who wonder if the march and its clearly one-sided violence in front of the media was part of a strategy. If so, it worked. It moved mountains. But you wouldn't know it by King's actions in the days that followed, as he flew to Selma, apologized to his followers, and quickly organized a follow-up march two days later—which he led to the bridge himself.

Unfortunately, no permit had been issued for the second march. A judge had to issue such a permit, and there was no way it could be reviewed and issued in less than three weeks. King was told in no uncertain terms that he and his fellow protestors had no legal right to stop traffic and cross that bridge. If they did, they would be arrested, and King knew that would not be good. He couldn't show the world that he was leading a bunch of people who broke the law. The goal was to get laws followed! So he did something no one expected. He led the marchers to the bridge, but once he got there, he stopped. He dropped to his knees and prayed.

Seeing what he was doing, everyone else dropped to their knees and prayed, too.

Then? He got up, turned around, and led the whole group back to where they started.

It was a powerful visual image that became known as "Turnaround Tuesday." It sent a strong message to the political leaders and to those who believed in the rule of law up North. But King made one big mistake: He neglected to tell his trusted subordinates about his plan. He didn't explain what he was doing and how it would be perceived. As a result, many of his followers thought the turnaround made them look weak—as if they were giving up and doing so after enduring such physical pain and sacrifice. Anger and division grew among some of his most-trusted subordinates. The Student Nonviolent Coordinating Committee, which was a big deal, said, "We're out of here." They left Selma altogether and took their people to Montgomery, where they organized a separate protest, signaling a weakness in the coalition.

You cannot be an effective delegator unless you have transparency with your people. You can't delegate to competent people unless you tell them what's going on. They have got to know the rest of the story. And if they don't, as a result of that, your actions are going to be much less effective.

Three weeks later, when the proper permit was issued, MLK finally led a group of 25,000 protestors over that bridge himself, all the way to the steps of the Capitol in Montgomery, where they urged Governor George Wallace to force the state's registrars to allow Black citizens to vote. And five months later, after all of the work he had done, all the delegating he had done, all the sacrifices that his fellow African Americans had made over the course of the prior decade in order to improve their fate and gain the rights they had been granted a hundred years earlier, MLK got his message through.

In August of 1965, President Lyndon Johnson passed the Voting Rights Act.

There would be many more battles to come, even then, to get that Act followed. Those in power would continue to find new ways—against the Constitution and against the rule of law—to keep the Black population from voting, in ways that continue to this day. But when it came to accomplishing his goal, his Vision, while sticking to a set of Values and Operating Principles (which included non-violence as a means of protest), MLK Jr. won the Civil Rights Movement's "creative war." And he did so by being an engaged leader, being widely known, and delegating effectively on a massive scale.

Oh, and don't forget. He did all of this according to a set of Values and Operating Principles he learned from his faith, which were carried forth into his leadership:

1 Corinthians 10:24: *No one should seek their own good, but the good of others.*

HOW DELEGATING GETS THE JOB DONE

Delegating can be much more than a one-on-one task. From a corporate perspective, one of the best companies I work with, which is constantly listed as one of the Best Corporations in America, makes delegating a part of its core business strategy. And they do this by focusing on centralized planning but decentralized execution.

This company has got so much trust in its store managers and in the fact that their store managers are committed to being successful, that they routinely give broad general guidance to the store leaders and then allow those leaders to apply that guidance however they choose to meet the needs of their local shoppers.

We all know of retail chains that look exactly the same, no matter where you are. You walk into one of their stores in Alabama, or New Hampshire, or California, and you know what you're going to get. The merchandise is displayed in the same areas. The checkouts are the same. The employees all dress the same. Those types of stores tend to operate on a centralized plan, without any sort of decentralized execution. They don't want people in different areas messing with their formula for "success."

Well, this company I work with does the opposite. Sure, the branding remains the same. The font and colors of the signs look alike. The company culture stays the same. All the big-ticket VVOP items are checked from location to location, to a T. But this company recognizes that different populations in different areas have different needs—and they trust their store managers to assess those needs. Not only through data, as a robot might, but as leaders who are human, who are on the sales floor, talking to customers, one on one, and getting feedback in real time about what they want, what they'd like to see, and especially what might be missing. By allowing their store managers to be the ones who determine how to meet the needs of the local residents who shop at their stores, it makes each individual store reflect the community that it's in. That's a big part of what makes them different from the big-box national chains *and* what keeps them thriving as the #1 store of its kind, wherever they grow. Number one! Against the biggest competitors imaginable. All the time.

Do things go perfectly all the time? No! Of course not. But this company develops its regional leaders well enough to be able to give them the freedom to fail now and then, to learn from their mistakes, and to do better next time—all in the interest of innovating and adapting to market changes in order to serve their local customers' demands.

They stay ahead of their competitors because they're a High-Performing Organization in many of the ways I've discussed in this book. But it's hard to argue that their commitment to delegating appropriately isn't one of their biggest strengths.

I'll say it again: The key to success, whether in the military or in corporations, is to surround yourself with competent people and delegate. Which means you've got to spend a lot of time making sure those people around you *are* competent; you've got to teach, coach, and mentor them; you've got to send them to school; you've got to give them on-the-job training and require them to develop *themselves*.

This particular company does all of that, and does it well.

And the results speak for themselves.

CHAPTER 15

SILO BUSTING: BUILDING STRENGTH THROUGH COLLABORATION AND TEAMWORK

As we work together in High-Performing Organizations to achieve our corporate goals, we have to step up, as leaders, and continually highlight the importance of teamwork and collaboration. If we're going to keep growing, and keep improving, and keep striving for higher and higher achievements, we need everybody to remain committed to the corporate goals and objectives. And the only way to make that happen, the only way to keep the organization from falling back into unhealthy patterns and behaviors that slow organizations down, is to demonstrate and insist upon teamwork and collaboration across all areas of the company.

Unfortunately, even in some otherwise very strong organizations, I see too many stovepipes in Corporate America. People get so committed to their particular branch of the company, or their particular segment of the company—be it R&D, marketing, sales, HR, whatever—that they wind up competing against each other for available resources, to the peril of the collective corporate goals.

We all know resources are limited. Hopefully they're not *too* limited, or the corporate goals are just hallucinations anyway. But assuming the corporation is providing the resources to get the job done, no matter how rich those resources are, they're going to be limited in some way, whether in terms of people, time, or money. And if you're an organization that doesn't advocate teamwork, everybody's going to be competing for those limited available resources. They're going to want more time, they're going to want more people, they're going to want more money. And that can cause the stovepipes to grow, with vast distances and walls between them, to the point where leaders of one division or section or another don't want to talk to the others, or worse: they want to outdo the others for the sole purpose of taking care of their own.

Those sorts of competitive attitudes and experiences do not serve an organization well.

In the Army, we realized this many years ago. Stovepipes had developed all over the place. So we started pushing the Enterprise approach, in which we stopped asking ourselves, "What's best for me, or my division, or my Corps?" or whatever we were in charge of, and instead started asking, "What's best for the Army as a whole?" We switched our overall mindset, and started collaborating on budget matters and everything else, in order to better serve our shared goals as an organization.

Achievement of a shared goal requires collaboration. And guess what? Collaboration includes a little something called *compromise*.

"Compromise" is not a bad word. I know it seems that way, especially if you've been watching what's happened in Washington for the past decade or two, where everybody seems to think that the only way to "win" is to pick a side and then dig in their heels. The unwillingness to compromise has brought nearly everything in Washington to a standstill, and that's not good.

We live in divisive times.

So what?

Let's do what we can to set a better example—to lead without letting divisiveness get in the way of progress in our organizations.

Compromise is necessary to reach big goals. Always. And don't tell me that you can't negotiate and make progress using compromise within your company, even with people who've got their heels dug in.

Progress and compromise are *always* on the table.

Back in Iraq, when my superior ordered me to "Go and negotiate with the insurgents," he asked me to read a book entitled *Getting to Yes* by Roger Fisher and William Ury before I did. *Getting to Yes* is all about the art of compromise. And compromise was definitely on my mind as I walked, unarmed, into a room full of armed insurgents every three months—and negotiated for exactly what we wanted.

You can read more about that intense experience in both of my previous books, but I'll just add this: When you're negotiating with a bunch of guys with guns who would love to see you dead, you don't walk in and say, "Here's what's gonna happen: Do it my way or else!"

That wasn't gonna work.

Let me tell you—that doesn't work in most civilian workplaces, either.

In Corporate America, I think it's clear that internal fighting is a just a killer of productivity and profits. It's the opposite of what collaboration can accomplish.

I mentioned earlier there was a company I worked with in which some of the bosses liked to walk into the hallway and openly berate employees in front of their colleagues. Now, what in the world does a company have to gain from that kind of behavior? Nothing.

I've seen companies pit divisions against each other in competition as well, and while competition can be healthy, more often than not, internal competitiveness drives behaviors that do not focus on the higher purpose of what corporate leadership intends. Rarely does it ever serve a corporate mission to launch an internal war, because guess what? At the end of the war to "win," the other team is left feeling like it "lost." And that means you've *all* lost, 'cause it's bad for morale.

Instead, encouraging all sides to win for the bigger purpose of bringing your company to the next level through collaborative endeavors will ultimately be much more effective.

True long-term thinkers, as in the smartest and more forward-thinking business leaders, the ones whose companies are outlasting and outliving companies stuck in old ways of thinking and acting, are already doing this. They're doing whatever they can to break down the silo walls and encourage cross-team collaboration in the best way possible. Nobody's perfect, and no company is perfect all the time. But they're *trying*. They're looking forward. They're sensing the changes in the business landscape and anticipating the changes that are happening in our society at the same time.

I am convinced that it is these leaders, the ones who do everything they can to eliminate internal roadblocks and competing interests, and instead seek out strong collaboration from their teams, who will become the truly great leaders in the decades ahead.

Some of them are even taking it a step further—to encourage collaboration outside of the organization, as a means not only to make their companies "widely seen," but with a higher goal of taking care of people and moving us all forward together. Even direct competitors can turn into collaborative allies when our missions are focused on a higher purpose.

A perfect example of this happened during the pandemic, when a bunch of Big Pharma companies laid down their swords and collaborated—actually worked together—to share patents and research—and even company secrets—in the interest of quickly developing a COVID vaccine. And guess what? They did it. They created a new vaccine in record time and have since all found ways to profit from those endeavors in a huge way. Nobody lost. Everybody won, including the American people and people all around the world.

Another case in point: In February of 2019, Elon Musk announced that he had released all of Tesla's electric car patents to the public as part of an effort to fight climate change.

You don't have to be a fan of Musk to be a fan of what that meant: In a blog post (followed by a press release on the Tesla website), the billionaire promised that the company "will not initiate patent lawsuits against anyone who, in good faith, wants to use our technology."

"Tesla Motors was created to accelerate the advent of sustainable transport," Musk said. "If we clear a path to the creation of compelling electric vehicles, but then lay intellectual property landmines behind us to inhibit others, we are acting in a manner contrary to that goal."

Musk said he was now skeptical of patents themselves, claiming they too often served "to stifle progress" and helped enrich giant corporations and lawyers rather than inventors. "We believe that Tesla, other companies making electric cars, and the world would all benefit from a common, rapidly evolving technology platform."

Think what you will of Musk and some of the other things he's done as a business leader. After years of holding tight to old-school competitive business practices, Musk appeared to have changed his tune. He exhibited in very clear terms that a more collaborative approach to using technological breakthroughs would be better for society, better for America, and better for our planet. (BTW: Tesla's sales went up after he did that—for the next four years straight.)

There are other examples of this in American history, too: The inventor of the computer language "HTML," the driving force that allowed the entire Internet to work and grow, released this potentially billion-dollar programming protocol to the public from the start, because he saw the value in everyone using it to create the Internet we know and rely upon today. The inventors of synthetic insulin released the formula free to the world, too, because they knew it could literally save the lives of every person on the planet with diabetes.

At the end of 2019, whether they were inspired by Musk's move or some other motivator, the hyper-competitive tech companies Amazon, Apple, and Google all announced that they were joining forces to create a common platform for smart home devices to be able to talk to each other, no matter which company makes the particular device you choose to buy. I'll admit, I don't personally want a device in my house that listens to my conversations, but a lot of people seem to really like the idea of turning their lights on with a voice command, playing music through their refrigerators, and leaving voice memos on their toasters. It's a rapidly growing market. And up until now, one manufacturer's "smart lightbulb" wouldn't work in conjunction with another's. Once they all work together on one standard platform, the hope is that even more companies will be able to get into the game of building a better lightbulb, as it were.

That's good for business. That's good for innovation. That's what collaboration and teamwork can do.

It's also what happened in the late 19th- and early-20th centuries when we standardized all sorts of things in this country. The width of railroad track lines, the synchronization of our clocks and time zones, 110-v electricity and three-prong plugs, the standard 33 rpm speed of LP records, the broadcast signals we use for TV and radio . . . if these things weren't shared and agreed to in a collaborative way, we'd have TV signals interfering with our firemen's radios; records that wouldn't have played on your friends' record player; toasters that might explode if you plugged them into a new outlet by mistake; you'd have to carry an electric converter with you if you traveled between states; and possibly transfer trains as you moved from state to state because the size of the tracks might vary everywhere you go.

Because of the spirit and history of collaboration that helped build this country, our corporations have been able to compete—in a healthy way—to create better and better products and services to serve the American people and people all over the world, all while growing tremendous organizations and generating profits that exceed anything our Founding Fathers ever could have imagined.

Fostering more collaborations now can lead us to more and more of the benefits of *healthy* competition—as we put out the best products, the best services, and continue to lead the world in innovation instead of crushing competitors with unfair practices, or holding tight onto great ideas that could benefit all Americans, or maybe even all of mankind.

You can either make history or read history. It is your choice.

Many High-Performing Organizations realize that once we're aligned with our company values and making sure our mission supports our people, and if we're engaged leaders, living up to our responsibilities and leading with integrity, then turning to collaboration and teamwork over any sort of unhealthy internal or external competition will lead us to a place of abundance.

THE POWER OF SHARED PURPOSE

Stomping on the rights of others, using unfair practices, and exerting power to keep a thumb on people who just want to live their lives freely rarely ever works out well for the oppressor.

Stepping back in history for a moment, I want to highlight the extraordinary collaborative efforts that led our country into the Revolutionary War—and would ultimately lead to our gaining America's independence from Great Britain. (This is a topic we cover in depth on our Leadership Tours to Boston.)

The year was 1775, and we as a nation had grown tired of suffering under British tyranny. We were tired of taxation without representation. We were tired of King George treating us as less-thans. So a bunch of revolutionaries got together and started talking about how we could gain our independence from England. Guys like Samuel Adams were part of this revolutionary group, and they kept talking and planning, while spontaneous reactions like the Boston Tea Party kept demonstrating our state of unrest.

In April of 1775, Lieutenant General Thomas Gage, the British governor in Massachusetts, was told, "Hey, there are munitions being stockpiled in Concord, Massachusetts. You've got to take those munitions away from the rebel militia."

Rather than negotiate or work to improve the root causes of the Colonies' unrest, on the night of April 18, General Gage ordered about 700 British soldiers to march to Concord and gather up all of those munitions. What he didn't realize is that the militia was already watching for that. This was the night when two lanterns were hung in Boston's North Church, and Paul Revere and William Dawes hopped on horseback and rode into the suburbs to warn the rebels, "The British are coming!"

Lexington is a town that sits in between Boston and Concord, and by the time the British soldiers reached Lexington, still under cover of darkness at around five in the morning, 70 members of the militia had already gathered on the Lexington Green to demonstrate to the British that their movement represented an untoward activity. The message was clear: "We're not going to accept it." But by no means did those 70 men want to get into a major conflict with 700 British soldiers. Their goal was to stop them from moving forward and, hopefully, to de-escalate the situation. (This also brings up the issue of conflict management, but I'll save that for the next Tour.) The confrontation didn't go well, and Major Pitcairn, who was the leader of the British group, took it upon himself to say, "Here's our chance to kill a bunch of rebels." So they did it. They killed eight and wounded many more, without taking any casualties themselves.

That was a terrible mistake, in both judgment and in action. And it highlights a lesson I always tried to teach my soldiers in the Army: "Don't make hasty decisions when unnecessary. Decide when to decide."

Pitcairn's haste to jump to violence became "the shot heard 'round the world"—the misstep that started the Revolutionary War.

Paul Revere was captured just outside of town, before he could warn his fellow patriots in Concord. But another man named Samuel Prescott picked up his mission and kept going. He reached Concord and warned the town's citizens. He also delegated the message-sending to others, who quickly rode off and spread the word about what had happened at Lexington. They also spread word of what the British were planning to do in Concord, which *now* included not only taking all of the militia's weapons and ammunition, but also burning the town to the ground.

Remember, there were no telephones or telegraphs in this era. And yet, less than three hours later, when the British troops arrived in Concord, they were met by militia from ten different cities—fifteen local militias who had never met each other in the past, who had no central leader or unified command structure in place, but were driven by one shared purpose: freeing themselves of British tyranny. And that morning, they very quickly formed a powerful coalition under a shared feeling of, "We're not going to tolerate them coming to our towns, taking our stuff, and burning down our houses!"

When the British got to the North Bridge at Concord, they were met by 450 militia men—and, as the story goes, the British were quickly defeated. Those who survived the bloody fight retreated to Boston, being shot at from either side of the road by *thousands* of militia men who had since gathered in Lexington and all along the route.

The casualties they suffered were only the start, as the collaborative effort of the rebels—driven by the power of their shared purpose—would eventually drive the British to surrender, and for the independent United States to be born.

Shared purpose alone can yield incredible results when collaborations are allowed to thrive.

THE WIN-WIN SCENARIO

Not everything in life should be a battle, of course. There is not always a need for war, or for winners to create losers. In the historical scenario described above, the militias formed only when there was no other way forward. But in business, and in most circumstances in life, there is always another way. And that's important for leaders to consider.

In my first book, *Adapt or Die*, I talked about how leaders should see "Opportunities, not Obstacles."

The basic idea is that there is opportunity in every roadblock. "Problems" are actually just "challenges." "Failures" are really just opportunities for learning and growth.

It's all about a change in mindset that allows leaders to adapt to challenges and changes.

That same sort of thinking is at the heart of what High-Performing Organizations do best: Lead with an "Abundance Mindset."

I can't take credit for that term. Stephen Covey came up with it. He talked about this subject in his 1989 bestseller, *The Seven Habits of Highly Effective People*, and what he said, essentially, is that leading with an Abundance Mindset is a lot like choosing to see opportunities instead of obstacles. It's about seeing abundance rather than scarcity in everything we do. And that changes the way we do business.

Covey wrote:

"Most people are deeply scripted in what I call the Scarcity Mentality. They see life as having only so much, as though there were only one pie

out there. And if someone were to get a big piece of the pie, it would mean less for everybody else. People with a Scarcity Mentality have a very difficult time sharing recognition and credit, power, or profit—even with those who help in the production. They also have a very hard time being genuinely happy for the successes of other people—even, and sometimes especially, members of their own family or close friends and associates. It's almost as if something is being taken from them when someone else receives special recognition . . ."

Sounds a lot like he's talking about the Type-B personality leaders I mentioned earlier in this book, doesn't it? An Abundance Mindset represents the very opposite. It's "a concept in which a person believes there are enough resources and successes to share with others," Covey writes.

Another name for it is a Win-Win Mentality—which gets back to the importance of collaboration and teamwork, especially within our companies. If we're all on the same team, we have to recognize that when one part of our organization rises, we all rise.

Covey writes: "In the long run, if it isn't a win for both of us, we both lose. That's why win-win is the only real alternative in interdependent realities."

Business guru Jim Collins refers to the Abundance Mindset as a shift in attitude, focusing in on the Win-Win Mentality as "the genius of the 'and' versus the tyranny of the 'or.'" And when we think of what we can do, as leaders and as organizations, if we stop seeing everything as "either/or" and "win/lose," some interesting ideas start popping up.

Especially in the minds of forward-thinking leaders who care about their people.

I love the concept. I just don't see enough leaders in Corporate America who seem willing to embrace it.

How about we increase profits *and* raise all of our workers' wages?

How about we increase efficiency to please Wall Street shareholders *and* offer increased profit sharing to the employees who pull off those miracles?

Why can't we make our brand #1 without toppling any of the mom-and-pop competitors in the towns we're moving into? Why can't we set up big-box/mom-and-pop partnerships to better serve customers instead?

These aren't radical new concepts. They're the types of concepts that served this country well through the great economic rise we witnessed in the U.S. in the wake of World War II, all the way into the 1980s. And I get it: Times have changed. So what? If we can't get back to those old ideas, then what are the new ideas that will serve our collective prosperity a little better than what's happening today?

Collaboration and teamwork, together, are two of the largest indicators and measures of success within any High-Performing Organization. And it's through collaboration and teamwork, both within and between these organizations, that our best companies gain the ability to thrive—no matter what big changes are right around the corner.

CHAPTER 16

IT'S TIME TO GO INNOVATE AND ADAPT

As a leader, I've already mentioned how important it is to ask yourself, continuously, "Are we doing the right things?" "Are we doing things right?" and, "What am I missing?" It's that third question which will lead you to being innovative as an organization—where you're always looking for better ways to do business; you're always trying to figure out, "What could we be doing to improve our profitability and our output? What could we be doing to become more effective? What could we be doing to make the most of our High-Performing Organization?"

Once you're there, once you're acting in full-time HPO mode, then the organization itself can, essentially, take on the traits of a strong Strategic Leader.

Remember: Strategic Leaders do four things: They observe and seek trends; they sound strategic when they speak; they ask the hard questions; and they take time to think and embrace conflict.

How does this translate into innovation?

By observing and seeking trends, your organization has a chance to pick up on good ideas that others have implemented and find innovative ways to apply them to your business.

By "sounding strategic," your organization can inspire change and innovation in others, by being widely known and standing out as the thought-leaders in your field, which will inspire even stronger, more forward-thinking applicants to come apply to work at your company.

By not being afraid to ask the hard questions, knowing that your teams have the competency and skills to go find the answers, the door to innovative solutions will open for you, again and again.

And because of your excellent time management—and plate management—everyone in your organization will have time to think, and think fearlessly: "What should we be doing that we're not doing? How can we become more effective, using innovative techniques? And how can we explore these new and conflicting ideas of how to move forward, and still get to the best solution?"

That last part, embracing conflict, seems counterintuitive, given that the entire last chapter was about teamwork and collaboration. But I'm not talking about the sort of conflict that comes from fighting over resources. I'm talking about the power of celebrating diversity—especially diversity of thought. I'm talking about the fact that conflicting ideas can be shared openly in an organization in which everyone is truly moving in the same direction. Conflicting ideas and viewpoints lead to *great* discussions, which ultimately lead to innovative solutions. Especially if you're open to "win-win" solutions, rather than "and-or" solutions.

Remember when I talked about the importance of Strategic Initiative Groups (or SIGs)? In a High-Performing Organization, your whole team can be looked at as one big SIG. High-Performing Organizations are places where ideas can flow in from everyone, top to bottom, and be heard—actually listened to and considered—because you already know that everyone who works for you can be trusted to have the best interests of the organization in mind.

Because you've already tackled the importance of leader and employee development, you know that your people are going to read this and study that; they're going to attend the conferences, call the organizations, go spend time with people who are smarter or more informed than them, so they can gather information to help answer the question, "What are we missing?"

And because you've instilled trust and active leadership throughout, everyone who does the work and comes to the office prepared to share what they've learned can rest assured that their senior leaders are going to listen—because they already know that their leaders are empathetic human beings. They already know that their leaders are good at focusing on the person who's talking, listening closely to what they have to say, and asking engaging questions. They're going to repeat what you tell them, to be sure that they heard it right. All those skills that I talked about in previous books about active listening come into play, on both sides of the equation. And we already know that the leaders are humble. They remember that they're not the smartest person in the room, and they're not afraid to let someone show them up in terms of how smart or knowledgeable they are—because it's all for the greater good of the organization.

Of *course*, an organization that exhibits these strengths is going to innovate. It can't help but happen, almost by default. And when it's not happening, the leadership of any HPO is going to spur it on. They're going to do what I did at the Pentagon with the "Stamp Out Stupid" campaign, and ask their people: "What do you think? Are we doing the right things? Are we doing things right?" And they'll listen when their people tell them, "No, we're wasting time doing this. We're not doing this the way we should."

And when leadership follows up by asking, "What are we missing?" the workforce will be ready and willing to answer. Because guess what? They've been around. They know things. I don't care if it's an 18-year-old kid right out of high school, or a 60-year-old former senior executive who just joined your outfit because of the turbulence in the marketplace: They know things. So HPO leaders *ask them*. They create great forums where they can share their thoughts and ideas.

What do those forums look like? Some of my clients hold a town-hall meeting for the entire organization, twice a year. I've heard of some corporations that refer to this as an "all-hands meeting." Like, "All hands on deck!" But whatever you call it, it should be a gathering of everyone, in which the C Suite executives get up and give a state-of-the-union type of address in front of every partner. Just as the President gives a State of the Union speech every year, in front of Congress and the nation, the leader or leaders at a company should speak to everyone, at the same time, on a regular basis, to let them know how the company is doing: What we're getting right, what we're getting wrong, what we've been through, what's next. There are companies that try to make these meetings fun, with visuals, maybe even bringing in musical artists or guest speakers to fire up the teams. But at all of these forums, there needs to be an opportunity for your teams to speak. To share new ideas. To comment. It can be done the old-fashioned way—standing up in the auditorium and speaking into a microphone. Or it can be done with virtual attendance, placing commentators and those with questions in a virtual line and then letting them through to speak one at a time. Or it can be done anonymously, with pencil and paper and a suggestion box, or whatever the virtual equivalent of that might be. (I, of course, always recommend that these meetings happen in person; that my clients budget for travel expenses, simply because the human, team-building payoff for handshakes and personal contact is so much greater than the effects of trying to communicate via videoconference. And audio-only conferencing is just a "No.")

The question-and-comments portion of the town hall will work, of course, only if the culture is there. Your people have to know that you're willing to listen. That their ideas are gonna be heard. They have to know that their senior leaders are going to take their ideas into consideration, even though it should be clear up front that not everything they recommend is going to get done. It's the listening and genuine consideration that matter. After all, leaders are supposed to be mentors. That's one of the Nine Leadership Principles that I've been sharing for more than ten years now. And being a mentor is a threefold task: you have to be accessible, you have to listen, and you have to truly care.

That's why robots can't lead. Sure, they can be available. Sure they can listen. They can take the information in. But a robot is a machine. Even if backed by AI, a robot cannot care. It doesn't care if a person is tired, fed up, anxious, worried, or sick. They cannot truly care for their people, because they are not one of them.

As a leader, don't do that. Don't be a robot. It just doesn't work.

THE RISK FACTOR

What *does* work? Creating a human-centered organization that works well together—so well that no one is afraid to take the risks required in order to innovate.

There is no question that being innovative involves some level of risk. I think every article ever written about being an innovator tells us that we've got to exhibit some risk-taking ability and be willing to try things that may not work.

It's all about being aspirational: What are you trying to accomplish? What do you see? I mean, this is where the strategic vision comes in.

What do you see the organization being able to do in a year, five years, ten years? If you want to lead a High-Performing Organization, you've got to be aspirational. And it's okay to dream big! Think back to President Kennedy's call back in 1962, when he said, "Let's go to the moon this decade." The man motivated our nation to *do that*. And then it *happened*. It's a perfect example of how a far-reaching vision is critical for setting an environment of innovation.

As hockey great Wayne Gretzky once said, "You miss a hundred percent of the shots you don't take."

The corporations that I've seen do this well always set in motion many more things than they can actually accomplish. They get lots of people working on lots of great options, just to see what's out there that's viable, or that could be pursued. Organizations that kind of constrain themselves from the beginning to "We're only going to look at one new idea or one new way of doing business at a time," are unnecessarily constraining themselves, and often wind up failing to innovate at all.

But you also have to remember to not take on too much all at once. As leaders, we have to remember that if we want to be innovative, we've got to build on past experience. We can't pursue everything, and it's often up to leaders to choose what to explore—or not. It can't always be done democratically, and there's often nothing but your gut between you and the right decision. If you're a forward-thinking leader who cares about your people, there is no focus group that can outperform your intuition and your experience. Trust me: When you've got a gut sensation that something may work, or may not work, that's not indigestion. That's years of experience and education that you have, because you've been down that road before. The only issue is this: You cannot be so wedded to the way it used to be that you can't see the way that it *should* be, now. But if you're going to lead and innovate successfully, there's got to be some level of choosing what you're going to pursue, given your own base of experience.

Once you've got those things in motion, then you've got to choose which ones you actually want to pursue. And the whole thing is an evolutionary process. So some of the big ideas, the new ideas, will fall by the wayside. And some of them will look like they've got some opportunity, so those will scale over time. And you'll accelerate the ones that you see are actually going to make a difference for your company.

So it's critical for a senior leader to be a person who builds on past experiences, and also tries to set an environment of innovation. And then you just have to demonstrate from the very top that you're willing to change. Your people have to know, to truly believe that they're not just wasting their efforts. I get so frustrated with corporate clients who administer surveys to their people but have no intent to change. They're not fooling anybody. Their people know. After doing it once or twice, they're not even going to bother responding to that survey. I've got some clients that, in a voluntary manner, get less than 50 percent of responses from their employees and associates, because the employees and associates know the organization is not going to change. "Why should I waste time filling out this survey when they're not gonna listen to me anyway?" So you've got to be *willing* to change; you've got to *demonstrate* that you're willing to change; and you've got to be looking for those opportunities to be innovative, based on your far-reaching vision of where you want the organization to go.

To do anything less is to fail the organization you've built.

You've come this far. You've done all this work to develop a High-Performing Organization. Please, please don't stop it from performing at a high level.

Again, that means you've got to be willing to take some risks, and you've got to provide an environment where people feel they can take risks, too—an environment where there's freedom to fail. To remain high-performing and innovative, you can't create an environment in which people are hesitant or concerned or overly conservative, thinking,

"If it doesn't work, it's going to be held against me." You have to be willing to expend the resources—time, money, whatever it might be—that need to be expended in order to try new things, otherwise, your people are going to be less willing to even *try* to be innovative.

I keep talking about "creating an environment," but what this whole idea of innovation really comes down to is your corporate culture. And I know people are going to argue about this, but once again, I'm just gonna say it: The best way to strengthen your corporate culture, to drive collaboration and teamwork, and therefore to create a culture that fosters innovation, is to bring your people back into the office as much as you can.

The essence of strong innovation is collaboration, and if people are working from home, and they're not getting together routinely around the coffee pot or around the water cooler or over lunch, they're not going to be able to pick up on each other's thoughts and ideas and capitalize on innovative ideas. Working from home is simply not the best way forward when it comes to building an innovative culture.

There's got to be time set aside for when everybody comes in and just brainstorms. And you have to do so as part of a Strategic Plan, because in the absence of a plan, all you have is chaos, random activity, and day-to-day activities that are unlikely to take you anywhere, and especially not to some lofty goal.

Just to break it down for those who don't have strategic planning as part of their built-in skill set: The first part of the Strategic Plan is a recap of the vision and mission; the "What are we trying to accomplish?" So everybody's on the same page and moving in the same direction. The second piece is basically the senior leader closing his or her eyes and projecting into the future. "What's our *Back to the Future* kind of deal, five to ten years from now?" so they can explain to everybody what this company is gonna look like in five to ten years. And then the real meat on the bone of the Strategic Plan is, "How do we get there? What precisely do we have to do to accomplish what this vision looks like?"

Unfortunately, what too many people miss is that the precision isn't the important part. The plan doesn't have to be perfect—because the plan is just a starting point. The importance of the Strategic Plan is what Eisenhower said back in World War II: "It's not about the plan. It's about the *planning*." (Emphasis added)

Right now, in the world, nobody has any idea what's going to happen next, with the various threats we face from Russia, China, and North Korea, or the effects of accelerated climate change, or the globally connected economy. Simply watching the TV news and thinking you're "well-informed" is a sad hallucination. You've got to stay active and involved in a broader education in your field, whatever it may be, so you can make the best assumptions possible.

But then? As I trained my leaders through Strategic Planning, I told them, "The first thing you've got to do is list your assumptions. And then every time your senior leaders get together, you've got to *challenge* those assumptions. Because sometimes, assumptions prove to be valid, and they become facts. And sometimes assumptions become invalid. And as a result of that, you've got to modify your plan."

In the corporate world, there are plenty of unpredictable futures that can rock your assumptions. The number-one issue in some of the industries I've dealt with are mergers and acquisitions. People fear that they'll walk in on a Monday morning and realize that their company is now owned by somebody else. Why? Because they've been through it before, and it happens all the time. We used to break big companies apart in this country, but for decades now, the trend has been one of constant mergers and acquisitions. So you have to have a branch or two in your Strategic Plan so you can deal with those big moves if they happen. There are also threats that come from changing regulations, or from unrealistic expectations from your own board. My pharma clients have all dealt with "the patent cliff," when one of their drugs reaches the end of its exclusive patent-protected period, and after which other drug companies are free to copy their product. The High-Performing Organizations have noted these upcoming cliffs in their Strategic Plans. Others? Sometimes they forget to make plans for that day until it happens, and how do you think that goes?

Every industry faces different threats and possibilities, and putting Strategic Plans into action will help any corporation get through them.

I can say with great pride that there are a number of clients I've worked with who've been very successful with this—where the senior leader took on Strategic Planning and did everything I just described. And therefore, as they were growing toward some very lofty goals, their organization was able to get through COVID and whatever else was going on.

Going back to my personal experience at UTARI, after retiring from the Army, the same thing was true: after pulling together a diverse SIG, together we developed a Strategic Plan based on facts and assumptions, and by the time I moved on, just four years later, we had already increased our research expenditures to $15 million per year. We were well on our way to accomplishing our goal of $100 million per year. Which is just to say: This stuff works!

I worked with another company that set a major goal of opening facilities in a large metro area, in which they had absolutely no inroads at the time I came aboard. They drew up a plan, and as part of that plan, they started buying real estate in that metro area—just to prepare for the eventual "what ifs?" If they didn't reach their goals and weren't able to build on that land, they knew they could always sell that land if they needed to raise cash. But they didn't focus on this. What they focused on was: What if they reached their goals and had the revenue and cash on hand to start building? At that point, if they *didn't* own the land, the land might be too expensive or might require some kind of lease deal, which would've cut deeply into their bottom line. Owning the land was therefore a strategic thing to do. It was all part of a broad Strategic Plan, and guess what? A number of years later, the plan came to fruition, and when they were ready to start building, the land was sitting there waiting for them, in prime locations that had gone way up in value during the interim years.

That was a perfect example of Strategic Planning in action.

I've seen things go the other way on a number of occasions in the pharma world—where a lack of strategic planning basically left those companies standing around with their hands in their pockets while a great opportunity passed them by. Like when a drug finally completed its long and difficult journey to FDA approval, but the company had not pre-planned a strategy for manufacturing and bringing that drug to market. So the drug just sat there, idle, for way too long, when it could have been turned into a nearly instant stream of new revenue.

A solid Strategic Plan would've avoided that catastrophe, every time.

In the hotel industry, I've watched as companies developed one high-end property and got the whole staff working like clockwork. They're catering to the highest-paying clientele, getting great reviews, selling out night after night—all the while driving straight toward a wall: They'd pushed their lowest price per night so high, they'd cut out an entire marketplace full of people who wished they could stay at that hotel, to experience the upside of that particular brand, but who can't afford to stay for even one night.

The solution? A five-year Strategic Plan to open another hotel, branching out from the name and reputation they've built, but catering to lower-paying clientele, while still living up to the high-standard mission of the original endeavor.

I've watched those in the construction industry develop strategic plans to move from low-end homes to high-end homes, and vice-versa, scaling all the while to take advantage of material costs by buying in bulk, allowing them to increase the number of builds while driving down costs. Strategic Planning was the key to making their goals a reality.

Strategic Planning was what allowed all of these companies to flourish, to adapt, and, most importantly, to innovate in their approaches and products.

Guess what happened to the companies that didn't?

They barely made it through COVID. Some went out of business. And a number of CEOs I knew lost their jobs—and then sat around scratching their heads, wondering what went wrong, even though they ignored so much of the advice that I'm sharing with you in this book.

So are you the corporate executive who's robotically living quarter to quarter, and at the end of every quarter, you're worried about what the results are going to be because your job is at risk? You might want to think about Strategic Planning. You might want to think about looking deeper. You might want to think about building a branch. You might want to think about having some empathy and properly taking care of your people, so then they'll, in turn, take care of you.

Believe me, if you just want to just keep living blindly, quarter-to-quarter, you're not gonna win in the long run, and your job's gonna be at risk every day.

Want to put an end to that chaos? Want to gain more control over how your organization responds to challenges, rather than live in constant fear? Then the way forward is through all of this—everything I've shared in this book.

WIN-WIN

I wrote this book with the intention of helping you to see the human factors that are necessary to help turn your corporation into a High-Performing Organization. I'm proud to say that no fewer than eight of the clients I've worked with on implementing and improving in these important areas in the last twelve years are now operating in the HPO stratosphere. There are eight to ten others that have struggled to implement much of what I've shared here, and it should come as no surprise that all of them are struggling to survive, every quarter. Everyone else falls somewhere in the middle, and I have no doubt that those who keep striving to improve will become HPOs in the next few years—while those that don't, won't.

Making these changes helps. It helps you, the individual. It helps the organization. And yes, it helps grow the kind of long-term shareholder value that pays off—big time, in some cases—while simultaneously making the company better for everyone who's there.

Win-Win.

In fact, working with that win-win mentality is an innovative step to take, in and of itself. Innovation isn't always about developing new projects. Sometimes, it's about seeing new ways forward, new ways to compete. A strong company culture that's focused on Taking Care of People will inevitably lead employees to want to find ways to Take Care of People, too—often outside of the workplace, in their communities, which are full of new potential customers.

For example, when one of my clients decided to open a new branch in Killeen, Texas, they took a few moments to look around—not only at the numbers, the demographics, the existing competition, etc., which any robot could do—but they looked around with actual humans in mind, and asked, "Who lives here? What do they need here? Who can we *help* here?"

The answers were obvious: Killeen is the gateway to Fort Hood, the largest Army installation in America. Therefore, the largest population of people who live and shop in Killeen are military families. Military families are also, by default, the largest population of people in need of *support* in the Killeen area—and thankfully, this particular company had always been ready and willing to support military families in all sorts of ways.

Killeen was not an easy market to crack. It's filled with all sorts of large corporate entities with dominant, long-established roots in the region, with names that military families were already well-accustomed to embracing. So in its first year open, facing competition from such well-established giants, my client was able to capture only about 10 percent of the Killeen market. But with each passing year, they focused more and more on a persistent pattern of providing assistance and support for military families in the area—giving back, as it were—and the military families started to notice. They not only fell in love with the company, its people, and its culture of putting people first; they realized that my client was the real deal. They weren't targeting military families in some short-term scheme to try to win over their business. It became clear that the leaders and associates actually *cared* about military families—and that changed everything.

This client now dominates 75 percent of its particular market in Killeen. They didn't get there by undercutting the competition, driving foot traffic through loss-leaders, or investing in more advertising or marketing than they did in any other town where they've opened a store. The only thing they did was to focus hard on giving back and doing good for the people in their community; because of that, they grew from a 10 percent market share to a 75 percent share—in a city previously dominated by big, national companies.

And it isn't a fluke. This company is one of those that plans centrally but decentralizes its execution, delegating responsibility to individual regional managers. Because of that, it has accomplished similar results by catering to the community needs of towns and cities all over. In survey after survey, they prove they have more loyal customers than any of their competitors, specifically because they are so client-focused. They invest in the people around them, who, in turn, invest their money in the brand, which keeps the brand profitable and able to give back even more. That's a pretty great system, isn't it? One in which everyone rises.

Another example of how values, caring, and a win-win mindset can lead to innovations that turn into new revenue streams happened when I was commanding Fort Hood—inspired in part by something that happened years earlier, when I was the commanding General at Fort Stewart in Georgia.

I think most people agree that recycling is a good way to deal with plastic waste, but we have to make sure we're dealing with it responsibly—that whatever we're putting in the recycling bin is actually getting where it's supposed to go. In my role at Fort Stewart, I made it a point to tell our people to recycle. Then one day, one of my family members followed the recycling truck and found out it was dumping our recycling at the same place where the regular garbage was being dumped. Nothing we were putting into our bins was getting recycled at all!

That recycling truck company got fired. That's just a matter of integrity and trust, and I would have had no integrity as a leader if I didn't fire that company and get a better recycling system in place. It didn't take long for news of what had happened to spread, and pretty soon every recycling company with an Army contract was put on notice.

Later, when I commanded at Fort Hood, we did one better. In order to make sure we had an effective recycling program, the previous Commander set up our *own* recycling plant on base. So not only were we able to see where our recycled items were going, but we were also able to recycle the items ourselves and sell the end product, which garnered $200,000 a year in income. That money went back directly to a morale and welfare program for our soldiers and their families.

Which just goes to show: It *can* be done. Whatever problem it is we want to solve, we can innovate and adapt, not only to solve it, but to generate positive results on both ends of the equation.

Innovation *matters*. Innovation will move you forward. Innovation will create your next great product or tee up your next profitable endeavor, whatever it may be.

Innovation will also allow you to adapt to whatever changes may come—including the sorts of changes even the best of us never see coming.

In a High-Performing Organization, the act of innovation is free to flourish due to the overwhelming sense of trust and competency, built on the shared values and vision of every person on the team, from top to bottom. And you will absolutely know when you're free to innovate as an organization, because you put in the hard work. You listened. You learned. And you never stopped reaching for the next higher goal.

So let me shake your hand.

You've done good.

There is no limit to where your High-Performing Organization can go from here.

CHAPTER 17

DON'T BE A ROBOT

As I bring this book to a close, I want to ask you to reflect a little bit on what you've read here. I want you to think about some of the new things you might have learned: some of the good things you noticed, which you may want to pat yourself on the back for embracing already, and some of the negative stories you heard, which may have hit just a little too close to home.

The fact that you made it this far means you care.

It likely means that you care about your *people*.

That's good. Because that shows empathy. And that means you're not a robot.

Now, please never forget: Your people aren't robots, either. They have needs. They have feelings. They want to know why we're doing what we're doing. And if all you're thinking about is the bottom line, those feelings and emotions and questions they have might seem like pesky annoyances. But I hope you now know that those human traits, when nurtured and developed, are the very traits that will lift your team into the stratosphere, by turning your corporation into the High-Performing Organization it ought to be.

Also, don't forget: Because you're not a robot, it's important for you to take a good long look in the mirror now and then, and ask yourself: "How am I doing. How are *we* doing?" And be honest!

Remind yourself, every chance you get, of just how important your empathy is—because when you take care of your people, they will take care of you. Especially when the chips are down, when the next unexpected event comes along. It's why we "Look down, not up," which is one of the Nine Leadership Principles you'll find in Appendix I, which I encourage you to embrace and to read more about in my earlier books.

Before you do anything else, you ought to ask yourself: have you established clear priorities in your own life, perhaps the way I did, with God, Family, and Profession, in that order? Have you established clear *values* in your life, guided by faith or whatever compass you follow? Because the separation between work life and real life isn't real. It's a made-up line. If you don't carry your values into *all* aspects of life, your chances of leading as part of a truly High-Performing Organization are slim to none.

And now that you've looked in the mirror, here's a little shortcut for you to come back to—to help you remember some of the key takeaways from this book:

LYNCH'S 10 STEPS TO CREATING AND MAINTAINING A HIGH-PERFORMING ORGANIZATION

1. Take Care of Your People

When you do, they will take care of you—*and* your company. How do you take care of them? Show them, with every decision you make and every action you take.

2. Define Your Values

If you don't know what they are, how can anyone else? Get your people on the same page and your teams all headed in the same direction. Lay out a Vision, and create Operating Plans. Define your Company Culture—so everyone is free to be the best they can be.

3. Get Your Leadership House in Order

Ask yourself, and, more importantly, ask others: "Am I being the best leader I can be? Am I active and engaged? Am I trustworthy? Am I leading by example?" Utilize the power of a 360 Assessment.

4. Be Humble.

Open your ears. Listen to criticism. Adjust and grow. Never assume you're the smartest person in the room, no matter who you are or what your title may be.

5. Define the Job

How can anyone be expected to do something well when they haven't been told what they're expected to do?

6. Practice Performance Appraisals

Learn to have the difficult conversations *now* in order to save the headaches and heartaches *later*. PAs aren't something to dread. They should be part of your company's greatness.

7. Embrace Routine Counseling

You can't take care of your people if you don't know them and they don't know you. Meet with them, talk with them; use the Form, and write it all down. **Bonus:** This simple step protects your company from post-firing lawsuits. A written record speaks for itself.

8. Trust Is a Must

And it goes both ways. Don't break it. Remember: Deeds are more important than words, and Integrity really does matter. If you say you're gonna do something, do it.

9. Delegate and Innovate

With Steps 1–8 in place, your company will break free from passive-aggressiveness, allowing the discovery of new opportunities and the exploration of new frontiers. **Bonus:** Gaining the ability to confidently delegate frees you to think, plan, and focus on the big picture—as a leader should.

10. Adapt and Thrive

Now that your company is free to be the High-Performing Organization it ought to be, go out and conquer whatever comes next through trust, collaboration, and teamwork.

Do these steps really work? It should come as no surprise that they do, since in every aspect of my life and career I've dedicated myself to serving with Integrity. Which means that if these steps *didn't* work, I wouldn't have bothered sharing them.

The truth is, turning your company into a High-Performing Organization is a mission you can accomplish—and a mission that will serve you well.

So I wish you well.

And I cannot wait to hear from you, and to see your results—once you follow these steps and get started.

Yours truly,

LYNCH'S LEADERSHIP PRINCIPLES

You can read more about these principles in the 10th Anniversary Edition of my first book, *Adapt or Die*, and in my second book, *Work Hard, Pray Hard: The Power of Faith in Action.* You and your organization can also see them through the lens of history on one of my Leadership Tours. Find more information at RLynchEnterprises.com

1. Focus on opportunities, not obstacles.
   "It can be done!"

2. Have fun!
   "If the boss ain't happy, ain't nobody happy!"

3. Achieve a work-life balance.
   "How are you living your dash?"

4. Decide when to decide.
   "Take the time to think!"

5. Look down, not up.
   "People don't care how much you know until they know how much you care!"

6. Be a mentor.
   "You must be accessible, you must listen, and you must truly care!"

7. Engaged leadership is important.
   "Love your subordinates like you love your own children!"

8. Be demanding but not demeaning.
   "Everyone must perform to his or her full potential."

9. Always celebrate diversity.
   "Don't surround yourself with people like you!"

APPENDIX II

LYNCH'S GO-TO SCRIPTURES FOR HIGH-PERFORMING LEADERS IN BUSINESS AND IN LIFE

Matthew 5:7—*Blessed are the merciful for they will be shown mercy.*

Matthew 5:20—*For I tell you that unless your righteousness surpasses that of the pharisees and the teachers of the law, you will certainly not enter the kingdom of God.*

Matthew 7:12—*Do to others as you would have them do to you.* (The Golden Rule) (also found in Luke 6:31)

Leviticus 19:18—*Do not seek revenge or bear a grudge against anyone among your people, but love your neighbor as yourself.*

Mark 12:31—*Love your neighbor as yourself.* (one of the two great commandments, as said by Jesus)

Luke 6:36—*Be merciful, just as your Father is merciful.*

Philippians 2:3—*Do nothing out of selfish ambition or vain conceit. Rather, in humility value others above yourselves, not looking to your own interests but each of you to the interests of the others.*

James 2:13—*Because judgment without mercy will be shown to anyone who has not been merciful. Mercy triumphs over judgment.*

1 Corinthians 10:24—*No one should seek their own good, but the good of others.*

1 John 3:17-18—*If anyone has material possessions and sees a brother or a sister in need but has no pity on them, how can the love of God be in that person? Dear children, let us not love with words or speech but with actions and in truth.*

Romans 12:9-10—*Love must be sincere. Hate what is evil; cling to what is good. Honor one another above yourselves.*

Romans 12:13—*Share with the Lord's people who are in need. Practice hospitality.*

Romans 12:15-16—*Rejoice with those who rejoice; mourn with those who mourn. Live in harmony with one other. Do not be proud, but be willing to associate with people of low position. Do not be conceited.*

1 Thessalonians 5:11—*Therefore, encourage one another and build each other up, just as in the fact you are doing.*

1 Peter 3:8—*Finally, all of you, be like-minded, be sympathetic, love one another, be compassionate and humble.*

Colossians 4:6—*Let your conversation be seasoned with salt so that you may know how to answer everyone.*

Ephesians 4:2—*Be completely humble and gentle; be patient, bearing with one another in love.*

Proverbs 31:8-9—*Speak up for those who cannot speak for themselves, for the rights of all who are destitute. Speak up and judge fairly; defend the rights of the poor and needy.*

Isaiah 1:17—*Learn to do right; seek justice. Defend the oppressed.*

ABOUT THE AUTHORS

Rick Lynch was privileged to serve 35 years in the US Army, retiring as a Lieutenant General. During his time in the Army he commanded at all levels, from a platoon of 30 Soldiers to a Corps of 65,000. His last job in the Army was commanding all US Army installations, with a workforce of 120,000 and an operating budget of $20 billion. After he transitioned from the Army. Rick was the Executive Director of the University of Texas at Arlington Research Institute (UTARI), which is focused on the use of advanced technology to help humanity. There he was able to utilize his graduate degree in robotics from MIT. He now is the President/CEO of R Lynch Enterprises, focused on building concerned, caring, adaptive leaders across our Nation.

Mark Dagostino is a multiple #1 *New York Times* bestselling coauthor who built his career by focusing on writing books that uplift and inspire.

Made in the USA
Columbia, SC
07 February 2025

52760732R00163